Crime and Measurement

Crime and Measurement

Methods in Forensic Investigation

Third Edition

Myriam Nafte
Brian Dalrymple

Carolina Academic Press
Durham, North Carolina

Library of Congress Cataloging-in-Publication Data

Names: Nafte, Myriam, author. | Dalrymple, Brian, author.
Title: Crime and measurement : methods in forensic investigation /
    Myriam Nafte and Brian E. Dalrymple.
Description: Third edition. | Durham, North Carolina : Carolina
    Academic Press, 2021. | Includes bibliographical references
    and index.
Identifiers: LCCN 2020049767 (print) | LCCN 2020049768 (ebook) |
    ISBN 9781531008529 (paperback) | ISBN 9781531008536 (ebook)
Subjects: LCSH: Forensic sciences—Methodology. | Criminal
    investigation—Methodology. | Crime scenes.
Classification: LCC HV8073 .N26 2021 (print) | LCC HV8073 (ebook) |
    DDC 363.25—dc23
LC record available at https://lccn.loc.gov/2020049767
LC ebook record available at https://lccn.loc.gov/2020049768

Carolina Academic Press
700 Kent Street
Durham, NC 27701
Telephone (919) 489-7486
Fax (919) 493-5668
www.cap-press.com

Printed in the United States of America

Contents

Part II
Death and Trauma

Foreword

" … And they took Joseph's coat and killed a kid of the goats, and dipped the coat in the blood … and they brought it to their father and said: This have we found: know now whether it be thy son's coat or no.… And he knew it and said: It is my son's coat; an evil beast has devoured him.…"

Genesis 37:31–33

This touching epigraph from the book of Genesis brings the story of the sons of Jacob, who after selling their younger brother, Joseph, to the Ishmaelites, wanted their father to believe he was dead. Jacob had no reason to suspect that the story was a fake, but a simple forensic test could have told him immediately that not only was the blood not his son's, it was not even human. Today, legal systems depend much less on human testimony. They can lean, instead, on the collection and scientific interpretation of physical evidence. Besides providing much more relevant information and being far more objective, these methods reduce the need for a "brilliant detective," who can resolve complicated crime mysteries single-handedly, leaning solely on his power of reasoning.

As a matter of fact, observation and interpretation have been the primary components of crime investigators since early times, but only in the middle of the nineteenth century have scientific methods become a significant tool in such investigations. The continuous refinement of analytical techniques often helps law officers in using the tiniest bits of physical evidence in their investigations, thus enabling them to decipher many crimes that would otherwise have remained unsolved, and provide solid and objective evidence to be presented in courts of law.

In this book, Myriam Nafte and Brian Dalrymple illuminate the concept of forensic science from a rather unusual angle: measurements. They show that measuring is actually "the core of almost every discipline in forensic science." Furthermore, *Crime and Measurement* provides readers a wide spectrum of topics pertaining to the application of science in criminal investigations. They start with basic definitions, followed by a short, evolutionary history of criminalistics and forensic science. They describe and discuss numerous forensic disciplines, from crime scene work to the interpretation of DNA results, the relationship between forensic scientists, law-enforcement agencies, and the legal system. Great emphasis is placed on death investigations.

Crime and Measurement is highly recommended both as a reference and as a textbook to be used in classrooms, as well as support material for police investigators, criminal lawyers, and anyone involved in the administration of justice.

Dr. Joseph Almog
Hebrew University of Jerusalem

Acknowledgments

The authors thank the following people for their professional insight, participation, and generous contribution of time, case material, and images.

Dr. Joseph Almog, Hebrew University of Jerusalem

Walter Baker, Eagle Investigations, London, Ontario

Alexandre Beaudoin, Research and Development, Sûreté du Quebec

Staff Sergeant Dennis Buligan, Toronto Police Forensic Identification Services

Carl Carlson, Supervisor, Fingerprint Identification Section, Kansas City Missouri Police Dept.

Derald Caudle, AFIX Technologies

Sergeant Scott Collings, Bloodstain Pattern Analyst, Hamilton Police Service

Brian Dew, Senior Consultant, Ron Smith & Associates, NC

Marc Dryer, University of Toronto

Dr. J. M. Duff, ret., Xerox Research Centre, Canada

Christine Farmer, Ph.D., Artist, Stourbridge, UK

Marie-Eve Gagne, Research and Development, Sûreté du Quebec

Lesley Hammer, Hammer Forensics, Anchorage, AK

Darryl Hawke, Forensic Analyst, Electronic Crime Section, Ontario Provincial Police

Michelle Hirson, Design/Layout Work

Scott Howard, AFIX Technologies

David Juck, Manager, Forensic Identification Bureau, York Regional Police

Kansas City Police Regional Crime Laboratory, MO

Dr. Anne Keenleyside, Trent University

Dr. Richard Lazenby, University of Northern British Columbia

Dr. Helene LeBlanc, University of Ontario Institute of Technology

Eugene Liscio, P. Eng., AI2-3D Animations

John Norman, Senior Forensic Analyst, Forensic Identification Services, Ontario Provincial Police

Andrew Nostrant, Buffalo Police Department. Crime Scene Unit

Larry O'Grady, Toronto Police Forensic Identification Services

Jo Orsatti, Toronto Police Forensic Identification Services

Dr. Michael Peat, Editor, *Journal of Forensic Sciences*

Christopher Power, Royal Canadian Mounted Police

Robert Ramotowski, Senior Scientist, U.S. Secret Service

Greg Schofield, Crime Scene Drafting Technician, Toronto Police Forensic Identification Services

David Sibley, Bloodstain Pattern Analyst, Forensic Identification Services, Ontario Provincial Police

Ron Smith, Ron Smith & Associates, MS

Dr. Della Wilkinson, Research Scientist, Royal Canadian Mounted Police

Dr. Brian Yamashita, Research Scientist, Royal Canadian Mounted Police

Jessica Zarate, Michigan State Police

About the Contributors

Joseph Almog was born in Tel Aviv in 1944. He obtained his Ph.D. in organic chemistry from the Hebrew University of Jerusalem and conducted research with Nobel Prize laureate Sir Derek Barton, at Imperial College in London, and with Sir Jack Baldwin at MIT. Dr. Almog joined the Israel Police in 1974, and in 1984 was appointed Director of the Division of Identification and Forensic Science (DIFS), the national crime-lab of the State of Israel. In October 2000, Dr. Almog retired from police service and joined the Science Faculty of the Hebrew University of Jerusalem, where he is currently Professor of Forensic Chemistry, at the Casali Institute of Applied Chemistry. His main fields of interest are: development of simple field-tests for crime-scene officers, explosives detection and identification, and the visualization of latent fingerprints. Over the past two decades, he has been active in advancing forensic science as a tool against terrorism. He has written over 100 articles and book chapters in chemistry and forensic science. In 2005, Dr. Almog was awarded the Lucas Medal by the American Academy of Forensic Sciences "for outstanding achievements in forensic science." In March 2009 he was appointed the first non-North American member of the editorial board of the *Journal of Forensic Sciences*.

Scott Collings joined the Hamilton Police Service in 1980 as a civilian member. In 1985 he embarked on a career as a sworn member and has worked in several areas of the police service. In 2001 he became a member of the Forensic Services Branch. Sergeant Collings is a member of the Canadian Identification Society (CIS), the International Association of Bloodstain Pattern Analysts (IABPA), and the International Association for Identification (IAI), and he is a past member of the Ontario Police College Forensic Advisory Board. In 2005 Collings became the course coordinator of the Ontario Police College-sanctioned Scenes of Crime Officer (SOCO) training program in Hamilton, where he instructs officers from Hamilton and other local police services. In 2006 he completed the training and mentorship required to become Hamilton's first Certified Bloodstain Pattern Analyst, one of approximately forty in Canada. He has been a co-instructor on the Basic Bloodstain Recognition Course and the Advanced BPA Course at the Ontario Police College, and has sat on the BPA Certification Board. He has been published in the Canadian

Identification Society journal and provided expert testimony to Ontario district courts on several occasions. With training in Forensic Post Disaster procedures and subsequent to the earthquake of January 2010, Collings was deployed to Haiti as part of a Disaster Victim Identification (DVI) team as coordinated by the RCMP. Sergeant Collings currently resides in Ancaster, Ontario with his wife, also a Hamilton officer, and his two teenaged children.

Wade Knaap is a part-time faculty member in the forensic science program at The University of Toronto where he teaches an introductory forensic science course and specific courses related to forensic identification. Prior to accepting his faculty position with the University, Wade was a Detective Constable with the Toronto Police Service and a Forensic Identification Specialist in the Forensic Identification Services Unit (FIS). In this capacity, Detective Constable Knaap served as training officer, providing forensic training needs to police and military personnel. Currently, Wade regularly lectures and conducts workshops at universities and colleges throughout Canada and the United States on forensic related topics, and is actively involved in presenting at conferences held on a yearly basis throughout North America regarding forensic identification techniques. He was past president of The Canadian Identification Society, and a former chair of The Ontario Police College Forensic Advisory Board. At present, he is an active member of the Forensic Advisory Committee at the University of Ontario Institute of Technology. His research, collaborations, and methods, on forensic identification concepts have been published numerous times in *The Journal of Forensic Identification* and *Identification Canada*. Since 2012, Wade has been the editor of *Identification Canada*. In 2002–2003, Wade Knaap was the recipient of The Al Waxman Award for "Excellence in the Field of Forensic Identification." Wade lives with his wife Charlene and family in Port Perry, Ontario.

About the Authors

Brian Dalrymple, formerly manager of the Ontario Provincial Police Forensic Identification Services, was personally responsible for deciphering some of the most challenging crimes that took place in the province of Ontario during the last quarter of the twentieth century. He co-developed the use of lasers to detect fingerprints and introduced the first police computer image enhancement service in Canada. He was awarded the John Dondero Award in 1980 by the International Association for Identification for "the most significant and valuable contribution to identification in the previous year." In 1982 he received the Foster Award from the Canadian Identification Society. In 1984 he was presented with the Lewis Minschall Award for "outstanding contribution to the fingerprint profession." In *Crime and Measurement* he presents a wealth of personal experience, applicable to the various phases of technical and scientific crime investigations.

Myriam Nafte is a forensic anthropologist and visual artist trained in anatomy. She received her Honors B.A. in medical anthropology from York University, followed by a B.Ed. degree in general sciences, an M.A. and PhD in physical anthropology from McMaster University in 1992 and 2013 respectively. For a number of years she has taught police workshops and university level courses in skeletal biology, forensics, and health sciences, while volunteering her services for criminal casework across North America. Myriam's present research interests focus on the worldwide traffic of human remains, and the use of the undisposed dead as material culture in contemporary societies. She is author of the book *Flesh and Bone: An Introduction to Forensic Anthropology.*

Introduction

"Every measurement slowly reveals the workings of the criminal. Careful observation and patience will reveal the truth."
—Alphonse Bertillon

All aspects of investigating a crime scene and its evidentiary material entail a science of measuring whether it is in the preliminary police sketch of the site, the counting of ridges and dots on a fingerprint, or observing the pattern and direction of blood spatter. Measuring for comparison, observation, analysis, and interpretation is, in fact, the core of almost every discipline in forensic science. In a pure sense, the science of forensics is the thoroughly objective mathematic search for the patterns, sequences, and traits left behind in the physical traces of a criminal and his crime.

A variety of identification systems have evolved over the past two hundred years that require lesser amounts of evidentiary material to measure but have greater and more vivid results. Forensic light sources, high-powered microscopes, and computer technology have opened up a new world in the extraction and examination of physical evidence from the once obscure 'dust' of a crime scene.

While examiners still look at the traditional array of latent evidence such as fingerprints, fibers, and blood, this can now include three-dimensional views of bullet striations, colorful genetic markers, and virtual crime scene reconstructions.

The justice systems of the world rely heavily on this continually evolving technology, a variety of which is offered in almost every discipline of forensic science. To keep up with increasingly sophisticated crimes and advances in technology requires constant resource and intelligence sharing. Hence, where once the relationship between science and the law was tenuous at best, good legal investigations now draw exclusively from a scientific methodology and an array of analyses offered by lab and criminalist technicians.

Accordingly, the forensic methodology detailed throughout the pages of *Crime and Measurement* can best be summarized as the ultimate and varied search for everything from mass, volume, texture, and length, to distance, height, shape, and sequence as revealed in the endless possibilities inherent in all forms and traces of physical evidence.

As an introductory guide, the goal of this book is to provide students in law enforcement, members of the justice system, law enforcement professionals, criminalists, and anyone interested in the field, a starting point in understanding the pivotal relationship between police, the investigator, and the scientist, in service of the law. From the first responder called to a death scene to the final analysis in the courtroom, *Crime and Measurement* outlines the processes, the rules, the protocols, and the principles of what it takes and what it means to measure and solve crime.

Beginning with the definition of all things forensic, chapter 1 outlines the various branches of the growing field of forensic science and offers a thorough discussion of what constitutes evidence, testimony, and an expert witness. Chapter 2 delves briefly into the history of criminology through a look at the emergence of uniformed police forces and the establishment of criminalists. In its exploration of the relationship between science and the legal system, this chapter also highlights the seminal work of pioneers such as Alexandre Lacassagne and Edmond Locard, founders of legal medicine, as well as Hans Gross, the judicial magistrate who officially brought science and the law together.

Going right to the scene of the crime, chapter 3 focuses on the primary role of police beginning with the requirements of first responders, the rules around barricading a crime scene, and a complete overview of the principles of search and recovery. The chapter also examines evidence collection and a special section on the use of forensic light sources in detecting latent evidence and reconstructing crime scenes.

Chapters 4, 5, and 6 discuss the events and protocols around encountering death at a scene, highlight various forms of trauma, and outline the processes of death and decomposition.

Three methods used by police and forensic scientists in assigning a positive identification to both victim and criminal are thoroughly outlined in chapter 7. The relatively short history and highly controversial use of DNA analysis is detailed from its first case in the 1980s to the current policies surrounding its use and storage in databases around the world. Following this section is a discussion of the much longer history of fingerprinting in pursuing and keeping track of criminals over the past two hundred years. Descriptions include the varying characteristics and features of the tips of our fingers that make us unique, and how technicians map these traits to identify and distinguish perpetrators. The chapter concludes with the popular and visually dynamic field of facial reconstruction.

Chapter 8 investigates an array of evidence, and the methods used by police to access, uncover, and highlight the latent (hidden) information in these items. Firearms, computer data, footwear, and tires all leave their mark on a variety of surfaces, and the challenges in documenting, retrieving, or reproducing these marks are presented in this last section.

Finally the appendix offers a series of high-profile cases provided by the authors and contributors. Each case highlights a variety of methods and tools that were employed to solve the crimes presented, and best illustrate the many areas of forensic analyses outlined in the book.

Throughout each chapter there are graphic photographs depicting human bodies that have sustained severe trauma or are in various stages of decay. The use of such images comes with an understanding that *mortui vivo docent*—the dead teach the living. To honor this process and out of respect for the victims and their families, the photographs published do not reveal their identity or the details of their case history.

Part I

Police and Forensics

Chapter 1

The Forensic Method

Defining Forensic

Traditionally, the term *forensic* referred to the place where justice was administered. The word is derived from the Latin word *forum* as in a public space like a market area, plaza, or meeting ground. *Forensis* literally means belonging to a public space, since in Roman times, legal trials, sentencing, and executions were *forensic* in nature—they were for the public to experience and view.

Today we define *forensics* as any research aimed at the analysis and interpretation of *evidence* (see later discussion) for a legal investigative process. The actual *forensic method* refers to a now-established systematic approach in documenting, collecting, interpreting, and presenting evidence for presentation in a court of law.

Since anything occurring in nature or manufactured may be considered evidence, forensic methodology draws from a diversity of disciplines ranging from accounting to zoology. With the integration of methods from such a diverse range of professions, the area of forensics has developed into a broad field of study referred to as *forensic science*.

Each area of forensic science integrates the same basic approach in its scope: research, analysis, interpretation, documentation, and presentation. These methods must all adhere to the *general acceptance clause* of the admissibility of scientific evidence in any court of law. In other words, the theories and technology used by scientists must be tested, recognized, and accepted by the legal and scientific community prior to any utilization. This ensures regulation and consistency in the field given the rapid pace of advances in science, and the legal profession's slow acceptance and understanding of these advances.

The application of scientific expertise and a forensic methodology to criminal investigation is most often the prerequisite for successful case outcomes. Science and the legal system (see chapter 2) have consolidated their resources over the past 100 years, creating a distinct field that has come to represent the essence of criminal investigation. Law is now fundamentally dependent on *expert testimony* (see the following discussion) through science and technology for more definitive answers and faster, more exact methods to provide information for use in courts.

A direct witness pointing out the suspect in a case at trial.

Evidence Defined

The term *evidence* refers to anything that can give or substantiate information in a legal investigation. The word is derived from the Latin word *evidentia*, "to be visible." The root word from Latin is *videre*, "to see." Therefore, evidence must be visible to be acceptable and provide information that may prove or disprove a point in question.

Evidence is crucial to all police investigations for three very specific reasons. First and foremost, it provides a clear direction for investigators who act on the nature of evidence to form *leads*. Second, the amount of evidence establishes a case's credibility once in court, affecting the positions of both judge and jury. Third, certain types of evidence bring with it the testimony of *expert witnesses* (see later discussion) that can determine or undermine the outcome of a case.

Testimonial Evidence

In the form of information, evidence can be abstract, derived from an individual's testimony (from the Latin word *testis* meaning witness). When individuals *testify*, it is assumed that they do so as witnesses with knowledge or information concerning the case.

Witnesses can be defined as being either *indirect* or *direct*. Indirect witnesses are beyond a crime scene, did not witness a crime, and may not be aware that a crime has occurred. A bus driver who can identify a regular passenger, for example, a neighbor who heard a loud crash, or a doctor who treated an individual for a head wound; all are considered indirect witnesses who could potentially provide crucial testimony by way of their firsthand knowledge or experience.

Direct witnesses are those individuals who witnessed a crime or are the victims of a crime.

Table 1.1 Physical Evidence

Type	Nature
Associative	any evidence that places an individual at a scene and/or with a victim
Class	evidence that requires classification into a more narrow range
Electronic	information and data transmitted and/or stored in any electronic device
Latent	any evidence that is not visible without the use of chemical, photographic, or electronic development/enhancement
Trace	evidence that has to be extracted from another substance and is in very small amounts, often invisible to the naked eye
Indicative	evidence that substantiates or proves that a certain period of time has elapsed
Circumstantial	facts, observations, activities from which the culpability of an individual may be inferred

Physical Evidence

Evidence that can be seen, touched, extracted, and exhibited constitutes physical evidence and represents a much broader range of items. Indeed, physical evidence can be anything manufactured or occurring in nature, from microscopic fibers, paint chips, and insect larvae to vehicles and machinery. Furthermore, due to the development of biological detection systems and more powerful isolation and separation methods, evidence can now be extracted from older, smaller, and more minute substances.

Generally evidence is divided into categories, determined by their source, content, and nature. Physical evidence is a very large category, which includes associative, class, trace, latent, electronic, and indicative classes of evidence (see following discussion and Table 1.1).

Associative evidence is any physical evidence that places an individual directly at the crime scene. It is a general category that may involve all or some of the other types of evidence listed next.

Class evidence includes any form of evidence that requires precise classification for it to be of use in court. Evidence such as hair, blood, urine, saliva, and semen, can be human or nonhuman, for example. If human, these items require further classification to narrow the range of possibilities within a given population.

Trace evidence is any physical evidence that has to be extracted from another substance or item and is in very small amounts, often invisible to the naked eye. Trace evidence can be class evidence as well as associative, and likewise associative evidence can be class evidence and trace in its amount.

Latent evidence includes DNA, palm prints, fingerprints, footprints, tread marks, and tire tracks. This type of evidence is considered latent (from the Latin word *latere*: "to lie hidden") because it is often not visible without some means of chemical, photographic, or electronic development. Police and/or lab specialists are usually charged with processing this class of evidence.

Electronic evidence is any information and data transmitted by or stored in an electronic device. This constantly evolving type of evidence is considered latent evidence in the same sense that fingerprints are. It is not visible until equipment or software makes it accessible. Testimony is often required to explain the examination process and any process limitations, much as it is with other classes of evidence.

Indicative evidence is any physical evidence that substantiates a certain period of time elapsing. This class of evidence is specifically for documenting rather than collecting. For example, the rate that a body has decomposed will be based on the state of the remains and the outdoor or indoor temperature. However, if the remains were found indoors in a cold basement during a hot summer, this information is vitally indicative in assessing an accurate time of death.

Temperature variations and location information cannot be physically picked up and bagged, but must thoroughly be documented. Likewise, the presence of newspapers and unopened mail piling up at a victim's door indicating that the individual has not collected this material over a particular period of time; the weight loss of a child in an abuse case; money withdrawal from an account or checks being cashed; and so on ... Indicative evidence ultimately outlines the crucial period of time in which a crime may have occurred.

All physical evidence is, by its very nature, fragile. It can be altered, damaged, or destroyed by improper handling and improper examination. For this reason, special precautions must be in place in its handling from its discovery and collection through its appearance in court. Failure to do so renders it unusable and/or inadmissible.

Circumstantial Evidence

The broad term known as *circumstantial evidence* refers to information that may be either physical or testimonial in its nature. Often circumstantial evidence is a collection of facts and observations that infer the culpability of an individual. These facts and observations may also be coincidental, hence the term *circumstantial*.

A defense attorney may on occasion casually dismiss a witness's testimony with the words "purely circumstantial" as though it were of little or no account. In fact, circumstantial evidence can be the most powerful and compelling component of a trial—the piece that decides the outcome.

Circumstantial evidence does not in itself establish guilt, nor does it establish that a crime has been committed. It presents a position that must be supported or corroborated by other forms of evidence. A fingerprint expert may testify that the fingerprint on a plastic bag of drugs

Collecting a broad array of physical evidence. Photos courtesy of the Buffalo Police Dept. Crime Scene Unit. All rights reserved.

was made by the accused. In cross-examination, however, the defense may establish any of the following:

- the witness cannot say when the print was made.
- the witness cannot say where the print was made.
- the witness cannot say what, if anything, was in the bag at the time of deposition.
- the witness cannot say that the accused was even aware of touching the bag, much less took any part in a crime.

All the expert witness can truthfully say is that, in his or her opinion, at some time, the finger of the accused came in contact with the plastic bag. The prosecution will rely on other corroborating evidence to attempt to form a picture of guilt and convince the court that no other reasonable conclusion can be reached.

"Physical evidence cannot be wrong, it cannot perjure itself; it cannot be wholly absent; only its interpretation can err. Only human failure to find it, study and understand it can diminish its value."

Paul Kirk, 1960

Processing Evidence

The standard protocol is for police, investigators, or a number of specialists to collect and recover as much evidence as possible from a prospective crime scene (see chapter 3). When physical evidence has been collected, police or investigators send certain types to a variety of facilities for processing. The evidence they maintain is what they process in house.

How evidence is processed depends entirely on what it is and what needs to be done to it for it to yield factual information. Some physical evidence, as in the case of severely decayed body parts, may need to be defleshed for better analysis, and other forms of physical evidence may require further extraction and closer examination, like bloodstains on clothing or hairs from a sweater.

Samples can be obtained from physical evidence that can yield many kinds of analyses during processing as in the case for blood, bodily tissues and fluids, hair, and fibers. These types of evidence are often sent to more than one lab for specific and further processing. For example, if blood is found, it will be sent to biology for classification to find out whether it is human blood and then more specifically whose blood. If there is a question around the contents in the blood, as in alcohol levels, prescription drugs, and/or poisons, the sample will continue to toxicology for processing and then to chemistry to analyze any drug or chemicals found (see forensic science layout).

Expert Witnesses

All physical evidence needs to be analyzed, test results interpreted, and accompanying information documented. The specialists who process physical evidence for a legal investigation are known as *expert witnesses*, because their handling, analysis, and expertise with various types of physical evidence is presented in a court of law.

An observer in court will usually watch direct evidence being tendered. A witness giving direct evidence requires no special training, no technical knowledge, and no unique skills. The only prerequisite is the ability to promise under oath to tell the truth. The person merely relates what he or she did, saw, heard, and experienced.

An expert witness is permitted to go further than simply what he or she did, saw, or heard. That witness is entitled to express an opinion on the work done, an opinion that can, as previously stated, decide the outcome. Neither the courts nor the practitioners take this privilege lightly, in the knowledge that their opinion could send someone to jail—or death row.

The court will thus want to be satisfied that

- the witness is of sound and unquestioned integrity.
- the witness is sufficiently trained and experienced to give evidence in this discipline.
- the science or technology being presented meets the criteria of acceptance through:
  ○ peer review,
  ○ testing and validation,
  ○ rate of error, and
  ○ general acceptance.

Who decides the status of an expert witness and whether they can be chosen to appear in court for testimony varies. Since specialists can be drawn from such a diverse group of people, it is often up to a judge, during the trial process, to determine the criteria needed to be declared or accepted as an expert witness in a specific field of forensics.

Evidence: Search and Seizure

In the United States, the Fourth Amendment to the federal Constitution, and in Canada Section 8 of the Canadian Charter of Rights and Freedom, state that all individuals have the right to be secure against an unreasonable (warrantless) search or seizure by government. In other words, the police cannot search a person's home or workplace without a *warrant*.

A warrant (from the Old German word *werent* meaning "an authorization") is a *writ*—a document from the court signed by a judge or

Judge signing a search warrant.

magistrate that outlines specifically what offense has been committed, the place to be searched, and the people or things that are to be seized.

The decision of the judge to sign a warrant is based on hearing sufficient reasons on oath, establishing *probable cause* (a U.S. term) or *reasonable and probable grounds* (a Canadian term) as to why a search and seizure should be issued. The judge must be in a position to assess this in a neutral and impartial fashion. Once a warrant is authorized and signed, it has to be executed immediately since there is an expiration date assigned. The judge may also limit the search and seizure to specific areas and items, and list these in the warrant.

Regardless of the search warrant parameters specifying or limiting what can be searched for and/or seized, items observed in plain view, relating to other criminal activity can also be seized.

This seizure authority is referred to as the *plain view doctrine.* As it implies, these seized items must be in plain view, and in areas within the proximity of the warrant limitations. It is not an acceptable practice for searchers to be intrusive or invasive in their search. For instance, if drawers or closets need to be opened to see contraband unspecified in the warrant, continuance of the seizure would be deemed unlawful.

There may also exist powers of seizure blanketed by multiple legislative authorities. An example of this would be where a domestic homicide has taken place in the matrimonial home. The residence would normally require a search warrant to be processed, however, legislation such as the Coroners Act and a *coroner's warrant* may override the necessity for a warrant and afford investigators permission to enter the premises and process the scene as it relates to the victim.

Areas of interest not directly associated to the victim or related to body removal may require a separate warrant to search. Ultimately, the presiding judge remains the gatekeeper in determining what level of search is deemed reasonable.

The rules surrounding search and seizure apply to individuals walking down a street, driving their cars, and at places of work. However, the expectation of privacy is diminished once the individual is outside his or her home. Police are permitted more access and certain rules protecting the individual are relaxed.

Chain of Custody

It is assumed that physical evidence will form a good part of an investigation and may in fact create the direction in which it goes. Since evidentiary material eventually ends up in court as part of an exhibit and/or expert testimony, it is necessary to safeguard its transport, handling, labeling, and constant whereabouts. The vital process of safeguarding physical evidence is referred to as *maintaining the chain of custody*. The formation of a chain of custody—also known as "chain of evidence," "chain of possession," and "continuity of evidence"—is to prevent unauthorized persons from accessing, tampering, adding, or altering evidence in any way, from its original discovery right through to its presentation in a court of law.

Maintaining the chain of custody or possession means a complete unbroken record of

- where it was located when it became evidence.
- who initially seized it.
- the date and time it became evidence.
- who has possession of the evidence.
- what has been done to the evidence.

This level of information ensures the integrity of all evidence in several ways:

- protection from dirt, moisture, abrasion, or other adverse conditions.
- protection from loss or misplacement.
- protection from tampering.

The collector and recipient of physical evidence must be prepared to keep it secure, account for any access to it, and assume responsibility for its labeling, handling, and transportation. Any indication that there has been an unaccounted-for access to evidence or if it goes missing for a period of time constitutes a "break" in the chain. A break increases the opportunity for evidence to be challenged or rendered inadmissible in court, no matter how damning or scientific it is.

Preventing breaks in the chain of custody has become top priority with police and forensic specialists. In the face of increased scientific input and more accurate test results, counsel can often only challenge

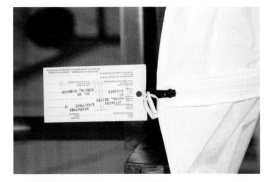
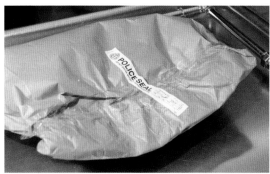

Evidence that has been sealed, bagged and/or tagged to maintain the chain of custody. Images courtesy of Toronto Police, Forensic Identification Services. All Rights Reserved.

the whereabouts of physical evidence, and the nature of its handling to create doubt in the courtroom. Since there are many specialists involved in the analyses of physical evidence, the question of who gave what to whom, how, where, and when is as important as what interpretations were made.

At issue is the fact that evidence handling, storage, and inventory are still traditionally manual efforts. There are many hands to keep track of material items, transfer them for analysis, and reference their location. The process of maintaining a consistent chain of custody using paper-based systems or computer logging is labor intensive and prone to misuse, inaccuracy, and error.

To address this matter, radio frequency identification (RFID technology) is quickly being adopted by law enforcement agencies throughout North America and Europe for use as a physical evidence-tracking device. From the time it leaves the crime scene to storage, transportation, and handling, the data, location, and date of all evidentiary material is recorded and monitored. RFID readers located in storage facilities, on doorways of evidence rooms, as well as in handheld devices read tags affixed to the material and provide a constant inventory reporting capability, thereby creating an electronic chain of custody. Who handled the evidence and when, its exact location, and its time of release are recorded and maintained without the repercussions of human error.

Fruit of the Poisonous Tree

Cross-examination is frequently based on what was *not* done, rather than what was done. A broken chain of custody or possession is an excellent example. If there is a breach in this chain, it cannot be established what was or was not done to any evidence in this unaccounted-for period, and it then becomes *tainted*.

There exists a doctrine in law referred to as *the fruit of the poisonous tree*. The theory is that the poisonous tree is the original tainted evidence, and that any fruit (evidence) that grows from it will also be tainted. An evidence technician, for example may develop and identify the fingerprint of the accused on a murder weapon, but if the integrity of the murder weapon has not been preserved through an unbroken chain of custody, or if the process was not properly documented, it may not be allowed by the court as evidence. At the very least, there will be doubts as to its integrity and meaning.

Corpus Delicti

The term *corpus delicti* translates literally as "the body of crime." This is a Latin legal term that refers to the establishment of proof through evidence that a crime has been committed against something or someone. For example, if an individual has been charged with arson, the corpus delicti must include any physical evidence of a fire and the subsequent damage to property. Likewise, if there has been a charge of homicide, an identified body must be present (although there are exceptions), with cause of death established and relevant evidence pointing toward the accused. A confession alone, accusations from another person, or testimony from an accomplice are not enough for a conviction.

The Forensic Specialists

There are different staffing models adopted by police agencies to conduct forensic identification duties. Generalists have historically completed the entire sequence of functions, from crime scene processing and evidence recognition, to detection, photography, optimization, interpretation and finally, presentation in court.

Other police agencies, large ones in particular, employ specialist sections, each of which is responsible for completing one or more of these duties. For example, the recording and examination of crime scenes, laboratory examination of exhibits, photography of impression evidence, and fingerprint comparison have become separate entities in many jurisdictions.

Each model or system has strengths. A generalist approach will obviously present less opportunity for disconnection between any of the functions previously mentioned, but in a dynamic technical world, it will be increasingly challenging for a generalist to stay current in all phases of the process, particularly when large caseloads are a reality. In contrast, specialists will find it easier to inform themselves of and act on, cutting edge developments in their respective disciplines.

Ultimately, all disciplines can be called on to provide information to solve a legal question or aid the investigative process. The most successful and vigorous analyses of data are those carried out by different, and comparative, means. This team approach requires multidisciplinary involvement with many individuals working on one case, collecting, processing, and examining evidence.

Whatever the discipline, if the work involves identifying or processing evidence for a legal investigation, it is called *forensic* work, for example, forensic anthropology, forensic odontology, forensic psychiatry, forensic entomology (see the examples on the following pages).

The goal in involving many specialists during an investigation of criminal activity is the thorough collection and analysis of an array of physical evidence. The more experts, the more a variety of evidence can be collected and analyzed. Specialists focus on their own strengths in an area but also rely on each other's expertise to enhance their understanding of the crime scene and to piece information together.

The choice and use of a forensic specialist or team is never random, as they are integrated according to the crime scene and the type of evidence analyzed. For example, in the case of a poisoning death, the toxicologist is called on; where a shooting occurred the firearm's expert is consulted; to identify skeletal remains, a forensic anthropologist is involved.

Their subsequent testimony as expert witnesses, however, must ultimately be determined by their own analysis and interpretation of the evidence gathered, not the team's perspective. It is their job to produce theories about this evidence based on the data, and the job of the investigator to assimilate these theories into a story of what happened and why.

PATHOLOGY

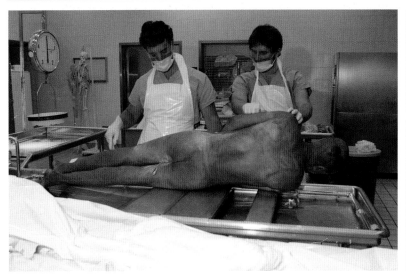

- **Pathologists** perform the post-mortem examination in order to determine or confirm identity, and to establish the cause, time, and manner of death.

BIOLOGY

Serology and DNA Profiling

- **Serologists** seek to identify class evidence such as human and nonhuman biological materials (blood, bodily fluids, hair and fibers) obtained from individuals, items or collected directly from a crime scene.

- **DNA** is found in every cell with a nucleus and includes bodily fluids, hair, teeth and bone. Profiling is derived from the analysis of this genetic material for comparative analysis and identification purposes.

- **Biologists** also interpret bloodstain patterns found on a range of items as well as at crime and accident scenes.

CHEMISTRY

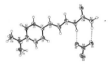

■ **Chemists** analyze materials like dyes, paints, explosives, drugs, soil, glass, petroleum products, and metals as well as synthetic and natural fibers.

TOXICOLOGY

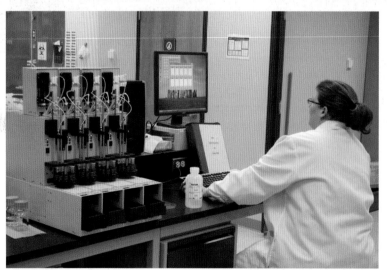

■ **Toxicologists** attempt to detect or determine the presence of poisons and drugs in blood, bodily fluids and tissues, as well as in non-biological material such as powders, liquids, and pills.

FIREARMS & TOOLMARKS EXAMINATION

■ **Firearms experts** examine and maintain custody of all evidence from the criminal use of firearms. They look at firearms, weapons, remaining live ammunition, compare fired projectiles and fired cartridge cases, as well as bullets, wound tissue, clothing from shooting victims, all tools and toolmarks.

PHOTOANALYSIS

■ Physical evidence is **photographed** for documentation, analysis, interpretation, and for presentation as court exhibits.

■ A camera and microscope along with infrared, ultraviolet, x-ray, or laser radiation may be used to highlight details invisible to the naked eye.

DOCUMENTS

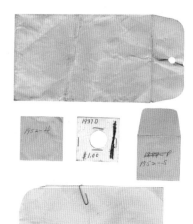

- **Document analysts** attempt to determine the legality, forgery and authenticity of handwriting in a range of items such as checks, anonymous letters, suicide, hold-up and ransom notes. For comparative and inventory value, they assess various types of ink and paper, machine-produced documents, and writing instruments.

ELECTRONICS

Electronics experts

- transport, recover, and maintain computer files, and any information or data stored in an electronic device including any material that has been erased or hidden.

- Retrieve call logs, texts, e-mails and contact numbers stored in cell phones as well as hand-held devices.

- Enhance the audibility of poor quality audiotapes.

- Examine stun guns and tasers to confirm their standing under the terms of the Criminal Code.

ODONTOLOGY

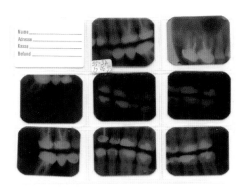
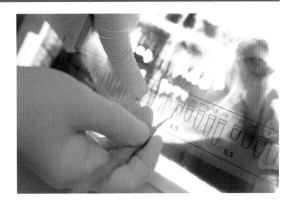

- **Odontologists** examine dental remains and premortem dental records for comparative and identification purposes, dental impressions, bite marks and injuries to teeth.

- These experts are also responsible for ensuring that bite marks on living or deceased victims be swabbed for DNA. This is the first process they perform prior to taking an impression.

- Working with unidentified remains, the odontologist must also be aware of the presence of DNA contained within the core of the tooth.

ENTOMOLOGY

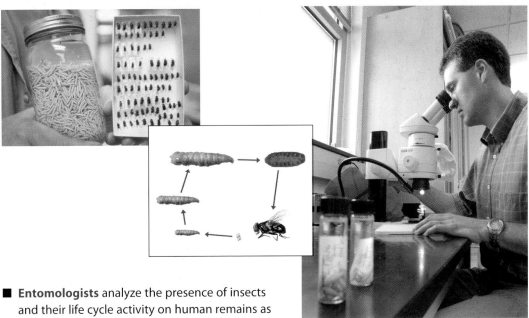

- **Entomologists** analyze the presence of insects and their life cycle activity on human remains as a method of estimating the time and location of death.

FORENSIC ANTHROPOLOGY

- **Forensic anthropologists** recover and analyze human skeletal remains to establish a biological identity (the age, sex, stature, and race of an individual).

- Human remains are also examined to determine any evidence of pre-, peri-, and post-mortem trauma, as well as any presence of disease.

PSYCHIATRY

- **Forensic psychiatrists** evaluate individuals prior to their trial in order to judge whether individuals are capable of standing trial (the Competency to Stand Trial assessment — CST), and to determine their state of mind, and their understanding of the crime committed (the Mental State at the time of the Offence — MSO).

- Psychiatrists in this sub-specialty make sentencing suggestions based on their evaluations and provide care of prisoners in jails and hospitals.

Chapter 2

Science and the Legal System

Police Forces

The 1800s heralded a major shift in the methods of understanding and approaching crime in Europe and North America. With violence and social unrest increasing in dense urban centers throughout Europe, came the formal establishment of uniformed and salaried police officers like the City of Glasgow Police (1800), the Sureté in Paris (1810), the Metropolitan Police in London (1829), and the Royal Irish Constabulary (1822). For the first time, these forces were charged with a preventive role: patrolling streets, maintaining a public presence, and investigating crime as part of a professional service. Indeed, the term *police* was borrowed from the French word *policie*, meaning, "to keep order."

Police in uniform, early 1900s. Image courtesy of the Ontario Provincial Police archives. All rights reserved.

The trend followed in North America, where major cities saw the benefits of keeping law and order and maintaining a uniformed police presence. Railroads needed securing, strikes were busted, horse thieving and rioting were prevented. What started out as handfuls of concerned citizen volunteers turned into formally trained and paid policemen. Toronto, Canada, saw the first municipal uniformed police department established in 1834, followed by Montreal and Boston in 1838. The New York City Police was formed in 1844, and Philadelphia followed in 1854.

Working alongside these newly founded organizations were the new *detectives* (from the Latin word *detectio-*, "to find"). Taken from the ranks of police officers, society's gentlemen, and military men, they became the specialists whose sole job was to determine who committed the crime and why. They established themselves within police agencies working less individually and more cooperatively to close cases.

Detectives at this pivotal time in the nineteenth century adopted the experimental science of the interview as a means of uncovering truths and commonalities, from the current trend in the new psychotherapy and psychiatry fields (see Merkel 2003). Getting to understand crime on an individual basis and through patterns of behavior, they recorded their observations, talked to witnesses, and interrogated suspects. The merits of this form of investigation, rather than the more traditional methods of spying and taking bribes, established and enhanced the detective's pivotal role in high-profile crimes.

Officer on the first cruiser radio, ca. 1947. Image courtesy of the Ontario Provincial Police. All rights reserved.

Criminologist Cesare Lombroso, 1835–1909. Image courtesy of Museo Criminologico. Rome, Italy. All rights reserved.

Doctors and Criminals

Two basic and contradictory philosophies pertaining to the criminal mind guided much of the police and legal systems at this time: *atavism* versus *positivism*. These philosophies had a long history, and by the 1800s were put forth largely by anthropologists, psychiatrists, and medical doctors who contributed to police investigations and sought to influence judicial practices.

Atavists insisted that criminals were born to commit crimes due to biological deviance, whereas positivists claimed that crime was the product of social causes. *Recidivism* (repeating crimes) was very high, prisons were overcrowded, and the costs of policing were rising dramatically. The nineteenth century emphasis therefore was to explain the deviant mind and predict who was more predisposed to commit crime (Broeckman 1996).

By the late 1800s, criminal anthropology conferences were being held throughout Europe to showcase research from the opposing schools of thought. Several charts and systems of identification were developed and displayed among the skulls, autopsies, and head casts of society's deviants. The two most prominent men in this field were both medical doctors: Cesare Lombroso (1835–1909) was an atavist (also a practicing psychiatrist) and considered the "father of modern criminology" (Mannheim 1972, 232). His positivist rival was a professor of legal medicine named Alexandre Lacassagne (1843–1924), whom many refer to as the "father of forensic medicine" (Renneville 1995).

With displays of the skulls of delinquents, specimens of conserved tattoos, photographs of epileptics and inmates, Lombroso argued that criminals were born deviant, as evident in the size and shape of their

Criminal heads: types studied by Lombroso, late eighteenth century. Images courtesy of Museo Criminologico. Rome, Italy.

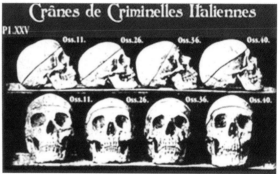

bodies (see Broeckman 1996). As an army physician he had observed and meas-ured height and size differences among soldiers; later, as the director of numerous asylums, he set out to collect a complete index of criminal traits. Visiting prisons, hospitals, and asylums in the mid-1800s Lombroso cast and measured the heads, arms, and legs of inmates and prisoners. He noted their facial asymmetries and peculiar head shapes, collected their writings and drawings, and photographed them in various poses.

This collection of data became the basis for his book in 1876 titled *Criminal Man* (*L'uomo Delinquente*), which sought to identify the physical characteristics "inherent in all criminals" (Lombroso 1876, 43). As he claimed in his introduction, " … Those who have had direct contact with offenders, such as members of their families or prison wardens, know that they are different from other people, with weak and diseased minds that can rarely be healed" (Lombroso 1876, 43).

Alexandre Lacassagne, on the other hand, pointed to charts and maps of crime statistics in France and the biographies of criminals to link crime rates with geography. Stating that "societies have the criminals they de-

Alexandre Lacassagne, 1843–1924, considered the "father of forensic medicine." Image courtesy of Institut de Médecine Légale. Lyon, France

serve" (Renneville 1995), he set out to prove that the behavior of criminals was dependent on their social environment.

Like Lombroso, Lacassagne had his start as an army physician and worked extensively in a military hospital. Gaining firsthand experience with the damage sustained by bullets and bayonets, he lent his observations to high-profile criminal cases in France creating an area of study called legal medicine (also referred to as medical jurisprudence).

Moving to Lyon, France, in the late 1800s, he established himself as professor of legal medicine and with coauthor Paul Dubuisson founded a criminal anthropology journal titled *Archives de L'Anthropologie Criminelle.*

To further expound his beliefs in the sociological aspects of crime, Lacassagne chose to research and write about one of the most notorious serial killers in France's history: Joseph Vacher. The collection of observations on this case, along with his pioneering work in blood spatter and knife wounds, quickly established Lacassagne as one of the major forefathers in forensic medicine.

Joseph Vacher

The case of the heinous Joseph Vacher, known as the French Ripper, captured the attention of the country when he was finally apprehended and executed in 1898 in the town of Bourg for the murders of more than twenty-three people. At the time of his execution by guillotine, he was twenty-eight years old (see *New York Times*, January 1, 1899).

Traveling the countryside with a large stick and a canvas bag between the years 1894 and 1897, Vacher approached young herdsmen and farmhands in rural areas of the country, grabbed them, and quickly slit their throats. Leaving their mutilated bodies by roadsides and in barns, he ventured off to the next village in search of more victims.

Joseph Vacher, ca. 1898. Image courtesy of Le Journal Illustré, Lyons, France.

In the summer of 1897, Vacher was taken into custody after a failed abduction attempt. Once incarcerated he immediately confessed to the murders of several young men and women. A host of criminal anthropologists, psychiatrists, and physicians soon descended on the town of Bourg to study Vacher and the nature of his crimes. It was the perfect opportunity for many of them to test their theories and prove the legitimacy of their professions. Vacher, like many serial killers, proved to be articulate and receptive to the attention.

Lacassagne attended the trial, researched Vacher's life, and interviewed him extensively while imprisoned. He wrote copious amounts on the details of the case, and provided expert testimony during the sensational trial. After Vacher's execution by guillotine, Lacassagne studied the morphology of Vacher's head and dissected his brain.

Vacher seemed to represent Lacassagne's belief that criminals are not born but made by society, specifically a society in which vagabonds are allowed to roam the countryside. In his long book on the subject, titled *Vacher L'Éventruer et Les Crimes Sadiques* (Vacher the Disemboweler and the Sadistic Crimes), Lacassagne describes a man who had no history of mental disease in his childhood and was an upright soldier until driven to attempted suicide by the rejections of a girlfriend. With a bullet still lodged in his brain caused by his suicide attempt, he was soon given over to "mental fits" and was confined to an asylum for a few months until being released for good conduct.

Thereafter Vacher was left to wander rural France as a vagabond. With "no place to work, no home and no attachments," Lacassagne claimed Vacher developed a hatred for society, and like all vagabonds, "they rape for sport and kill for money … they are pariahs and manifestations of anarchy" (Lacassagne 1899, 308).

The book was a warning of an imminent social crisis in France concerning the "scourge of vagabondage" (Lacassagne 1899, 308) as were many other reviews and articles at the time (see also *Revue Des Deux*

Mondes 1898–99; Smith 1999). What distinguishes this work from many of the other publications on Vacher was its medico-legal context. Lacassagne wrote as a physician involved in the legal process with an interest in society and judicial outcomes. He referenced other physicians' research, contributed illustrations of the crime scenes and the execution, photographed autopsy details, gave the perpetrator's history, and recounted the judicial process including future recommendations. The highly praised book set the standard for research in medical jurisprudence, and established a niche for doctors involved in criminal casework.

At the same time Lacassagne was debating biology versus sociology, he founded a school of criminology in Lyon, where scientific methods of observation played a prominent role in solving crime. There he practiced and refined autopsy methods, noted patterns of blood spatter in relationship to the position of bodies, and soon became famous for his expertise in bullet and knife wounds before the field was formally established. Thus he was given the title "father of forensic medicine" (Renneville 1995; also Artières and Corneloup 2004).

By the end of the 1800s both Lombroso's and Lacassagne's methods were hugely popular and formed the basis for gathering empirical data on crimes and the people who committed them. As a result of the opposing schools (atavism versus positivist approaches) led by these and other prominent physicians and anthropologists, a variety of measurements and identification systems were soon established. Police and legal investigators adopted many of these systems, or used them as a basis on which to develop their own. These are explored in the following sections.

Alphonse Bertillon

Relying on early methods in classifying criminals according to size and shape, criminal anthropologist Alphonse Bertillon (1853–1914) created the first system of physical measurements combined with photography and record-keeping that police could use to identify recidivist criminals.

While working for the Paris police in the 1870s, Bertillon documented individuals by eleven measurements of the head and body, including the shape of the ear, mouth, and eye, limbs, scars, tattoos, and personality characteristics. The measurements were compiled into a formula and recorded onto individual cards, and with the recent invention of photography it neatly bore a frontal and side profile image of the suspect or the charged.

Bertillon first described this identification system in his detailed book titled *Photography: With an Appendix on Anthropometrical Classification and Identification,* published in 1890.

Before this system of identification was introduced, the earlier methods of recognizing repeat offenders entailed cutting off their ears or branding them with hot irons. Since these established methods had been abolished by 1832, suspects could only be identified through eyewitness descriptions and unorganized files of photographs (see also Caplan and

Alphonse Bertillon, ca. 1890. Image courtesy of Musée de la Préfecture de Police, Paris.

Torpey 2001). As Bertillon stated, "Up to now, the police, and behind them the courts, moved in a vicious circle; one photographed people to be able to find out their name, but in order to locate a previously taken photograph, we needed the name of the offender" (see Bertillon 1883).

Where Lombroso and Bertillon parted ways was in Bertillon's emphasis on creating an immediate identification system as opposed to understanding the inherent morphology of criminals. His primary goal was to develop and maintain a comprehensive photographic archive of offenders that could be readily pulled to show witnesses and be displayed by police. By 1883, Bertillon identified the first repeat offender and by the following year, he had identified at least 241 criminals (Bertillon 1890). The nature of policing and record-keeping changed dramatically during this pivotal stage—from an inefficient disorganized scheme to one that was more systematic and methodic in its approach to criminal apprehension and crime prevention.

Bertillon's system came to be known as the *signaletics* (or the *bertillonage* method) and was adopted by many if not all European and North American police agencies. By 1887, it was formally introduced in the United States through the Illinois State Penitentiary, Joliet, by Major Robert W. McClaughry, warden, and Gallus Muller, records clerk (see McClaughry 1922).

Rigorous training by competent technicians was required to get consistent results, yet problems soon became apparent. When the same person was measured twice by different individuals or even by the same technician, measurements varied dramatically. Likewise young criminals grew, and many older ones shrank, creating wild ranges of numbers and preventing any conclusive identification. Matching measurements on file became increasingly difficult, and a number of people were wrongly identified. Thereafter, questions of accuracy and misidentification made the

Early identification photos. Image courtesy of Musée de la Préfecture de Police, Paris.

Learning the Bertillonage method with overhead images of mug shots. Image courtesy of Musée de la Préfecture de Police. Paris, France.

rounds among police and prison wardens, most often in cases where prisoner's names and measurements were closely matched (McClaughry 1922).

Due to the amount of time and expense in performing Bertillon's measurements, combined with the degree of inconsistency and defective measuring devices, police eventually abandoned the method. Though the basic elements were maintained like the inventory of features and brief descriptions of the criminal, the comprehensive set of measurements was taken over by a simple set of photographs. Thus, out of Bertillon's vast archived system emerged the concept of the rogue's gallery and what has come to be known as the mug shot (see chapter 3).

The Bertillon system was used for at least thirty years and was eventually replaced by a new and consistent method of measuring variations within a population. The relatively new science of fingerprinting had begun to emerge about the same time the Bertillon system was fully integrated (see chapter 7).

In 1904, Sergeant John Kenneth Ferrier, who worked for the fingerprint branch of Scotland Yard, was at the World's Fair in St. Louis, Missouri, assigned to guard the British Crown jewels. He was a fervent believer in fingerprinting as the new form of measurement and he rallied police who

Another one of Bertillon's contributions in the late 1800s was the use of photography to document the contents of a crime scene. He devised a method whereby a camera was mounted onto the top of a tripod and used to photograph victims of homicide, and other forms of physical evidence, as 'proof' that a crime had been committed. He also developed metric photography which used wire grids to highlight the dimensions of an object within a particular space. Images courtesy of Musée de la Préfecture de Police. Paris, France.

attended the World's Fair to formally instruct those who were interested in learning. Once again, ever eager to learn new methods of identification for his prison, Warden McClaughry met with Ferrier and ultimately appealed for fingerprinting to be the official identification system at his prison in Joliet (see Hambridge 1909).

Though fingerprinting was used sporadically in Canada and the United States at this time, Ferrier is considered to be the first fingerprint instructor in the United States. Many of the people he trained went on to train others in this new science of measurement (see chapter 7). The ease and process of rolling fingers and thumbs produced a readily identifiable mark of a person's uniqueness, officially putting an end to the use of the Bertillon system.

Edmond Locard

Where Lombroso and the school of criminal anthropology had a direct bearing on Bertillon, Lacassagne's school in Lyon directly influenced his young assistant, a medical doctor by the name of Edmond Locard (1877–1966).

As Lacassagne's assistant in Lyon, Locard slowly developed a methodology for examining cause of death and any associated physical evidence. Encouraged to study law alongside his medical work, he acquired a law degree by 1907 and began to surround himself with newly established identification systems and various legal cases.

Locard's research and work in the areas of death, injury, and criminal investigation were part of a rising trend in legal medicine whereby many physicians, statisticians, anthropologists, and mathematicians created and contributed various forms of classification and identification. The late 1800s and early 1900s saw the establishment, for example, of fingerprinting methods by noted physician Dr. Henry Faulds (1880) and statistician Francis Galton in 1892; a blood grouping system by Austrian biologist Karl Landsteiner in 1901; a postmortem (autopsy) methodology by pathologist Karl Rokitansky (1850s); and the categorization of bullet striations by chemist Paul Jesrich (1898) and more comprehensively by Dr. Victor Balthazard (1912). Many such advances formed the basis of what was referred to as *criminalistics,* the science of solving crime. Much later (by the 1970s) it came to be known as the field of forensic science.

What differentiated Locard from many of the more prominent scientists and doctors of his time was his vision and approach to crime solving. Traveling around Europe and North America in the early 1900s, and even stepping in on Bertillon in Paris, Locard experienced firsthand the advantages of cooperating with a variety of experts and applying various identification systems, along with a microscope, to criminal cases.

Arriving back in Lyon by 1910, and armed with a more coherent methodology and structure, Locard took the next step that would establish his name in history. (See Locard's Dust, page 34.)

Hans Gross, ca. late 1800s

The Rise of the Criminalists

Hans Gross

While physicians and scientists were busy establishing advanced measurement and classification systems for use in solving crimes, and the police were happily engaged in assisting them, the legal profession was playing catch-up. Though individual scientists and lawyers did work together on specific cases, there was no formal cooperation between the professions.

Throughout the late 1800s and early 1900s there existed a mutual distrust between science and the justice system derived largely from the rapid pace of advances in science and the legal profession's lag in accepting and understanding these advances. Likewise, scientists considered it beneath them to appear in court to present years of their research findings only to be challenged by nonscientists. In fact, most "preferred to offer only their conclusions in curt reports and ultimate opinions" (Cleary 1972, 524).

Despite the trend, some legal experts, jurists, and professors of law encouraged an interaction between scientists and lawyers. They recognized the pivotal role that a scientific methodology could have in determining legal outcomes.

Some recognition of "science in service of the law" began to circulate in European courthouses and magistrates' offices by 1898. Hans Gross (1847–1915), an Austrian professor of criminal law, published a handbook that year titled *Handbuch fur Untersuchungsrichter als System der Kriminalistik* (Handbook for Examining Magistrates as a System of Criminology), which detailed among other things the need for legal investigators, lawyers, and jurists to understand the scientific study of crime or, as he coined it, "*criminalistics.*"

Microscope, nineteenth century.

Integrating this relatively new area of study into the justice system according to Gross was the only way of ridding the legal system of "bias and misunderstanding": "We must agree that to establish scientifically the principles of our discipline alone is not sufficient. If we are to make progress, the daily routine also must be scientifically administered. Every sentence, every investigation, every official act must satisfy the same demand as that of the entire juristic science" (Gross 1898; see also Gross 1909, 328).

The model of criminalistics as a subfield of legal medicine became a feasible concept after Gross's publication. Whether one was a chemist, a physician, an anthropologist, or a mathematician, one could be considered a *criminalist* if one was involved with or conducting scientific studies to help solve a crime.

In many ways Gross unknowingly but officially unified the use of scientific inquiry for the legal profession (now known as forensic science) at a time when there was no such recognition. Most important, he promoted a systematic approach over the use of intuition and uninformed experience (Turvey 2008, 25).

Nineteenth Century Microscopy

As stated, there were a lot of advances and contributions in many areas of science throughout the 1800s, and the new field of criminalistics reflected this in its broad variety of disciplines. Primarily the field was determined and limited by one's ability with a microscope, a novelty item at the time but with much practical use.

Throughout his book, Hans Gross discussed the microscope as a vital tool for crime solving, describing cases where it had been used successfully. In so doing he encouraged a wary justice system to keep up with the latest

Using a microscope to analyze firearms ca. 1940s. Image courtesy of Buffalo Police Dept. Crime Scene Unit.

advances in its use, and work cooperatively to understand how it could solve a crime.

At the time of Gross's nineteenth century publication, the field of criminalistics was based largely on what could be observed under a microscope, for example, fingerprints, toolmarks, shoeprints, soil composition, fibers, glass, paint, serial numbers, some chemicals, bloodstains, inks, documents, explosives, certain poisons, and biological fluids like semen and urine.

Criminalists with good lighting and the best equipment (as in a medical microscope) had the advantage and a steady stream of work. However, physicians and chemists were restricted to the use of their own private lab or office to examine evidence. At the time there was no central lab or building where experts could gather together to extract and look at a variety of items. Rather, police and investigators had to move evidence to various locations for different types of analyses, always with the risk of damaging or losing evidentiary material altogether. A combination of a crime wave and a few available rooms would eventually solve this problem.

Locard's Dust

By the turn of the century, a good decade before World War I, France was experiencing what would be described as a "social crisis" (see Smith

1999; Caplan and Torpey 2001). Violent murders occurred across the countryside; thievery and "vagabondage" were creating turmoil in both urban and rural areas. The newspapers expressed a level of hysteria and writers for the abundance of criminal journals seized on high-profile cases to demonstrate the downfall of French society.

Responding to a crime wave in Lyon, Locard persuaded the police prefecture to let him use two empty attic rooms above the law courts. By 1910, he moved into the tiny space armed with a medical microscope, a spectroscope (an optical instrument with a prism) and two assistants. He was immediately challenged by the Lyon police to take on one of their most difficult cases.

Though Locard was a physician, his primary interest increasingly turned to extracting and analyzing trace evidence then referred to simply as "dust." The illustrious German chemist Justus von Liebig (1803–1873) had greatly influenced Locard through his own research in organic chemistry, as well as physician George Vuillemin of France, who had written his thesis on dust from the "medico-legal point of view" (see Locard 1930). George Popp (1867–1928), another German chemist, was solving arson-related cases in the late 1800s looking at soil samples and ash under his microscope. The concept of trace evidence and its direct link to crime solving was fast becoming the foundation of the newly emerging field of forensic science.

Throughout the early part of the twentieth century, Locard studied "all things" contained in dust. He tweezed out fibers, turned out pockets, scraped fingernails, and even examined earwax (comparing millers' earwax with coal miners' earwax, for example). He identified and catalogued hundreds of particles found in the build-up of daily life, claiming "the microscopic debris that covers our clothing and bodies are the mute witnesses, sure and faithful, of all our movements" (Locard 1930, 276).

Years of examining crime scenes, the bodies and clothing of victims, perpetrators, and dead soldiers during World War I in the context of collecting their microscopic debris led him to establish the exchange principle named after him (see Locard's Exchange Principle). The principle was based on his claim that "it is impossible for the law breaker to act without leaving traces of having been on the scene. These traces are extremely diverse" (Locard 1939, 126).

When any two objects come into contact there is always a transference of material from each object onto another.

Locard's Exchange Principle

Cynical about what mere dust could determine, the police largely ignored Locard, occasionally peering in while he beat clothing and examined its contents under the microscope. He explained and wrote copiously on the topic that "dust taken from the clothing of an individual can indicate what the person was doing prior to the crime" (Locard 1939, 4).

A young Locard tweezing out fibers from a hat in the early 1900s. Courtesy of Institut de Médecine Légale. Lyon, France.

To demonstrate his theory, he requested the clothing of a group of suspects in a counterfeiting ring. Police were stumped, and the suspects refused to talk. Back at his attic lab, Locard shook their individual clothes in separate bags, turned out jacket pockets, and tweezed samples from their shirtsleeves and cuffs. Under the microscope he found the presence of tin, lead, and antimony in all of their clothing, the exact components of the coins they were accused of counterfeiting. When presented with Locard's array of trace evidence contained in little paper packets, the group immediately confessed, and the police were suddenly curious (see also Ruffell and McKinley 2008).

Trace Evidence and the Case of Marie Latelle

In 1912, the Lyon police brought the case of a young woman named Marie Latelle to Locard for assistance. They wondered what dust could determine about her death. She was found dead in her parent's home in a state of rigor mortis (see chapter 6), indicating she had been dead well before midnight the previous night. Her boyfriend, a bank clerk named Emile Gourbin, claimed he had been at a friend's house miles away playing cards until well after midnight. His friends confirmed this, insisting he could not have done such a horrendous thing and in such a short period of time.

Locard examined Latelle's body at the morgue, noting the strangulation marks on her neck and bruising around the head and face. He ventured over to the prison across the street from his attic lab and scraped the fingernails of Gourbin, who was being held as a suspect. Locard returned to his lab with the small packet of scrapings.

The search for trace evidence that Locard was perfecting entailed the examination of very small amounts of substances in human crevices, hair, and clothing. Based on his theory, these substances would need to be identified and compared to their sources of origin. Doing so would establish a link between the crime scene, the criminal (suspect to scene), and the victim (Locard 1939).

In the case of the young Marie Latelle, this involved a trace amount of skin cells and clinging to them a pink dust made up of magnesium stearate, zinc oxide, rice starch, bismuth, and an iron oxide pigment known as Venetian red—all identified in Gourbin's fingernail scrapings. Locard also happened to be a great fan of the theater and knew that the mix of such pink dust was a type of cosmetic (see Wagner 2006, 149).

Requesting a search of Latelle's room, the police returned with a jar of cosmetic powder, which matched the combination of substances under Gourbin's nails. Locard also contacted a local druggist who had mixed the batch for Latelle.

As in the previous case, when faced with a bizarre array of little packets of evidence, the suspect confessed to having strangled his girlfriend in a fit of rage. To his shocked friends, he admitted turning forward the hands of the clock to fool them into thinking he had stayed later than he actually had.

The end of the Latelle case marked the beginning of the Locardian lab. In 1912, the Lyon police bureau officially recognized his little attic space, and as it grew in size and scope, a protocol to submit all physical evidence was carried out. With increased space, Locard invited scientists from other disciplines, such as biology, chemistry, and toxicology, to analyze a range of materials, share resources, and reconstruct crime scenes. Locard's lab was soon internationally renowned for its cohesive strategy and subsequently became the model for police and crime labs around the world.

> *To write the history of identification is to write the history of criminology.*
>
> **Locard, 1931**

The Crime Lab

Dr. Wilfrid Derome

The success of Locard's crime laboratory led to the establishment of many others throughout Europe during the early twentieth century (Spitz 1993, 8). In North America, Montreal was the first to establish a criminalistics laboratory in 1914 following the Locard model. The early lab was run by physician Dr. Wilfrid Derome (1877–1931), who had attended Locard's lectures in Paris and had studied the works of Bertillon and Balthazard.

Dr. Wilfrid Derome, early 1900s.

Based on his experiences in Paris combined with a degree in legal medicine, Derome pursued the Locardian concept of a lab (for the police) with the latest microscopy equipment and assistants. Like his predecessor, he understood the merits of specialists analyzing evidence in one place. The lab earned an enviable reputation in North America staffed with "dedicated and competent" individuals who were known for accepting difficult casework (Côté 2003).

Since it was a medico-legal lab, a subspecialty of medicine, doctors supervised by Derome analyzed the presence of poisons, bloodstains, knife and gunshot wounds, and the increasingly popular science of fingerprints for criminal investigations. The lab's motto was to "refrain from assertions you cannot prove" and with its share of high-profile crimes, word of its structure traveled across North America, bringing visitors and journalists from afar (Côté 2003).

The success of the Montreal lab (officially named Laboratoire de Sciences Judiciaires et de Médecine Légale) inspired the first such laboratory in the United States in Los Angeles in 1923 by the L.A. Sheriff's Department. Soon after, the newly established Federal Bureau of Investigation set up a crime laboratory in 1932 after J. Edgar Hoover (the first director of the FBI) visited Derome's Lab in Montreal. Unlike the Locard lab in France, however, contributions from areas of science like biology, chemistry, and physics were minimal at this time. It was well into the mid-twentieth century before crime labs in North America grew in size and scope.

The Full-Service Crime Lab

The modern full-service crime laboratory, now more commonly referred to as a *forensics lab*, has evolved quite substantially since the two-room attic. The medico-legal structure is no longer the predominant

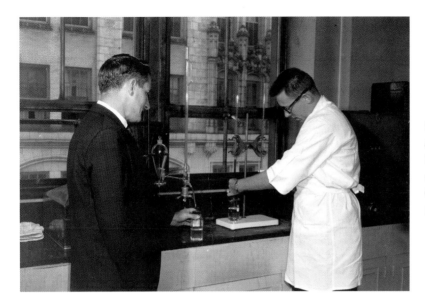

Science and the law in an early criminalistics lab, ca. 1950s. Courtesy of the Buffalo Police Dept. Crime Scene Unit.

standard as scientists in areas of physics, chemistry, toxicology, biology, and electronics have replaced the good doctor and his microscope.

As illustrated in chapter 1, a full-service crime lab consists of the following departments: pathology, toxicology, biology, firearms examination, questioned documents, photo analysis, electronics, and chemistry.

Police labs are also referred to as crime labs but are often smaller units depending on their proximity to full-service laboratories. Many maintain some of the more traditional criminalistic services, like fingerprint collection and identification, as well as toolmark-footwear analysis and tire track examination (see chapters 7 and 8).

More recently larger police forces have established *forensic identification units* that take on the exclusive task of crime scene management, that is, collecting, analyzing, interpreting, and documenting a range of physical evidence. Once the domain of the detective or civilian field personnel, with the bulk of evidentiary material housed in state or provincial crime labs, the forensic identification unit further establishes the uniformed police officer's role and presence throughout the preliminary investigation.

Crime laboratories in the United States and Canada that are without these facilities, and police stations in more remote parts of the country, often send evidentiary materials to regional crime laboratories or to major labs such as the RCMP crime lab in Ottawa or the FBI Criminalistics Laboratory in Washington, D.C.

Presently, the structure of crime laboratories in the United States varies considerably from state to state. Technically, crime labs are under the jurisdiction of the state's law enforcement agency or a federal agency. But there are privately run laboratories that provide a variety of services, as well as labs operating in universities, public defender's and prosecutor's offices, as well as in hospitals and private clinics.

Using laser lighting to highlight fingerprint evidence on a tin can.

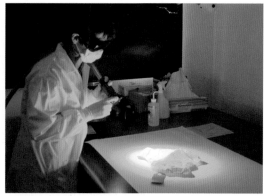

Using an alternate light source to examine biological evidence not visible in ambient lighting.

Police Crime Lab

A forensic anthropologist examining human remains.

In an effort to keep track of advances in the field and establish appropriate standards for crime laboratories across the United States, practicing forensic specialists from around the country formed various organizations and committees. By the early 1980s for example, FBI Director Clarence Kelley and Laboratory Director Briggs White organized a group of forensic lab personnel that became known as the American Society of Crime Laboratory Directors, which was soon followed by the American Board of Criminalistics.

Crime laboratories that wish to be accredited (legally recognized when certain standards are met) must submit to extensive reviews and examinations by these organizations. The credentials of their personnel, their administrative practices, their use of evidence controls, and the type of examination methods employed are some of the key areas reviewed for accreditation. However, in the United States, this process is voluntary because crime labs do not have to be certified to be operational (see the National Institute of Standards and Technology Handbook 1998).

Chapter 3

At the Scene
of the Crime

I: The Crime Scene

Crime

The word *crime* is defined as an act punishable by law. The Latin word is *crimen,* meaning an offense or charge. As such, a crime scene can be defined as any place where an act has taken place that is contrary to law.

Physically a crime scene can be anywhere and may be as large as a park, house, or business, to something as inconspicuous as a computer or the corner of a room. It can also include large-scale disasters, terrorist violence, aircraft or train crashes, explosions, mass murders, and other violent incidents on a large-scale.

Crime scenes are spaces requiring control, maintenance, and documentation because they are assumed to yield physical evidence. Locard's exchange principle (see chapter 2) is the one constant that applies to every crime scene. A crime scene must therefore be excluded from public access until it has been thoroughly processed.

The immediate area where the crime took place, as in the room where the homicide occurred, the street where the abduction took place, the alley where the assault began, is considered the *hot zone*. This area determines and designates other possible sites to search, investigate, and collect evidence.

Special attention is paid to all adjacent areas called *warm zones* surrounding the hot zone, which may turn up more evidence and often point to other possible crime scenes, for example, if the kidnapping took place at one location, the victim was killed at another site, and then was buried or dumped in yet another. Hence the scene of the crime not only defines where the criminal act took place, it often determines where else to search.

The Role of the First Responder

Duties of emergency first responders vary in complexity and are continuously evolving. Government policy, often influenced by societal de-

The primary or hot zone at crime scenes before barricading. Courtesy of Toronto Police Forensic Identification Services.

mands, dictates the roles and responsibilities that each branch of their emergency services are assigned. It is important to consider that the content of this section provides a general overview and a best practice approach. It is not intended to override policies instilled by individual agencies.

Many jurisdictions rely on a "three-tiered response" to emergency calls for service. This term refers to the dispatching of all three branches of emergency response, including Police Departments, Emergency Medical Services (EMS), and Fire Departments. It is imperative that all three of these agencies react in sync with one another. Attending personnel from each of these organizations has specific knowledge, skills, and abilities to effectively aid in situations of emergency but must be aware of their own limitations and respectful of the specialty training others may have to offer.

Although police, EMS, and firefighters are regularly dispatched to emergency medical and other types of calls, not all of these requests for service relate specifically to crime scene attendance. Regardless of the initial details being provided by witnesses, dispatchers, or 911 call receivers, all incidences could potentially have a *criminal origin* and therefore should be approached as criminal investigations. This approach can be modified or downscaled as further information becomes known. Common sense remains the best filter for ensuring that the integrity of a crime scene is maintained.

The safety and physical well-being of officers and other individuals at or near the scene are the responsibility of the initial officer and should be the first priority. The first officer arriving on scene identifies and initiates the appropriate response to dangerous situations or persons.

Once the scene has been deemed safe, the next priority for all responders is the preservation of life. Providing first aid to victims and suspects suffering life-threatening or grievous injuries must be attempted, even at the expense of potentially degrading, contaminating, or destroying evidence. Preservation of evidence and crime scene examination practices remain secondary considerations in these instances. This is not to minimize their importance or suggest that personnel ignore these topics, but it is a reality that the scene often changes between the time of the incident and when it is later documented by forensic investigators.

Where possible, responders should avoid altering the scene. This aside, the initial response to any incident must be effective, efficient, and methodical. Police officers receive instruction on crime scene preservation as part of their training, the degree of which varies from one department to another. Other first responders may not have received any formal training in crime scene management, so it is incumbent on police to take the lead role. If the scene is altered or damaged by responders prior to being documented by forensic investigators, it is crucial that those involved note what they have changed as they may be expected to articulate what they have done later in the investigation or in court proceedings.

Altered Scenes

It does not pose a problem when a possible crime scene is altered, providing a reasonable explanation exists to justify it. Examples of these alterations may include:

- damage caused to gain entry.
- items being relocated within the scene to facilitate medical treatment to the victim and/or suspect.
- damage resulting from suspect apprehension.
- environmental effects like rain, snow, and wind.
- time lapse prior to determination that a crime has taken place.

The acronym LOSER may assist in formulating a decisive and practical approach to scene management:

Listen to victims and/or witnesses.

Observe the scene and surroundings—including the approach.

Search for potential victims, suspects, witnesses, and physical evidence.

Evaluate the scene and information obtained—does it add up?

Record information in a memorandum or casebook.

A common error made by first responders is the desire to race to the incident without following these simple guidelines while en route. Crime scene management begins long before arrival at the scene. Valuable information could be overlooked or compromised if officers are not prepared and observant.

Procedures to Consider

- Officers should respond promptly while exercising extreme caution on the approach and entry to the crime scene.
- Remain observant of any person(s), vehicle(s), potential evidence, environmental conditions, and other events in the surrounding area.
- Note or log all dispatcher information (address/ location, time, date, type of call, parties involved).
- Be aware of any persons or vehicles at or leaving the scene.
- Scan the entire area thoroughly to access the scene, making note of any possible secondary crime scene(s).
- Make initial observations (look, listen, smell) to properly assess the scene.
- Ensure officer and/or victim safety before proceeding.
- Ensure there are no immediate threats to other units responding.
- Remain alert and pay attention; assume the crime is ongoing until you determine otherwise.
- Treat the location as a crime scene until it has been determined otherwise.
- Scan the area for sights, sounds, or smells that may present a danger. For incidents such as clandestine drug labs or those of a chemical, biological, radiological, or nuclear (CBRN) nature, notify the appropriate unit or agency immediately and proceed cautiously.
- Approach all scenes in a manner that will reduce the risk of harm to the first responder and other officers, while maximizing the safety of potential victims, witnesses, and others in the area.
- Survey the scene for dangerous persons and take control of the situation.
- Notify and update supervisory or investigative personnel and call for assistance or backup as required.

Securing the Scene

Determining the parameters of a crime scene is often difficult. When descriptors of the incident are not readily available, officers may be required to estimate the breadth of the crime scene with little or no input or understanding. In cases such as this, it is highly recommended to oversize the scene perimeter to minimize contamination or degradation. The scene can be reduced later as further information is received, however, it is far more problematic to enlarge. Generally, there is only one opportunity to do this right, so it must be done correctly from the beginning.

Securing the scene is necessary to maintain control of events that follow the incident and to ensure its integrity is preserved. Further examination of the scene and its contents may be conducted by *forensic investigators* (see below). Where and whenever possible, identify primary and secondary security zones.

The term *primary* or *hot zone* implies the area of greatest investigative interest. This area is most often where the actual event unfolded and where physical and trace evidence is most likely to be compromised by the presence of nonforensic personnel.

The *secondary* or *warm zone* identifies the larger perimeter surrounding the primary zone and is generally where police line tape is used as a barrier to signify the crime scene perimeter.

These two distinct zones enable police to maintain order and keep unwanted public and media out while protecting the area of interest for forensic investigators to properly conduct their work. Continuity or chain of custody of evidence must be maintained and proven in court for a successful prosecution. As a result, scene security is of utmost importance. Failure to maintain a sufficient level of security may potentially minimize or eliminate the evidentiary value of anything found in or related to the scene.

There are several means available to maintain security of the scene or evidence; the more commonly accepted are as follows.

- Physical presence: police officers guarding the scene.
- Police line-tape: barricading perimeter.
- Police or evidence tamper-proof security seals: placed on or around physical evidence.
- Locks or barriers: preventing public access, theft, and unauthorized entry.
- Evidence logs: maintains a consistent record of all physical evidence.
- Tamper-proof property evidence bags or boxes: for transportation, protection, and storage.

Assigning a *scene security officer* to the access point of entry into the scene will prove useful. The officer only permits entry of persons authorized for admittance. All pertinent information is documented by the recording officer in a log or memorandum book including (but not limited to) who entered, when, why, and for how long.

Crime scenes, particularly those of a horrific nature, attract curious civilians, media, and other police officers. If entry is not required or authorized as part of the investigative process, these persons should not get in. Information of any person entering a crime scene, regardless of

Barricading a crime scene, first responder present.

Crime scene barricaded with evidence markers in place.

The perimeter of a crime scene encompassing both primary and secondary areas of interest.

the purpose, is subject to disclosure laws. That individual may be subpoenaed to court and ordered to testify as to the reason for being in the crime scene.

Rules for Protecting Evidence

The forensic principle of crime scene examination has evolved from the initial research conducted by French criminalist Edmond Locard (see

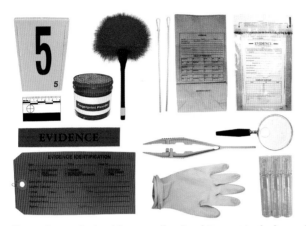

Above: **A practical evidence collection kit must include a ruler, a variety of containers and bags, tags, gloves, swabs, evidence markers, and standard fingerprinting brush and powder.**

Right: **Delicate hair and fiber evidence marked and numbered at a crime scene.** Courtesy of Toronto Police Forensic Identification Services. All rights reserved.

chapter 2). As one of the early pioneers of forensic sciences, Locard developed a scientific approach to crime scene examination. The basis of the theory provides that every contact leaves a trace. When this is applied to crime scene examination, it suggests that a suspect leaves a trace of him or herself behind and takes something away from the scene when leaving. For forensic investigators, this principle is the basis for their job function, linking the suspect to the victim and/or the crime scene.

The old adage of "Keep your hands in your pockets and don't touch anything!" is no longer a viable methodology for crime scene management and evidence protection. At one time, this was the accepted instruction given by seasoned police officers to new recruits. The intent was to minimize contamination within the scene by following this simple rule. Although it has merit on some level, it is abysmally inadequate to maintain the integrity of a crime scene given current forensic technologies.

It is not, as a general rule, the responsibility for nonforensic personnel to collect and preserve physical and trace evidence. Crime scene examination should be left to trained forensic investigators.

Access to and from the scene should be by one route, or path of contamination, ideally a path least likely traveled by suspect and victim, and cleared of any potential evidence awaiting collection. Where practical, this path is used for all emergency response personnel to minimize further contamination to the scene.

Crime scenes must be vacated and secured pending arrival of the forensic team. However, there are exceptions to this practice, such as:

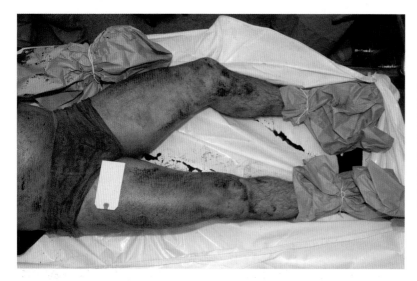

Hands and feet of homicide victim are bagged to protect and preserve trace evidence during transport.
Courtesy of Scott Collings, Hamilton Police Service. All rights reserved.

- safety: leaving the evidence in situ (in its original location) poses a danger or safety concern for responders and public, especially when a scene contains biohazardous materials.
- destruction or degradation of evidence: leaving the evidence in situ may result in it being compromised in some way (through environmental means, a suspect's deliberate action, mishaps during medical treatment to victim or suspect).
- public interest: scenes in open view that may be disturbing or horrific in nature, some require closure out of respect for victim and his or her family.

It may be diligent to protect evidence pending the arrival of forensic personnel. As noted, environmental challenges are common at outdoor scenes. Fingerprint, footwear, and tiretrack impressions, as well as DNA evidence, are particularly susceptible to the environment. Rain, snow, wind, extreme temperature, and ultraviolet rays can quickly and effectively destroy, degrade, or in some way compromise these and other forms of evidence.

Protecting evidence may require creative thinking. Whatever means appropriate to ensure the evidence is left intact may be used. Containers or covers must be new or in clean condition and least likely to add foreign objects, materials, or sources of DNA to the exhibit. Items should be handled in ways least likely handled by the suspect or victim.

When evidence is to be moved or the scene altered in some way, these changes must be documented to assist the forensic team in re-creating the events. Once an item has been relocated, the responsibility of describing its origin rests on the person who moved it; this will be beneficial to attending forensic officers and later during court proceedings. The court will expect the involved officer to describe the moved item, how it was handled, and why moving it was necessary.

Extensive note-taking is just as crucial as photography for documenting crime scenes prior to evidence collection. Image courtesy of Her Majesty the Queen in Right of Canada as represented by the Royal Canadian Mounted Police. © 2009. All rights reserved.

Before entry into a scene and/or the seizure of evidence is contemplated, consideration must be given to what legal authority supports the action. Local, state/provincial, or federal laws may vary from one jurisdiction to another. Failure to comply with arrest and search and seizure legislation may result in the exclusion of evidence and/or an unsuccessful prosecution in court.

II: Documenting the Scene

Police Photography

The importance of visually documenting physical evidence found at crime scenes, processed in labs, or in the identification of criminals cannot be emphasized enough. In fact without photography, most physical evidence, including fingerprints would not be visible to the naked eye or exist for presentation in court.

It can definitely be said that photography evolved alongside the police; both were firmly established by the 1800s and many of the innovations in photography were first adopted by police for illustrating crime and identifying criminals. In this way, photography continues to be the cornerstone of every police and forensic investigation.

Historically, police took photographs primarily to understand, pursue, and depict criminals. When photography was finally implemented to document crime scenes, in the early 1920s, police took very few pictures of the crime scene, and then only to prove the presence of a body, and portray the onset of an autopsy. The overall emphasis of police photography remained on portraying criminal types.

Fragile physical evidence marked and photographed in situ.

It was not until the 1960s that many rolls of film were taken for major scenes. The film (black and white and, by the 1970s, color) required processing in a darkroom, immersion in a series of chemical baths, followed by washing and drying, before any preliminary viewing of the results could be made. After drying, the film would be printed on photographic paper, which also required immersion in a series of chemical solutions, washing, and drying, before any final assessment.

Color film required a sophisticated, complex, and expensive system to transform unexposed film to final print. This system was extremely sensitive to temperature and chemistry quality and costly to maintain.

Police photographer with camera and a light meter photographing a fingerprint chart, ca. 1940s. Image courtesy of the Ontario Provincial Police. All rights reserved.

For many decades, film, chemistry, and darkroom equipment represented significant ongoing expenses as well as serious storage issues, which rose commensurately with the volume of photographs taken.

Today police agencies use a variety of equipment for documenting crime scenes, photographing evidence, and detailing injuries and wounds, as well as looking for and booking criminals. The current trend is for police photographers to use a digital camera, a 35-mm single lens reflex (SLR) camera, and a digital camcorder. Unlike its film counterpart, a

Police photographer documenting body found in canal, ca. 1940s. Image courtesy of the Ontario Provincial Police. All rights reserved.

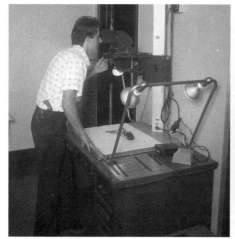

Photographing evidence, 1970s.   **Developing photographs in a police darkroom, ca. 1970s.**

forensic photographer knows within seconds if the image is satisfactory and can begin to use it in the time it takes to transfer the digital file to a computer. Furthermore, using digital photography entirely eliminates the need for darkrooms.

Because digital photographs are computer files, they need only be printed if and when they are required. While high-volume digital file storage presents other challenges, the physical storage requirements are not nearly as great, and they can be archived and searched more easily.

Right: **Photographing exhibits.**

Below: **A 35mm single lens reflex (SLR) camera.**

The change from 35-mm film to digital has been an epic shift in police photography. It has radically altered the ways in which photographs are taken, processed, and filed. As well, the volume and storage capacities have sizably increased, with immediate results available for viewing and downloading. Where once hand-developed images took many days to send out, they can now be sent to computer-equipped police cars, offices, media, boats, and other police agencies across the world in seconds.

As the cornerstone of all police and forensic investigations, police photography is still pivotal in capturing actions and events in time. However, it is no longer the single cop with a camera at a crime scene. Today the types of police photography range from surveillance photography, aerial photography, and crime scene photography to laboratory imaging and criminal identification. These are all highlighted in the following discussions.

Surveillance Photography

Surveillance photography is the act of establishing the identity and behavior of suspects. It also serves to provide evidence for a search warrant and ideally document crimes in the act of commission. In this way, surveillance photography has identified many arson suspects, captured images for terrorist investigations, caught many people disposing of murder weapons, and some in the act of crimes they later vehemently denied.

Due to the invasive nature of this type of photography, and because most of it is covert, little room can be left for error. Images of the suspect's facial and body features as well as their behavior must be made visible. All street locations, addresses, and other identifiers such as buildings, parking lots, car tags, and the like must also be clearly captured.

To ensure that surveillance is thorough and comparative, police often employ still images taken with a digital (SLR camera) along with footage from a digital camcorder.

Surveillance photography.

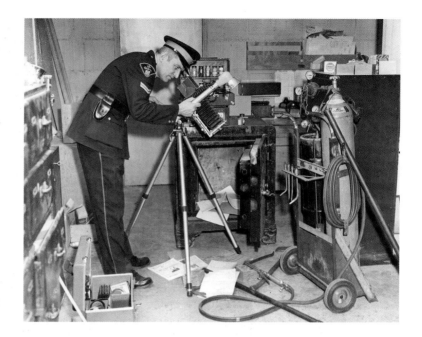

At the scene of the crime. Photographing evidence after a safe has been cracked, ca. 1940s. Image courtesy of the Ontario Provincial Police.

Crime Scene Photography

Any individual who has processed a crime scene knows that photography is one of the most critical functions. At all death and crime scenes, photography serves to capture the scope of the site, the focal point of the scene, and all associated physical and material evidence found and subsequently taken from it.

Crime scene photography is also a photo narrative with important references to context. Though the crime scene is the focal point, the surrounding area and the physical environment are as important. Good police photography aims to tell the whole story; it highlights all entrances and exits to the scene, captures physical evidence in situ and presents a range of images that describe the physical environment of and surrounding the scene (piled-up newspapers, disarray, presence of pets, orderliness, etc.).

Hundreds of images are often taken of the overall scene, along with detailed photos of individual areas, and evidence such as footprints, fingerprints, wound details, and trace items. This lengthy process is vital in recording and documenting the scene before it's dismantled. Video recordings are usually made to accompany these images.

At death scenes, the body is photographed from many angles along with close-up (micro) images of any wounds or injuries that may range from bullet holes, slashes, contusions, and dismemberment to bite wounds and ligature marks. These often shocking photographs should only be displayed when they can be shown to be relevant to the facts of the case. An exception, however, is when the prosecution wants to illustrate to a jury how heinous a crime was.

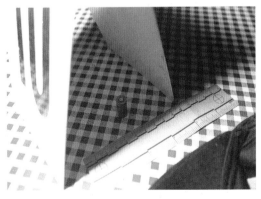 

Police crime scene photography aims to tell a whole story; it highlights all entrances and exits to the scene, captures physical evidence in situ, and attempts to describe the physical environment.

Photographs, most especially of vicious crimes and injuries to people, shock juries and sway verdicts, and there are often many objections to their use in court. They must therefore be shown to be relevant to the charge, and the photographer must be able to testify that the photograph was not altered or manipulated in any way; moreover, that the images or footage are accurate representations of the victim and/or scene.

In the age of digital photographs, which can easily be altered, proving an image was not manipulated hinges on how the images are taken and stored. To deal with this issue, photography sections in all police departments archive images as RAW files (the camera creates a header file which contains all of the camera settings, including sharpening level, contrast, and saturation settings, color temperature/white balance, and so on). The file holds exactly what the imaging chip recorded. An image captured in RAW format cannot be altered in any way and is subsequently saved under the same file name. Furthermore, a RAW file carries embedded information, including the time and date of capture.

Aerial Photography

➘ Any photograph that is taken with a camera not situated on ground level is considered to be aerial. Images taken with cameras on rooftops, ladders, raised platforms, balconies, and office tower windows or fixed to airplanes and helicopters are all considered aerial photographs. Police also have access to miniaturized, remotely controlled aircraft ranging from the simplest of model planes to sophisticated drones that are equipped with digital cameras.

Aerial photography is ideal for outdoor areas that are extensive and large indoor areas where an overhead view is important. These images provide good coverage for gathering data with an overview of the crime scene and its surroundings. Surveillance and crime scene photographs can include aerial photographs for these reasons.

Aerial photograph of intersection.

Laboratory Photography

With all of the technological advances and sophisticated processing systems in forensic science, none would be of any use if it were not for the highly specialized images resulting from laboratory photography. Photographs produced in the forensic lab are the sought-after images that propel a case forward, influence juries, and create the weight of physical evidence. The few strands of DNA that identify the culprit, the invisible microfiber teased out of a victim's sweater, the subtle striations along the case of a bullet are some of the most powerful images presented in court.

⌐Though not the realm of police photography per se, lab photography (or photo analysis) works closely with police agencies to provide images of any physical evidence for trial purposes. Forensic labs primarily use a camera and a microscope along with infrared, ultraviolet, x-ray, or laser radiation to highlight all the details of an object or structure that would normally be invisible to the naked eye.

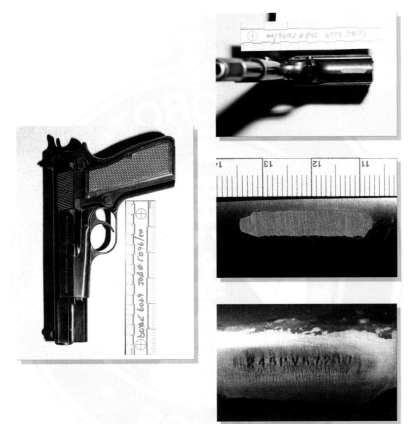

Lab photography highlighting the details on a gun that has its serial number reconstructed, presented as a jury exhibit.

Impression Photography

Photography of scenes, involving overall, midrange, and close up recordings of crime scenes are different in nature from the capture of impression evidence. Images of latent fingerprints, footwear impressions, tool marks and blood pattern will ultimately be carefully analyzed and compared to known standards, and in the case of fingerprints, searched in large digital databases. Such images must possess a range of attributes in order to meet the standards required for material evidence. These attributes are as follows:

- The impression must fill the frame, taking full advantage of the camera's resolution.
- A scale must be included so that the image may be accurately calibrated.
- The subject, scale, and image planes must be parallel.
- The subject must be in sharp focus and correctly exposed.
- The area of interest must be evenly illuminated.

Images of impressions like fingerprints and shoeprints will be meticulously scrutinized in great detail, seeking either agreement or dissimilarity with known standards. These impressions are frequently challenging, with detail of limited extent and clarity. It is vitally important to the success of this process that all impression detail be recorded as clearly and completely as possible. Also, these images may be enlarged significantly and digitally optimized to facilitate the comparison process, and subjected to search in AFIS—Automated Fingerprint Identification System. For all these reasons, all detail in impression images must be recorded as accurately and faithfully as possible.

It is strongly recommended that impression images be recorded in camera RAW, for the following four reasons: First, the RAW file can be thought of as a digital "negative." The integrity of that record remains intact, because it cannot be resaved under the same file name if any changes have been made. Second, all of the subject detail received by the camera sensor (CCD or CMOS) is recorded, without the kind of editing that is completed when JPEG or TIFF format is used. Third, there is a significantly higher "bit depth," or brightness resolution in RAW than with TIFF or JPEG formats, for example. Data capture is 12 or 14 bit, which translates into thousands more levels of brightness. This is particularly vital when recording impressions with a compressed dynamic range (low contrast).

Fourth and last, the photographer controls what editing will be done in creating a TIFF image which may be subjected to optimizing procedures in Photoshop, or other editing software. This will simply result in the highest quality possible for that image.

Focus Stacking

Aperture Priority

There are two exposure controls on a camera—aperture and shutter speed. In other words, one controls the amount of light entering a camera by the size of the opening (aperture) and the other controls how long the opening stays open. Shutter speed is a critical control for photographers who record moving subjects, and wish to "freeze" them without motion blur, or must take hand-held photographs in low light situations. Forensic photographers are not usually required to record moving subjects, nor is there a need to hand-hold the camera. For this reason, aperture priority should be the preferred mode when determining exposure.

Although any camera lens includes a range of aperture (f-stop) options, each will result in different image properties. The largest opening will require the shortest shutter speed, but offers minimum depth of field, and maximize the effects of negative factors, such as chromatic aberration. Conversely, the smallest opening will allow diffraction to reduce image sharpness and resolution of fine detail. It must be said that these undesirable effects can be quite subtle, but there are several reasons why forensic photographers should strive for the best quality possible in their recordings.

Scale and Calibration

Simple insertion of a scale in the field of view does not necessarily ensure the value of the recording. First, the scale must not obscure any other vital image information, including the identifying markings. As previously stated, it must be parallel to both the impression (fingerprint) and the image plane in the camera. Fingerprint images submitted for AFIS search are first calibrated to ensure that they are exactly the same size as the fingerprints in the database to which they will be compared. There are millions of minutia sets (coded fingerprints) in any such database and small errors in sizing, such as would be the result of a scale which was not positioned parallel to the fingerprint, could result in the miscoding of that impression. The search algorithm could then easily fail to place it on a list of possibilities for subsequent human comparison.

Chromatic Aberration

There are several optical aberrations in lenses that affect image quality. Lenses have different refractive indices for different wavelengths of light. Blue wavelengths are "bent" more than green, and green are bent more than red. This means that the lens cannot bring all wavelengths of light to focus on the same plain. The result can be a fringe of color at the transitions between light and dark areas of the subject. The effect becomes more extreme as the light enters further from the axis (center) of the lens, and is therefore partially mitigated by using only the central part of it. In fact, the effects of all lens aberrations are reduced by using only the central part of each element of a lens.

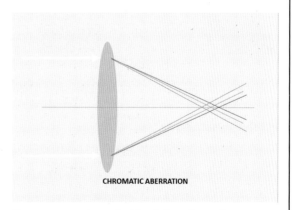

CHROMATIC ABERRATION

Component colors of white light refracted to different degrees.

Chromatic aberration—green and purple fringing can seen on transitions between light and dark areas of image. Shot wide open with a nikon d7000 camera and an af-s nikkor 50mm 1.8 lens.
(http://en.wikipedia.org/wiki/Chromatic_aberration)

Diffraction

Although stopping down will lessen the effects of aberrations and increase depth of field, there is a price to pay as the aperture size is reduced. Diffraction is the bending of light when it encounters an obstacle, in this case, the edge of the iris diaphragm which controls the aperture size in a camera. This disruption has a negative effect on image quality and sharpness, and as the aperture gets smaller, the disrupted light becomes a larger percentage of the light entering the camera. Fine detail is lost.

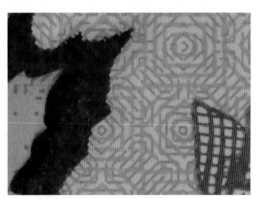

Aperture F-8   Aperture F-40

Detail of Canadian currency photographed with Nikon D90 Camera and Nikkor 60mm F2.8 lens.

The Sweet Spot

Professional photographers have long been aware that every lens has an aperture setting that optimizes image quality, by minimizing the effects of lens aberrations and diffraction, while offering an acceptable depth of field and acceptable shutter speed. This is something of a balancing act. Certainly, there will be no hesitation in using other reciprocal settings when the situation requires it but all other factors aside, professional photographers will have one aperture setting as the default choice for most images. Opinions among professionals vary, but it is generally agreed that this preferred aperture or "sweet spot" is in the range of 2 to 4 stops from wide open. The selection of this optimal aperture is particularly critical in impression photography.

Depth of Field

The concept of depth of field is illusionary. Light rays come to a point of intersection (focus) at one plane. The human eye cannot discern lack of sharpness in objects situated a short distance in front of or behind the plane of focus. This distance range in front of and behind the point of focus that appears to be in focus is known as depth of field. The depth of field is dependent on several factors:

- Focal length of lens — the shorter the focal length, the greater the depth of field
- Camera to subject distance — the greater camera-to-subject distance, the greater the depth of field
- Aperture — the smaller the aperture opening, the greater the depth of field

Shot at F-22

Focus-stacked at F-11

Thresholds

The process of finding latent fingermarks and bringing them to a final optimized condition for comparison or search in an AFIS system consists of a series of progressive, interdependent steps, the number and extent of which can vary considerably:

1. Detection
   a. Light
      i. Reflected
      ii. Fluorescent
   b. Physical techniques
      i. Powders
      ii. Suspensions
   c. Chemical techniques
      i. Stains
      ii. Fluorogenics

2. Photography

3. Digital optimization
   a. Grayscale conversion
   b. Contrast adjustment
   c. Noise reduction
   d. Pattern removal

All actions are conducted to comply with the Best Evidence dictum (see Chapter One). There are sound reasons for such compliance. Only by deriving the clearest image of a fingerprint destined for comparison or search can one ensure that an accurate evaluation and interpretation will be made.

Threshold situations (those for which there are not familiar, unambiguous, and/or exclusive choices) occur routinely at each of the steps outlined above. They are also found in other areas of forensic identification, requiring difficult but pivotal decisions to be made. At the straightforward end of the scale

Exemplar fingerprint with extensive clear and continuous detail.

Same fingerprint photographed by laser, with barrier and narrow band filters.

for example, procedures for processing a paper document are well established and documented, and the professional is trained to apply proven techniques used within his/her agency without uncertainty or hesitation. However, for other exhibits (composite items, those suspected of bearing blood transfer, water exposure, items requiring other forensic tests), the assessment path can be much less obvious, possibly requiring "either/or" processing decisions, and may depend on the practitioner's personal opinion as to the best likelihood for success in *each specific case*.

Threshold fingerprint impression of questionable comparison value.

Similarly, many fingermarks developed at crime scenes and on exhibits are of sufficient quality, clarity and extent that competent photography will suffice, with little or no adjustment in Photoshop or other image processing software. They are frequently comparison ready with no further adjustment necessary. Equally and inevitably, fragments and obscured impressions are revealed in the detection process. These are also unambiguous, quickly and easily designated as valuable only as indications of contact with friction skin and possibly touch DNA. In many cases, these impressions will not be photographed. In both extreme situations, a trained fingerprint professional will spend little time and have no difficulty in determining the potential worth of such impressions.

Threshold impressions, however, are not easily evaluated prior to photography. It is simply not always possible to visually determine with accuracy whether these impressions contain sufficient clear and continuous detail for evaluation, comparison and/or, search. In other words, it is sometimes necessary to take a photograph to determine if it is necessary to take a photograph! Impressions in this category are prime candidates for post-photography optimization.

Several decades of detecting and photographing friction skin evidence (in the film domain) and compilation of the unit statistics, has taught the writer to expect that approximately 10–15% of impression photographs recorded prove to be of no comparative value, comparable to difference between one's gross salary and the amount actually taken home. Digital recording of fingerprint evidence has reduced that percentage, attributable to the range of powerful, post-photography computer techniques that can be used to recover marginal impressions existing at the very brink of significance.

Silver Emulsions (Film)

With the use of film, a fingerprint photographer's skill and experience needed to be focused on actions up to the tripping of the shutter, including exposure, lighting strategy and focus. Little could be done to increase the amount or clarity of ridge detail (beyond contrast adjustment) in the darkroom. On viewing the negative, what you saw was quite literally what you got. The recording medium for fingerprints (and virtually everything else) for the 19th and 20th centuries was film, which consisted of a sheet of plastic with a layer of gelatin containing small crystals of light-sensitive compounds called silver halides. When the photograph was taken and the film developed, the crystals that were exposed to light formed the image on the film. When the shutter is opened to take a photograph, they are either exposed to light or not. Gray scale values in the finished print are dependent on the number and density of the exposed crystals. The eye sees a range of gray values between black and white, based on the concentration of the exposed halide crystals, a kind of grayscale pointillism, comparable to that seen in French Impressionist paintings. There is no "depth" to the analog data stored in this layer, no hidden information. The data are fixed and rigid, not amenable to meaningful optimization, beyond contrast adjustment.

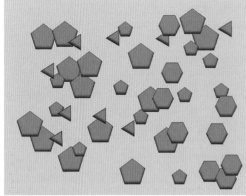

Silver halide grains in film emulsion.

After exposure to light some of the silver halide grains are activated, the rest are not.

The Impact of Digital Imaging

The digital revolution introduced dramatic changes to the world of forensic imaging. Suddenly, there were powerful techniques that could make tangible increases in the clarity and extent of fingerprint detail. The huge advantage offered by digital imaging lies in two key factors—***control and sensitivity***. The digital image is composed of rows and columns of what are essentially building blocks, each representing an area of the image. They are referred to as picture elements, "pixels" for short. Each pixel consists of digital information, including its address (location in the image) and the color/ grayscale values. Although the component pixels of the image are viewed in their entirety, each one is a separate entity from its neighbors.

The user has control over the display of the image data in much the same way we can control the way we view our email. Messages in an inbox are typically displayed ***chronologically***, showing the most recent message first, and the previous ones behind it going back in time, but we are not limited to this view. With a click of the mouse, the inbox contents can be displayed ***alphabetically***. This might be advantageous in quickly locating messages received from a specific sender. When that task is completed, another click of the mouse will return the display to the one most practical for daily use. It is important to note that in the display conversion, the component data were not changed in content, but simply arranged differently. This action exemplifies control over data that is simply not possible in the analog domain.

The sensors in CMOS chips (the image capture device in digital single lens reflex cameras) are arranged in rows and columns, comparable to the pixel grid in a digital image. Each is responsible for capturing the light information for a specific area of the image. The color mode typically used in forensic image capture is RGB (red, green, blue) and the preferred file format either RAW or TIFF, both uncompressed, lossless formats. The human eye is capable of discerning roughly 30–32 shades of gray. An 8-bit grayscale TIFF image has the potential to display up to 256 intensities of gray at each pixel. A 16-bit RAW image may contain up to 65,536 separate gray values. To the computer, each of these gray tones is a discrete and separate value, as different and distinct from each other as black is from white.

There are several other key differences between the human eye and the digital camera. The capture strategy of human vision is not quantitative, but comparative. For example, we cannot identify an image area we see as exactly 18% gray, but we can see that it is darker than the adjacent area. Also, we cannot file and store exact image data for effective retrieval at a later date, a function easily completed by a digital camera which in 24-bit RGB color mode can detect, capture, display and store up to 16.7 million colors, each one different and distinct from the others.

It is immediately apparent that a digital image may contain detail unseen by the viewer, detail that can be rendered visible using computer techniques. Much more is possible in the digital realm for recovering the full value of fingerprints that exist at the very threshold of significance because of **control** over each pixel in the image, and hugely extended **sensitivity** to grayscale.

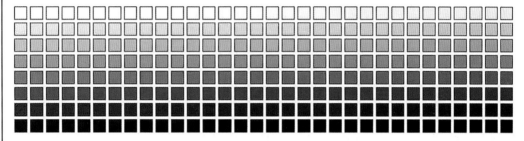

256 Tonal values possible in an 8-bitgrayscale image.

File Format

It is strongly recommended that a lossless uncompressed file format be used to record impression evidence. Recording in RAW provides both unsurpassed image quality and integrity. The example below shows a partial fingerprint in which the lighting is grossly uneven. It was captured simultaneously in RAW and JPEG. The JPEG image was opened in Photoshop and optimized to the degree possible. The RAW file (16 bit) was opened and adjustments were made, clearly illustrating the value of RAW as a recording file format.

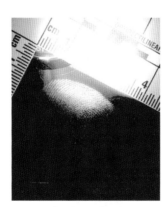
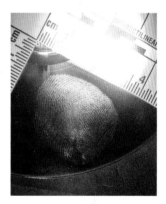

Fingerprint with significantly uneven lighting recorded simultaneously in RAW and JPEG.

Best attempt to correct lighting in JPEG image.

Lighting successfully corrected in RAW image.

Fast Fourier Transform (FFT)

FFT is a post-photography computer process that can reduce or eliminate repetitive patterns that obstruct fingerprint detail. It is often said that there is rarely, if ever, only one way to accomplish a task. Nonlinear thinking can often result in alternative roads to success. That said, the writer is aware of no other procedure, computer or otherwise, capable of removing repetitive patterns in a grayscale image as effectively as FFT. Routinely, fingerprint impressions are found and photographed on surfaces covered with repeating pattern elements—dots, parallel lines—which pose a serious obstruction to the evaluation and comparison of ridge detail. This computer program converts the data in an image from the spatial to the frequency display. We capture and view the image data in the spatial domain, seeing a recognizable reproduction of what we saw in life, but bearing in mind that this digital image is composed of numbers, enormous quantities of zeroes and ones, in an unlimited combination. This is not the only display of the image open to us, just the one that is practical for everyday use.

When the image data are converted to the frequency domain, there is no change to the image content. The data are simply organized and displayed as a function of their frequencies rather than their position in space. Repetitive patterns, such as rows and columns of dots or lines, will generate spikes that appear quite prominently in the frequency display, where they can be removed. This array of spikes, or "noise signature," can be surgically removed by a trained user. This can be done without altering the fingerprint data. When the edited display is converted back to the spatial domain, the interfering pattern will be greatly reduced in presence or eliminated entirely.

FFT has been applied successfully and introduced in court in many criminal cases since 1991. It should be considered in cases where evaluation and comparison are impaired by persistent pattern interference which cannot be removed by other strategies.

For more detailed information on digital imaging, color mode, file format and FFT, see *Forensic Digital Image Processing* (Dalrymple and Smith, 2018).

Narrow Band Filters

Another threshold situation frequently encountered is a fingerprint revealed by a forensic light source that is difficult to assess because of weak fluorescence and/or substrate interference. Narrow band filters (described in Chapter Three) can be used in sequence with digital techniques to transform a suggestion of ridge detail to a viable, valuable fingerprint.

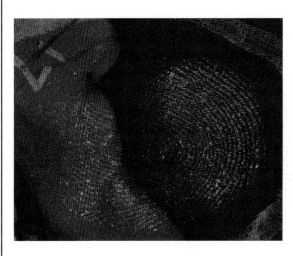

A finger impression has been marked on a printed magazine page treated with 1, 2 indanedione and photographed with the standard orange barrier filter. At this stage, the impression lacks sufficient clear and continuous ridge detail necessary for comparison.

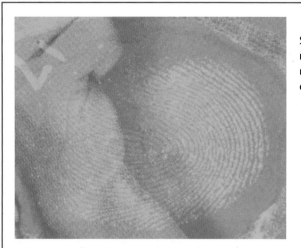

Same fingerprint photographed by adding a narrow band filter (Arrowhead FF 1.0). The ridge detail is now clearer and more extensive.

Same fingerprint in grayscale, revealing printing pattern obstruction. When the image is converted to grayscale and inverted, the ridge detail is still partially obstructed by the printed pattern on the background.

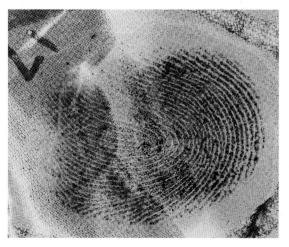

Final result after editing in FFT, revealing clear continuous ridge detail. FFT was used to eliminate the pattern and the result is a fingerprint ready for evaluation and comparison.

Infrared Detection

The use of infrared reflection scrutiny presents another option for sequential, nondestructive evidence detection that should be mentioned. Although most forensic photography is conducted in the visible spectrum, niche detection and recording of physical evidence in the infrared had been exploited in the film era. Since the human eye has no sensitivity in this range, it was a blind search, requiring a photograph to be taken and then examined for evidence rendered visible. Infrared-sensitive emulsions were temperamental and required considerable time for capture and development before the results could be viewed. Many types of physical evidence present a different appearance against their substrate when illuminated by infrared reflection, including gunshot residue and the presence of blood transfer on different substrates. A range of filters, blocking the visible spectrum and transmitting different ranges of the infrared were in use with film cameras and work just as well in the digital domain.

During laser examination, an area of faint ridge detail was observed and marked on an untreated rail ticket. The image, taken with a standard orange barrier filter, reveals no trace of ridge detail.

A second photograph was taken, adding a narrow band filter to the camera lens.

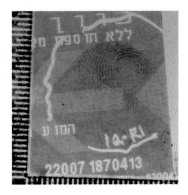

When this image was converted to grayscale and inverted, the ridge detail was readily visible but seriously obstructed by the printed pattern on the ticket.

Editing in FFT eliminated the pattern noise and revealed a clear continuous fingerprint, suitable for evaluation and comparison.

The CMOS (complementary metal oxide semiconductor) image sensor is the de facto "retina" of the digital camera and is sensitive to wavelengths in the infrared beyond a micron. Cameras used for conventional photography contain a filter to block unwanted infrared, but in 2007, Fuji introduced the *IS-Pro*, a DSLR camera intended for ultraviolet/infrared photography without a filter, which featured live view, the ability to preview the result in real time without having to take a photograph. There are currently a wide range of options for recording evidence by infrared reflection, including camera conversion by removal of the IR filter, which would obviously negate any warrantee on the camera. Infrared examination offers another nondestructive step to detect evidence in sequential processing prior to any chemical treatments. This applies particularly to exhibits suspected of bearing blood transfer. In the example below, blood transfer on a black cotton shirt is virtually invisible in ambient light. Photographed with an infrared-sensitive DSLR, electronic flash and an 87C filter, the blood is immediately observed.

Black t-shirt bearing blood transfer, photographed in white light.

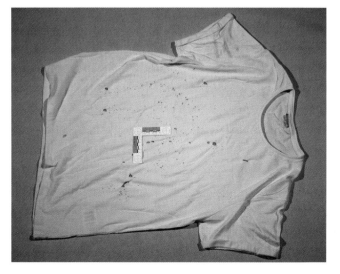

Reflected infrared photography reveals blood transfer

(Images courtesy of R. Rigole, Ontario Police College.)

Investigator looking for a suspect among mug shot files.

Modern mug shot format.

Mug Shots

Prisoner photos were once known as a rogue's gallery, which featured images of criminals and those who had criminal tendencies. Taking many hours to develop on glass or tin, the first grainy images of prisoners began to appear in the latter part of the nineteenth century. They were generally taken after the arrest of a suspect with photographic prints attached to the fingerprint record as a positive form of identification.

This system had obvious limitations. There was wide variation in quality, lighting, head size, and the background behind the subject, depending on the location and the officer taking the photograph. Also, the photograph was physically locked in the subject's file and was available only through a manual search.

More currently, prisoner images are called *mug shots* ("mug" refers to the face) and are restricted to individuals who have been charged with a crime. New digital technology has allowed for the creation of Record Management Systems (RMS), an all-inclusive approach to recording and tracking police activities, of which the mug shot database is only a part.

All actions taken by a police agency, including all criminal occurrences, investigations, associated exhibits, and vehicles, are documented as they happen. When a digital mug shot is created, it is automatically entered into the master database and associated with all existing file information on that individual. The locations in each detachment or station for taking mug shots have been standardized (same lighting, background, and distance), to ensure consistent quality.

When a photo line-up is required, any number of appropriate mug shots can be accessed quickly by searching the database for similar subjects. Features like hair and eye color, facial hair, glasses, tattoos, and body piercing can all be searched. The photos can then be individually viewed, and a final selection made for the photo line-up. Other police forces using the same RMS systems may access other agencies' databases on a courtesy basis.

Using Light to Detect Evidence

Implementing Lasers

In 1976, Brian Dalrymple, a forensic analyst working for the Ontario Provincial Police (OPP), was attempting to solve an exhibit treatment problem. Several dozen shiny black cardboard boxes had been submitted in a drug investigation. The only fingerprint reagent for paper in use at the time was ninhydrin, a chemical used to detect the presence of amino acids sloughed off in fingerprints. Although it is superb on light-colored papers, it is not visible on a black surface (see chapter 7).

Dalrymple tried iodine fuming, followed by silver plate application, in an attempt to transfer any latent fingerprint impressions to the smooth, shiny surface where they could be seen and photographed (see chapter 7 for methods). The first few exhibits processed in this way yielded nothing. He then placed his own fresh fingerprint on one of the boxes and repeated

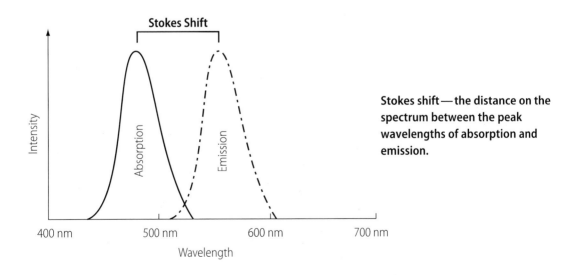

Stokes shift—the distance on the spectrum between the peak wavelengths of absorption and emission.

the silver plate application, to determine if any transfer—even in a fresh print—was made. Again, the results were completely negative.

Finally, Dalrymple considered the possibility of inducing iodine to fluoresce, that is, to absorb light of one wavelength and emit light of a longer wavelength. He turned to a friend and neighbor for assistance. James Duff was a research chemist with Xerox Research Centre in Ontario who had a great depth of knowledge concerning the reaction of chemical compounds to light. Permission was obtained from both the OPP and Xerox for Dalrymple and Duff to explore this possibility. E. Roland Menzel, a physicist, was also consulted. His research at the time centered on picosecond spectroscopy, a way of measuring complex sequential photosynthetic reactions by varying the pulse time and wavelength of light generated by a combination of argon-ion and dye lasers (Menzel, personal communication 1976).

The attempt to induce iodine fluorescence in a practical way was a failure. Although iodine does fluoresce, it has a very short Stokes shift, which is the distance on the electromagnetic spectrum between the wavelength of the exciting light and the wavelength of the resulting fluorescence (Duff and Menzel, personal communication 1976). This means that no filter could possibly isolate the iodine fluorescence by blocking the reflected excitation source.

During the research, however, the work of Robert Olsen (Olsen 1978) was consulted with particular attention to the composition of sweat. An extensive list of potential organic substances and inorganic salts led to the question: with so many different compounds potentially present in fingerprints (see chapter 7), is it possible that one or more of them might exhibit intrinsic fluorescence, that is, without the need of adding chemistry?

Menzel stated knowingly that *spectroscopists* (those who use light to study matter) had known for years that care had to be taken when handling

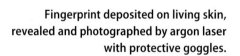
Fingerprint deposited on living skin, revealed and photographed by argon laser with protective goggles.

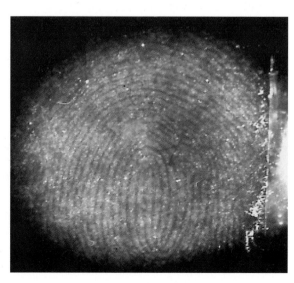

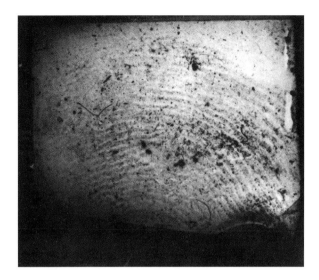

Untreated fingerprint revealed by argon laser on adhesive side of black tape led to identification of suspect.

thin-layer chromatography plates and all associated equipment, because fingerprints deposited on them fluoresce and spoil the results. Immediately, samples of perspiration were taken from a number of individuals and subjected to spectroscopic analysis.

The results were encouraging, with clear evidence that some component of the perspiration (in the fingerprint deposit) was absorbing blue-green light and emitting yellow fluorescence. Fingerprints were placed on a number of surfaces and examined under the light of Menzel's argon-ion laser.

Large lasers are very hazardous to the eyes, and those who use them must wear protective goggles that have a very high optical density at laser wavelengths. Fortunately, the goggles performed two functions. As they protected the eyes of the researchers, they also transmitted and isolated the fingerprint fluorescence, an unexpected result. Hence, the first inherently fluorescing fingerprints in history were observed and photographed (see Dalrymple et al. 1977).

First Case Use of Laser

During the research period of the late 1970s, Dalrymple was approached by a colleague from the Royal Canadian Mounted Police regarding a problem exhibit. He had a piece of black electrical tape that had been used to secure a packet of drugs. He could see a small fragment of three-dimensional ridge detail on the sticky side of the tape, but no technique at the time, either chemical or photographic, would improve its visibility in room lighting.

Dalrymple took possession of the exhibit, and his team received permission to examine it under Menzel's laser at Xerox. Extremely faint yellow-orange fluorescence was observed on the sticky side of the tape, just at the threshold of visibility. No ridge detail could be seen. The pho-

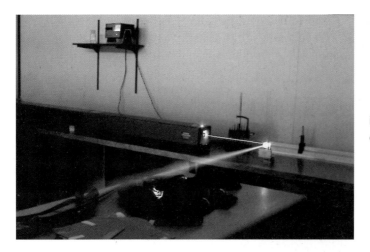

The first operational police laser in Forensic Identification Services of the Ontario Provincial Police.

tograph required a long exposure time (an exposure of f8 for forty minutes), and the developed film revealed a clear finger impression. Dalrymple was supplied with known fingerprints and subsequently identified a suspect who had not previously been charged (see Dalrymple 1979). Within months, the first fingerprint identification by laser was tendered and accepted in court.

In April 1977, the Ontario Provincial Police became the first police agency in history to acquire an argon laser and examine evidence for inherent fluorescence.

Light Sources

What we refer to as light is but a very narrow slice of an enormous energy spectrum beginning with the shortest wavelength on the left, and the longest on the right.

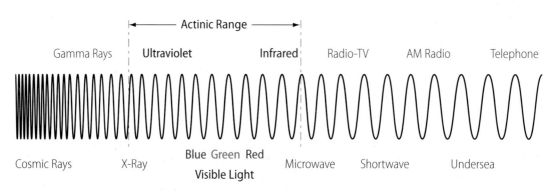

The electromagnetic spectrum—a vast array of radiated energy, only a small range of which is useful in forming images. NB: This is schematic—not accurate in linear relationship.

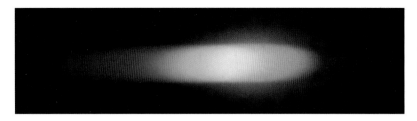

The visible spectrum, from 400 nm to 700 nm.

The only part of the electromagnetic spectrum (EMS) of forensic interest to us is the section referred to as *actinic*, a term meaning the capability of radiation to form images.

X-rays are valuable in medicine and pathology because they pass through soft tissue and give excellent images of bone, including injury and trauma, but the radiation of greatest importance to the identification photographer comes from the *ultraviolet*, *visible*, and *infrared* portions.

Although our eyes are not sensitive to the wavelengths of ultraviolet and infrared, these types of radiation are extremely useful in imaging. Firearm residue patterns that were invisible in white light have been revealed under ultraviolet light, while document alterations are routinely detected by infrared techniques.

Both lasers and forensic light sources have become essential detection tools in the laboratory and at the crime scene. Fortunately, many types of organic-based evidence, such as semen, ingredients of sweat, and saliva (riboflavin and pyridoxine; see Guilbault 1973)—not to mention hair, fiber, and trace evidence—fluoresce to some degree and may be visible by inherent fluorescence, depending on the surface they occupy.

Also, many chemical reagents have been created to fluoresce on contact with fingerprint deposits (see chapter 7). In fact, three decades of exhibit examination by laser and forensic light sources indicate convincingly that the vast majority of inherently fluorescing fingerprints are due to some sort of contamination, including cosmetics and pigments transferred from objects that have been touched.

In 1976 lasers were very costly, fragile, and high-maintenance devices. Few police agencies were initially positioned to add this technology to their program delivery. Three decades later, a techno-revolution has placed robust, powerful, and relatively inexpensive light sources in the hands of virtually every police force.

Luminescence/Fluorescence

Luminescence is the umbrella term for the radiation of any light generated by means other than heat. A luminescent substance releases light energy after absorbing another form of energy. There are two sources of luminescence that are forensically important. These are identified as *chemiluminescence* and *photoluminescence*. Luminescence is classed as

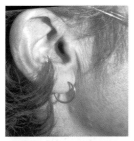

Ear photographed in ambient light displays warmth and life due to penetration of skin by visible wavelengths.

Ultraviolet wavelengths exhibit almost no penetration of the skin, giving it an opaque, lifeless appearance. Concentrations of melanin (the pigment determining hair, skin, and eye color) absorb ultraviolet more readily than visible wavelengths (see freckle).

Writing obliterated by black marker cannot be seen in white light.

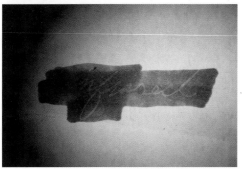

The writing is clearly seen by the reflected infrared technique.

fluorescence if the light goes out as soon as the generating source is turned off. It is called *phosphorescence* if it continues after the light source is turned off (like the numbers on a watch face that glow in the dark).

Products for use by forensic investigators are based on light-emitting sources. For example, Luminol and Blue Star™ are extremely sensitive blood detection (chemiluminescent) chemicals. They are sprayed on a crime scene in total darkness and emit light after reacting with blood. Both reveal the slightest trace of blood even after careful cleanup has been attempted.

It was recognized in the 1970s that lasers were valuable laboratory tools. Expensive, temperamental, and nonportable, they were well outside the means of all but the largest police forces. Circa 1980, Milutin Stoilovic, formerly of the Australian Federal Police, was the force behind the Rofin Polilight®, a white light source that, through the use of exciter filters, isolated specific bands of the visible spectrum.

With the filter centered at 450 nm in place, the Polilight® emits virtually the entire blue component of the visible spectrum. The 505 nm filter transmits only green wavelengths. These two filter options allowed the user to detect almost all of the physical evidence previously located by laser alone. Other filter options were available for specific applications. A less expensive, portable, and more robust light source was now available and affordable to many more police agencies.

At about the same time in Canada, John Watkin, then of the National Research Council, was developing what became the Lumilite®, another filtered lamp source.

When light is emitted from a substance after it has absorbed another wavelength of light, it is known as *photoluminescence.* This is the best-known and most widely used form of luminescence to those in search of forensic evidence. Police use lasers and forensic light sources to excite photoluminescence in fingerprints and other evidence including (but not limited to) hair, fibers, body fluids, and trace chemicals. Lasers and light sources have also been used to reveal alterations and obliterations in documents through both visible and infrared luminescence (see Dalrymple 1983).

Fixed versus Variable Dynamic Range

We typically see and photograph objects by their reflection and absorption of light. Light-colored objects reflect most of the light that strikes them and absorb much less. Dark-colored objects do the reverse. They reflect much less light and absorb much more. Objects viewed in this way have a *fixed dynamic range.* A light gray fingerprint, for example, on white paper has a narrow or compressed dynamic range, while a black fingerprint on white paper has a much wider range (see Dalrymple 2000).

No matter how much light is directed onto a surface, we don't change the dynamic range. Absorption/reflection viewing, therefore, creates a fixed dynamic range.

When we view objects by luminescence, we are not using reflection of light to see them. We are creating and seeing a new light source. Viewing items in this way is much more sensitive than reflection because it offers a variable dynamic range, which is potentially much wider. This wider, variable dynamic range is critical when detecting fingerprints

 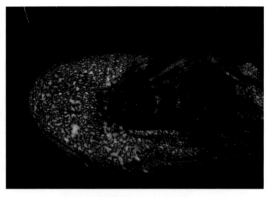

The use of a chemical blood detection agent highlights the evidence of blood on a perpetrator's running shoe long after it had been cleaned up.

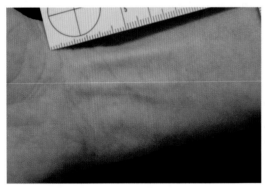 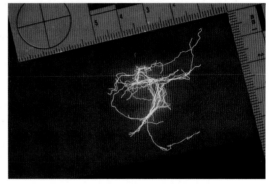

Fibers on the arm are not visible under ambient light.

These once invisible fibers are now revealed by inherent photoluminescence.

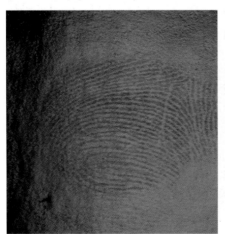 

Left: **An image with compressed dynamic range exhibits low contrast, with little difference between the lightest and darkest tonal values.** Right: **An image with wide dynamic range has much greater contrast.**

that contain minute quantities of material. It explains why so many of the cutting-edge methods for detection of evidence now rely on fluorescence.

The Use of Filters

Filters are both common and critical tools in the photographer's bag. Photographing luminescence is photographing a new light emission generated by the light source. It is undesirable for any reflection from the subject to pass through the lens. This approach to imaging has brought three types of filters into prominence.

1. **Exciter filters.** Exciter filters are an integral part of a forensic light source. When in position in front of the light, each allows the passage of a specific band or color of light—ultraviolet, blue, or green, for example—while blocking the rest. When using a forensic laser, no exciter filter is required because all of the emission is monochromatic (one wavelength).

2. **Barrier filters.** A barrier filter is required at the eye and the camera whether one is using a forensic light source or laser. It isolates the desirable fluorescence while blocking the reflection, allowing the user to see and photograph fingerprints and other evidence.

3. **Narrow band pass filters**. In most situations, the barrier filter works well in revealing fingerprint fluorescence, but on occasion, when the *substrate* (the surface on which the evidence sits) also fluoresces, the barrier filter is not specific enough to give satisfactory results. A narrow band pass filter has the ability to further isolate the fluo-

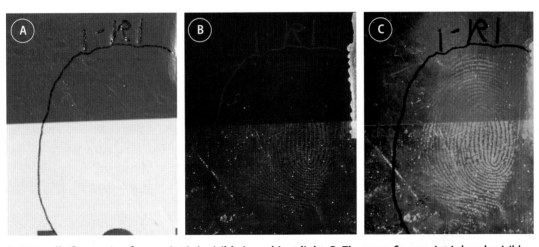

A: Naturally fluorescing fingerprint is invisible in ambient light. B: The same fingerprint is barely visible when illuminated by Coherent Tracer® and viewed with the orange barrier filter. C: Now it is optimized with narrow band filter Melles Griot® 03 FIV 008.

rescing target, even from a fluorescing background. The transmission curve of the narrow band pass filter fits over the fingerprint emission like a glove on a hand, blocking most of the background luminescence (see Dalrymple 1982).

In 1977, when laser-excited luminescence became a mainstream detection strategy, a new use for viewing filters emerged—to block the reflected light or the laser (or forensic light source) and allow the passage of the desirable fluorescence. It was serendipitous that the mandatory safety goggles protecting the eyes from laser emissions would also perform this function. An examiner would be required to wear goggles to see any evidence that the laser had revealed. However, the goggles as personal safety equipment had never been designed or intended for use in evidence detection. At first, when it was necessary to photograph fluorescing evidence, a filter was removed from the goggles and affixed to the camera lens, often with a piece of tape. As the technique expanded and became a regular component of exhibit examination, barrier filters designed for attachment to cameras were introduced.

Laser scrutiny revealed a periodic challenge. Some substrates fluoresced at wavelengths similar to those of the desired evidence, fingerprints for example, and the barrier filter was not specific enough to isolate it. Narrow band filters presented one solution. If a filter with a narrow transmission spectrum (10 nm), centered on the emission wavelength of the fingerprint, was placed at the camera lens in combination with the barrier filter, the obstructive background fluorescence could be reduced or eliminated, and thus clearer detail in the fingerprint could be seen.

As with the initial barrier filter, narrow band filters were atypical, in that they had never been originally intended for photographic use in revealing evidence. Consequently, there was no easy way to attach them to a camera lens for photography. This process required both filters to be attached, resulting in a large filter factor—a huge reduction in all light entering the camera. The consequence of this was a very long exposure. In spite of their displayed value as a niche solution for recording fingerprints on troublesome fluorescing substrates, narrow band filters were not immediately adopted as conventional equipment.

In 2012, a procedure was introduced to facilitate the use of narrow band filters as an occasional solution to the problem of substrate fluorescence. An assembly of stepping rings is constructed to facilitate the easy and rapid attachment of the barrier filter, or the barrier filter—narrow band filter combination, when required.

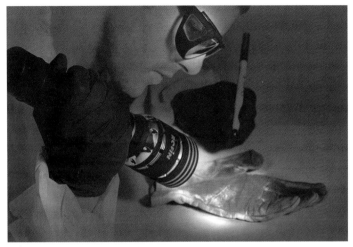

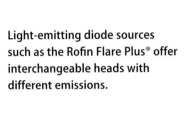

Light-emitting diode sources such as the Rofin Flare Plus® offer interchangeable heads with different emissions.

Light-Emitting Diode (LED) Sources

LEDs have emerged as a viable alternative to filtered lamps. Light is produced as a function of electrons moving through semiconductor material. LED sources are available in a range of different spectral outputs, including peak emissions in the ultraviolet, blue, green, yellow, red, and infrared. They are robust, long-lasting, efficient, and relatively inexpensive.

Semiconductor Lasers

One of the best new introductions (in the writer's opinion) is the semiconductor laser. Having the same properties as the LED sources (economy, long life, low operating cost), it offers high-intensity monochromatic output. The predominant version emits green light (532 nm), but the output can be engineered. Other models emit blue (460 nm) and yellow (570 nm) light. This laser has displayed a propensity for revealing on occasion untreated, inherently fluorescing fingerprints.

There exists an inconvenient truth here—one of many in the forensic identification discipline. In the attempt to develop a less expensive, more practical, and universally available alternative to lasers, another complimentary technique has emerged. While there are many detection tasks that are performed equally well by lasers and filtered lamps (or LEDs), each source has the capability and the proven record of finding evidence missed by the other. Because current lasers emit a single wavelength of very high intensity, and the other light sources offer a chosen band of wavelengths (as much as a third of the visible spectrum), this should not be too surprising.

Of paramount importance, however, is that detection by fluorescence is now standard practice both in the laboratory and at the crime scene, and our forensic reach in time, sensitivity, and range of amenable substrates has been substantially extended. Police agencies, based on their

Lasers such as the Coherent Tracer® emit a single wavelength of light and do not contain exciter filters.

resources, can now make informed decisions about acquisition of this powerful evidence detection technology.

Measuring the Crime Scene

Once the crime scene and its environs are photographed and described through notation, accurate measurements of the scene must be taken, recorded, and transformed into scale drawings. Once again, this is done to preserve the intact crime scene before any evidence is removed. These drawings are intended both for use as visual aids to the investigator and to help witnesses recall what they observed.

Various electronic devices supplement measuring tapes, paper, and pencils and have taken crime scene drawing to a different level. Surveyor's tools, including a total-station device that automatically plots and measures evidence and a laser-guided three-dimensional scanner, are now common items and in use in many police forces.

Forensic Reconstruction

Three-dimensional (3D) computer applications and animation programs have been growing in popularity in the digital world since their inception more than two decades ago. Their dominance is evident everyday in movies and television, video games, advertising and graphics. Almost

The completed sketch or plan drawing of a crime scene. Image courtesy of Greg Schofield, Toronto Police Forensic Identification Services. All rights reserved.

all design, whether it is automotive, architectural, or electronic or any one of a million products, utilizes some degree of 3D technology.

Shortly after the introduction of 3D digital technology, it began to appear in niche industries such as medical diagnostics and imaging, virtual training, artificial intelligence, and law enforcement. The latter use can be referred to by many names, including re-creations, animations, 3D crime scenes, forensic virtual modeling, and reconstruction.

Forensic reconstruction can be defined as the physical and graphical reenactment or re-creation of objects, situations, and events from accident and crime scene occurrences. Today, this is commonly accomplished by utilizing 3D digital technology. It must be noted, however, that forensic reconstruction has been around for many decades through analog methods like physical model building, scene measurement and drawing, video reenactments, and event reverse engineering. These are and were labor-intensive pursuits. Digital techniques in contrast, offer speed, ease of use, increased accuracy, clarity, and increased productivity.

Many of today's law enforcement agencies use 3D digital technology in investigative and forensic capabilities. Common applications of this 3D technology can include:

- crime scene investigation and survey,
- motor vehicle collision analysis,
- postmortem examinations,
- accident reconstruction,
- crime scene reconstruction,

- blood spatter analysis,
- bullet trajectory analysis,
- injury reconstruction, and
- scenario testing.

These reconstructions are typically generated by means of computed aided drawing (CAD), 3D digital modeling, computer animation, and other digital graphics software. In recent years, manufacturers of 3D digital technology, realizing the influx of their technology in these niche markets, are producing specific flavors of their applications geared to specialize in a specific market. This is evident in many areas of law enforcement.

Software such as Crimezone and Crashzone are designed and marketed specifically for the reconstruction of scene evidence for crime and collision scenes, respectively. EnCase digital forensic application is software designed to copy and extract digital evidence from electronic equipment—it is marketed strictly to law enforcement and forensic electronic crime agencies. This trend in marketing is not limited to software. Survey equipment used widely in civil engineering, such as total stations and laser scanners, are also being advertised as crime scene survey and documentation devices. Cameras typically used in the graphics and print advertising market (known as high-definition imaging) are being used as image capture devices for crime scenes.

The process of forensic reconstruction starts with gathering information. The most important aspect of reconstruction is accuracy. "Garbage in, garbage out" is a well-known computer axiom; detailed and precise measurements are crucial to the success of any reconstruction. Measurement gathering sources include:

A laser scanning system collecting data at the scene of a bridge collapse. Image courtesy of Leica ScanStation. All rights reserved.

- tape measure,
- laser measuring devices,
- total station,
- 3D scanners, and
- photogrammetry.

Other information commonly used in the reconstruction process includes:

- photographs,
- professional/expert reports,
- collision reconstruction,
- bloodstain analysis,
- shooting incident experts and engineers,
- climatology (weather conditions),
- witness statements, and
- surveillance video.

The level of accuracy obtained through digital measurement capture is impossible to reach through traditional measurement techniques. In many cases, scene data can be digitally captured and stored, then downloaded into a 3D software application that will allow for the 3D viewing of a 100 percent measurement accurate scene—all with no human influence or error on the measurement data. This is all accomplished in a fraction of the time it would take using traditional analog methods.

An accident scene can be accurately depicted from the driver's point of view. Image courtesy of Eugene Liscio AI2-3D Animations. All rights reserved.

The accident scene can be shown from virtually any viewpoint—another driver involved in the accident, a witness on the sidewalk, or even a bird's-eye view. Image courtesy of Eugene Liscio AI2-3D Animations. All rights reserved.

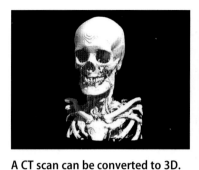

A CT scan can be converted to 3D.

The path of a bullet, in relation to objects relevant to the scene can be accurately depicted. Images courtesy of Eugene Liscio AI2-3D Animations. All rights reserved.

The sophistication of the software applications used in forensic reconstruction is remarkable. 3D animation programs used in reconstruction follow all the rules of physics. Objects can have weight, and they can be affected by wind and gravity. Many software applications also have built-in collision detection, friction control, sun generation based on geographical location, date and time, and automatic shadow mapping.

Forensic reconstructions are produced with a purpose in mind. The reconstructions are used to visualize and demonstrate a point-of-view and/or opinion pertaining to events that have occurred at a particular crime or accident scene. A common misconception of forensic reconstructions is that the creator can make a reconstruction demonstrate whatever the client wants it to. Although this technology can be used in a misleading manner, it is highly unlikely such an attempt would withstand the scrutiny of the courts.

The greatest benefits of forensic reconstructions can be summarized in two main points. The first very important factor is clarity. Forensic reconstructions help illustrate complicated scenarios in a simple and easy-to-understand manner. This benefits both the court and jury members, as they are not forced to remember abstract concepts and technical terms.

The second important factor is its retention value. Visual evidence can certainly aid in one's ability to retain complicated information. Forensic reconstructions provide the ability to place the audience into the environment that is being shown. The audience is not only exposed to a realistic 3D environment, but with the creation of real-time reenactments, they experience the feeling of time. There is an old saying that "a picture is worth a thousand words." With 3D animation, a moving picture is probably worth much, much more. One can experience how long a scenario would take to complete or how fast an object was moving. These important factors are virtually impossible to convey through verbal dialogue or still images.

Forensic reconstructions can be output in different presentation formats, including printed, video, and interactive formats. Printed formats may incorporate plotted CAD drawings, full-color still images, and charts. The creator of the reconstruction finalizes the scenario and incorporates this into an animated movie that cannot be altered. The various movie formats allow for playback on either a television or through a computer movie player.

In a sense, a reconstruction gives the court almost superhuman powers. A judge and jury come as close to seeing the event as it is possible to achieve. They can "see" the multiple stab wounds in a victim's torso, including the penetration depth, without the graphic obstruction often created by photographs. They can "witness" the car crashing into the guardrail at the exact speed that other evidence has designated. They can "observe" a vehicle collision as the driver of either car experienced it, as a witness on the sidewalk, or from an overhead perspective.

A highly detailed 3D forensic reconstruction that supports the position of expert witnesses (of either side) can be a powerful and valuable piece of evidence. A thousand words for an accurate and relevant forensic picture is a very conservative estimate.

III: Collecting the Evidence

Best Evidence Rule

There is a dictum descended from British common law referred to as *best evidence*. It states that the law does not permit a man to give evidence when there is better evidence within his reach, which he does not produce. In simple terms, it is better to produce an original piece of evidence than a copy. The law could not be more lucid.

We can therefore see two principles that should be used as guides and touchstones for all professional forensic activities. The first is that any zeal or passion must not be allowed to influence and potentially damage the search for, and interpretation of evidence, and consequently, diminish the process of law. The second is that there is an obligation placed on the proponent of evidence to deliver the best, truest and most complete evidence possible, in both quantity and quality.

Tendering in situ photographs and lifts of a fingerprint removed from a crime scene complies with the spirit of best evidence. If prints are lifted from a piece of glass, for example, the taped print as well as the glass should be retained along with all photographs taken. This is also advised when chemically developing prints on documents, notes, tickets, and letters.

In the case of large pieces of evidence, for example, the wall in a factory, heavy machinery, or a vehicle, the rule cannot always apply. One must then be prepared to show photographs of the original source of the evidence and an explanation for why it cannot be introduced in court.

The spirit of Best Evidence has broad implications in how forensic professionals should conduct their activities. It clearly directs that **all** possible evidence be detected, collected, recorded, evaluated for relevance, and interpreted. The "low-hanging fruit" approach—gathering only the easiest, most obvious pieces of evidence perhaps to display cynically that the attempt has been made—is in direct contravention to the Best Evidence dictum. Therefore, compliance with the Best Evidence rule requires professionals to be cognizant of and competent in the most current and effective technologies for detection and recording of the physical evidence for which they are responsible. After all, can it be imagined that, in a trial that will determine the future life of an accused person, the attitude of the judge or the jury would be that a half-hearted attempt to find evidence would suffice? In fact, many effective cross examinations in court have been based on what was not done—completely, competently or at all.

Mission Statement

With any career, but in forensic identification in particular, it is essential to have and follow a clear and accurate agenda, one that is not only discipline-compliant, but one that pursues ethically and morally defensible goals. Taking criminals off the streets and putting them in prison is an occasional *outcome* of these duties done well, but it should not be seen as an objective. Other equally admirable goals, including keeping the streets safe and maintaining law and order have no place in the *direct* mission statement of forensic professionals. Again, these should be viewed as desirable outcomes rather than objectives.

Objectives will be reflected in the job description of any worker, a statement of expectations the employer holds of each employee, but in no other profession is it more vitally important that all of the specific objectives are not only known, but applied to all professional activities.

The following are suggested as goals for the forensic identification specialist, all of which reflect the need for a consistent methodology in crime scene investigation, and which comply with the laws of Best Evidence:

- Secure and protect crime scenes for the processing of all types of physical evidence;
- Diagnosis and triage of exhibits and crime scenes to determine the most effective sequence of detection processes for each;
- Maximum detection, extraction, visualization, and recording of physical and impression evidence from exhibits and crime scenes;

- Documentation of all procedures undertaken to preserve the integrity and continuity of evidence;
- Objective, clear, neutral, supportable and complete interpretation of findings, and tendering of said findings, in court; and
- Protection of one's personal safety, as well as that of others, by an understanding of the hazards associated with crime scene and evidence processing, and employing the appropriate precautions and countermeasures.

Appraising Constraints

On the receipt and confirmation of search warrants (see chapter 1) forensic officers (the number of which depends on the size and scope of the crime scene) undertake an initial sweep of the area. This allows them to formulate an investigation plan and secure any transient or fragile evidence. It also allows them to appraise any challenges or *constraints* that may affect subsequent evidence recovery and collection.

Police execute an underwater search. Image courtesy of the Buffalo Police Dept. Crime Scene Unit. All rights reserved.

These constraints may be *legal* or *jurisdictional,* as in the case where a crime scene extends beyond the provincial or state boundary; they may be *geographic/physiographic* in that the scene may involve an underwater, underground, or a highly modified ground search. Constraints may also be *technical* and/or *financial* in that recovery may require certain equipment or gear that the agency does not have. Searches may also require helicopter or fixed-wing aerial surveillance, which may be unavailable at the time. Seasonal and weather constraints also factor into the initial search phase and in some areas of the country prevent them altogether.

Principles of Evidence Recovery

Only after the crime scene has been thoroughly documented through photography, notation, measurements, and sketches can evidence then be collected and retained. Evidence collection, however, is not simply a task of picking things up but a skill developed after several years of experience. It combines knowledge of criminal law, an understanding of the rules of search, the value of evidence, and proper collection and analysis techniques. Therefore, only qualified forensics officers are able to collect physical evidence in a manner that complies with forensic science principles.

Prior to removing any evidence, it must be photographed in place (in situ) using close-up and wide-angle shots. Usually a ruler is placed alongside the artifact in the photograph as a reference point to the size of the exhibit.

An important next step is referred to as establishing *spatial controls,* which is to measure the location of the evidence as it relates to other pieces of evidence in the room or space. Understanding the spatial relationship is to know how physical evidence has been distributed at a crime scene, which can indicate the nature of the crime, the activity and intent of the perpetrator, as well as the direction to other possible crime scenes. The scattering of clothing, the direction of footprints, and the distribution of human remains, for example, may reveal more about the physical evidence than the evidence itself. Its position among and between other items is crucial to identify and record before it is removed from the scene.

Because physical evidence is vital to all investigations, the requirements are summarized as specific principles that guide its recovery and collection.

The distribution of physical evidence often reveals as much as the physical evidence itself. Image courtesy of Toronto Police Forensic Identification Services. All rights reserved.

Police searching for evidence. Image courtesy of Her Majesty the Queen in Right of Canada as represented by the Royal Canadian Mounted Police. © 2009. All rights reserved.

Principles of Evidence Recovery and Collection

1. The collection of evidence entails the loss of information. Crime scenes are invariably destroyed through the collection process and can never be revisited for more recovery once the police perimeter is down and the public has been allowed access. The certainty of a complete recovery will ensure that the officer or specialist understands the *significance of an absence*. For example, if a body has been recovered with the head and arms missing, was this due to incomplete recovery? Was there animal scavenging? Were the arms and head deliberately removed by the perpetrator to prevent identification?

None of the questions can have a definitive answer without a degree of certainty in the collection process. Therefore, it is up to the forensic officers involved to document and recover as much information as possible the first time in.

2. Potentially significant evidence may not be physically retrievable. Information that can explain certain factors and types of evidence are not things that can be picked up and bagged, for example, the weather, the position of body parts, the location of a car, the exposure of certain items to sunlight or extremes in temperature. This is the sort of information that is crucial and must be included in all notes, photographs, and documentations.

3. Not all recovered evidence has been intentionally deposited. In many crime scenes, this is the case in the collection of fingerprints, DNA from a victim or perpetrator, discarded cigarette butts and cans, bottles, hair, fabric, and all other trace evidence. It is also the case in the presence of certain insects, plants, soil, and faunal deposits, which provide vital information in homicide cases such as location and time of death.

4. The evidence may not be obvious. In cases where items are scattered in different areas, throughout a large space, and/or the crime scene is outdoors, the relevance of certain features and their proximity to other items make the relationships between and among items very difficult to assess or immediately appreciate. Combined with the presence of roads, highways, interstates, water, rocks, trees, and animal dens, spatial controls are often the most readily dismissed or lost. Often the distribution and placement of physical evidence can only be understood once it has all been documented and mapped. As such, it is necessary to record and collect everything at a scene even if it appears unimportant or irrelevant. It is never advised to make assumptions based on previous experiences or with cases that appear similar.

Once the scene has been recorded, evidence may be collected. It is important to remember that much of what is collected is intended for further analysis either by forensic officers or forensic scientists. Hence, proper labeling of evidence packaging is of immense value, especially to those who have not attended the crime scene. In addition, the chain of custody begins once the evidence has been handled.

Rules for Packaging and Transporting Evidence

Forensic evidence packaging containers are readily available from crime scene equipment suppliers. These systems provide a variety of packaging options to accommodate most types of evidence when preparing for transportation and short- or long-term storage.

Before packaging and transportation is investigated further, the following issues should be explored to ensure that the best options are selected. Although standardized packaging and associated protocols may pre-exist within police departments, a review of these topics may lessen or eliminate potential problems. These are as follows.

Safety

Police work generally, and crime scene examinations especially, involve contact with many hazardous and biohazardous materials. Personal safety and the safety of others is paramount. Biological evidence is, in all probability, the most common hazard associated with crime scenes (blood, semen, vaginal discharge, saliva, decomposition fluid, human tissue, etc.). Investigators must be aware of the ease in which hazardous materials can be transferred, absorbed, ingested, or inhaled. Wearing safety equipment (gloves, masks, protection suits, etc.) suitable for sustaining

The suited-up team of the CBRN Unit: Chemical, Biological, Radiological and Nuclear. Image courtesy of Toronto Police Forensic Identification Services. All rights reserved.

Safety equipment is worn for protection during evidence collection. Image courtesy of Her Majesty the Queen in Right of Canada as represented by the Royal Canadian Mounted Police. © 2009. All rights reserved.

an acceptable level of safety is essential. Proper selection and labeling of evidence packaging can minimize accident or injury.

Note: The following topics—continuity and contamination or cross-contamination—are two of the most contested issues facing forensic investigators today. These issues are closely interconnected in the courts' view. While examining a crime scene, investigators must be cognizant of these issues and judge their approach accordingly.

Continuity

As discussed in chapter 1, continuity or chain of custody of evidence must be accounted for. From the time an item is located within the crime scene until it is tendered as an exhibit in court, the prosecution must account for every moment of time. Questions pertaining to the movement and handling of physical evidence are constantly conveyed as in the following questions.

1. Where has the exhibit been?
2. Who has had control of it?
3. Who, if anyone, had access to it?

It is not adequate to simply answer these questions verbally; one must be able to corroborate it through physical presence, notations, log books, evidence seals, tamper-proof packaging, and records. The court must be satisfied with the authenticity and validity of any and all evidence produced for trial.

Contamination or Cross-Contamination

The judicial system places trust in the competency of forensic investigators and a great deal of weight to physical and trace evidence being presented. This is particularly so with DNA evidence (see chapter 7). It is crucial to sustain this trust by ensuring the integrity of the samples.

DNA and other such physical types of evidence must be pure and unaltered. If the samples have been compromised or contaminated by incompetence or improper handling, the entire analysis, comparison, evaluation, and verification (ACE-V; see chapter 7) process is flawed, and therefore the results will be as well.

Wearing clean latex or nitrile gloves and changing them between collections assist in preventing transference of DNA evidence. Each item must be packaged individually, again to minimize transference. Avoid actions that may cause one's own DNA to be added to the sample collected (as in coughing, sneezing, sweating, spitting, etc.) on the exhibit.

Wet or blood-soaked items require air drying prior to long-term storage or laboratory submission. Initial packaging for transport, and short-term storage should be in paper bag or similar packaging, to allow for air drying. Plastic packaging is not advised primarily because it retains moisture and does not permit air movement to facilitate drying. DNA degradation and mold issues may arise if the exhibits are left for too long in such packaging. Many forensic laboratories have accredited drying lockers available for controlled drying of exhibits and should be used.

Laboratory Prerequisites and Protocols

Packaging, handling, and submission procedures vary. It is imperative that investigators familiarize themselves with local, state/provincial, and federal laboratory protocols. Failure to abide by these regulations may result in disciplinary action, improper analysis performed, rejection by the laboratory, or exclusion in court.

Presumption of Innocence

Remembering the presumption of innocence in the courts of North America, one guiding principle known to the medical community comes to mind, "First, do no harm," commonly ascribed to the Hippocratic Oath. It is directly applicable to forensic science because in the past, tragically, harm has been done. The Criminal Code of Canada (6 [1]) for example, states that a person shall be deemed not to be guilty of the offense until he is convicted or discharged under section 730 of the offence.

There are three representative entities participating in criminal courts appearing before the trier of fact, a judge, and frequently a jury. The question is, who is obligated to presume the innocence of individuals convicted of a crime? The first entity are the police investigators. They do not maintain this presumption. Investigators pursue and gather evidence, through a deductive, inductive and eliminative process until they become certain that a person has committed a crime. During this investigative process, it is reasonable to assume that they will become more certain that the evidence points to a specific individual(s), to the exclusion of all others. Charges would not have been laid unless the investigators were convinced of the accused person's guilt.

The second entity is the prosecutor. Equally, the prosecutor, in partnership with the police, would refuse to proceed, unless he or she was equally persuaded that sufficient evidence pointed to guilt, and that a trial would offer a reasonable chance in court for a guilty verdict. Prosecutors can and do believe that, on the basis of available evidence, that the person is probably guilty, but may elect not to proceed on the basis of insufficient evidence. The law clearly does not require a presumption of innocence from either the investigator or the prosecution. Indeed, a prosecutor has discretion over what evidence is tendered, and is not required to search for and present evidence that does not point to the culpability of the accused. The defense position speaks for itself, and is unequivocal in its presumption of innocence. All witnesses called by the defense will appear based on their presentation of exculpatory evidence.

The third position is the witness box, in which all evidence is introduced, and it is here that expert witnesses granted the privilege of tendering opinion evidence, must be strictly compliant with the principles of neutrality and objectivity. There is neither presumption of innocence or guilt. Answers must be the same regardless of who asks the questions, and the findings must never exceed the evidence. The testimony of an expert witness is only reflective of what the science has revealed—nothing less, nothing more.

Perception in Court

In addition to previous discussions, investigators should be aware of court perception, or how the court envisions their role. Other topics are more tangible and concrete, but perception is relevant and deserves further note.

Forensic investigators routinely employ a systematic or methodical approach to crime scene investigation, and how evidence is documented and collected. What sometimes goes unrecognized is how the court perceives what methods are used. For example, when a forensic investigator collects multiple pieces of physical evidence to be submitted for DNA analysis, one may ask, "Is it necessary to change gloves to avoid cross-contamination?" Many will argue that it is necessary. Others will say, "Only if the area contacted is being considered for DNA analysis, otherwise it is not." Who is right? The discussion then leads to further debate with terms such as "possibility" or "probability" of transference. If items are dry, and contact using the same glove is made, what is the likelihood of transference, possible or probable? If the exhibits are blood-soaked, does that change the perception?

Forensic investigators cannot go down that path of possibilities and probabilities. The court will not care whether it is more or less likely that transference occurred. The court only acts in absolutes. "Is it possible?" "Yes." "Is it probable?" It doesn't matter. If the possibility of transference exists, the courts will exclude or at least minimize the evidentiary weight put on the item. It is best to eliminate the perceptual argument by changing gloves each time. Remember, it is the responsibility of the forensic investigator to explain what he or she did and why.

Costs

Some careers are dollar driven, with the ultimate objective of revenue generation. This is both honorable and necessary for such business to prosper and continue to exist. After all, if a business doesn't generate sufficient revenue to cover its costs and show profit, it will cease to exist. All adopted business strategies will be subordinate to this goal.

Forensic science is diametrically opposed to the philosophy of generating profits. It is, or ideally should be, event driven. However, "budget restrictions" and "fiscal responsibility" are phrases frequently used by management within the police and forensic communities. Being conscious of these concerns is a necessity, but the reality exists that crime scene investigations can be expensive. Hourly wages and overtime pay aside, forensic equipment and supplies are costly. But they are necessary to perform the job task efficiently. Appropriate funds must be supplied to the program in order to comply with, and deliver the program, without any aspirations of generating revenue or mitigating costs by reducing effectiveness. That said, all forensic science is dollar dependent, meaning that those who manage the service delivery of forensic identification units have a responsibility to ensure that the allocated funds are used responsibly and well. Above all, the mission objectives must be clearly identified, understood, and followed.

In any case, the courts expect a competent level of forensic investigation to be conducted, regardless of the associated costs. Investigators and ultimately their agencies will be criticized for inadequate training and lack of personnel, equipment and supplies in which to conduct a thorough investigation.

Evidence Identification

There are countless soda cans in existence, and they all look very much alike. It is essential that the one soda can vital to an investigation is individually identified and identifiable. This is achieved partly through preserving chain of possession but also through *exhibit numbering*.

In general, the following is a useful protocol.

- Photograph the item *in situ*.
- Describe the item. It does not have to be a detailed description, but should be sufficient to differentiate the item from any other similar seizures.
- Document the time, date, and location of the seizure.
- Exhibits should be numbered sequentially as they are seized. If there is an additional item that will be removed from an exhibit for separate examination (e.g., a letter from an envelope), it can be given an extended number like 1-1 or 1a.
- If practical, mark the item with initials, case number, and exhibit number. If not, mark on exhibit packaging.
- Package item in a way that will protect it, and mark the packaging.
- Transport to lab or to a secure exhibit storage.

An excerpt from a sample exhibits list might read as follows.

1. One white envelope, addressed to Mary Brown containing:
   a. One page handwritten document beginning "Dear Mary."
2. Diet Coke can, flattened
3. Diet Coke can, intact

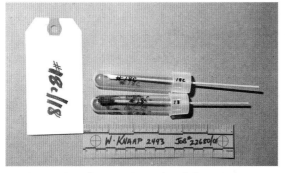 

Evidence identification through exhibit numbering. Images courtesy of Toronto Police Forensic Identification Services.

Successful crime scene management is a highly cooperative effort between law enforcement front-line personnel and specialized forensic investigators. The outcome of criminal investigations often hinges on the first responder's approach in protecting the perimeter right through to the forensic identification officers' collection and recovery methods. A consistent team approach with few deviations, ongoing training, and meticulous notes, photographs, and strict adherence to chain of custody solidify the quality and strength of any investigation.

IV: Cleaning the Crime Scene

Once the evidence is collected and the investigation is done, police and forensic identification officers leave and release the scene. In the aftermath, many individuals (next of kin or owners of the property) step into the disarray of the processed crime scene.

Often, where the death was violent or undiscovered for a period of time, this presents immense challenges. Invasive smells (death odors), bodily fluids, exposed tissues, and deep staining to furniture, floors, and walls are some of the major issues that confront the survivors at a scene.

It is often assumed that crime and/or trauma scene clean-up is provided by police or other emergency services. This is not the case, and

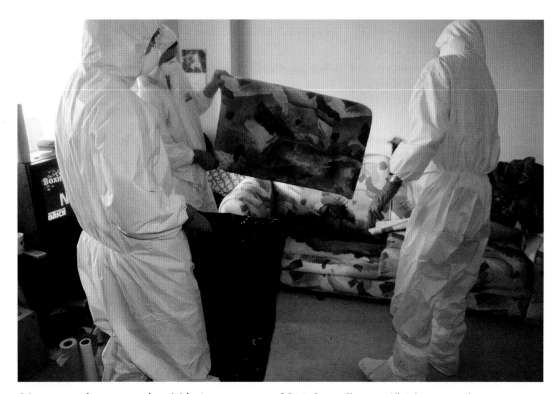

Crime scene clean-up at a homicide. Image courtesy of CrimeScene Cleaners. All rights reserved.

Scenes from a clandestine drug lab in the basement of a house. Images courtesy of Toronto Police Forensic Identification Services. All rights reserved.

private companies who have become highly specialized currently run the process.

Clean-up teams often employ former paramedics, police officers, and funeral service workers who are accustomed to the sights and smells of unnoticed or bloody and violent death scenes. Family members or insurance companies may contract their services, which are critical during unpleasant and often tragic circumstances. This relieves family members or employees of the emotional and traumatic task of having to clean, wash, and dispose of biohazardous wastes and contaminating substances.

All companies must follow strict guidelines set out by government agencies to deal with the handling of contaminated waste. For many, this includes the cleaning and removal of waste from suicides, homicides, decomposition, disease, and human and animal feces.

Since biohazardous waste and animal feces can lead to a range of human illnesses, badly contaminated items that cannot be cleaned are packaged in biohazard containers to be disposed of by medical waste disposal companies.

These cleaning services are not confined to crime or trauma scenes but may include hospitals, police vehicles, holding facilities, and jails. Detainees and/or prisoners sometimes have contagious diseases or defecate, vomit, or bleed while in transport or in their cells. Clean-up requires full protection gear and a variety of chemicals to restore these areas.

Specialized cleaning also extends to buildings or properties that have housed clandestine drug labs or grow-ops. Many of the residual chemicals in meth and ecstasy labs can cause severe respiratory damage, burn eyes and skin, and still be at risk for fire and explosion.

➤ These chemicals contaminate the indoor environment of a building as in its drywall, flooring, air ducts and plumbing, as well as the outdoor environment including the soil, well, and septic systems. The property is usually quarantined until it is thoroughly cleaned and inspected.

Although the chain of custody at a crime scene is not in effect once police release the scene, cleaners are guided by a highly regulatory process and are trained to inform police of the discovery of evidence if it was missed during the initial investigation.

Part II

Death and Trauma

Chapter 4

Death at the Scene

Pronouncing Death

When police arrive at a trauma scene, they are trained to give their first priority to preserving life. Individuals who are wounded are given immediate first aid by paramedics and/or quickly taken to hospital.

In the case where two officers are present, one accompanies the victim to the hospital and remains with him or her until instructed otherwise. The other officer must remain at the scene. The accompanying officer must take note of any statements made by the victim and the preservation of evidence during the entire process, especially if the individual succumbs to the injury and dies. The chain of custody surrounding the victim is vital especially when he or she is removed from the initial crime scene.

Chain of custody is also the main priority of the officer remaining at the scene. The scene cannot be left unattended until advised by a supervisory officer.

If an individual dies at the scene, the *coroner* is called. The terms *medical examiner* (ME) and *coroner* may be synonymous or might have significant differences in job function; in either case, they are usually the persons responsible for determining death. The *cause of death* is the task of the forensic pathologist (see autopsy section).

The coroner attends all death scenes, whether at the crime scene or medical facility, and in some jurisdictions conducts the preliminary examination of the body. It is the coroner's responsibility to issue a death certificate. The coroner may also order that the body be transported to a forensic medical facility for an autopsy, which is the order given as a *coroner's warrant* directing that an autopsy be performed and certain medical testing be carried out.

Police and forensic investigators are not authorized to pronounce death. However, there are three general exceptions to this standard. In instances of *decapitation*, *trans-section* (body is severed in half), and advanced *decomposition*, police can assume death; otherwise life-saving protocols must be enacted until relieved or discontinued by a qualified person. This standard appears to be common in many areas. However, jurisdictional variances exist, particularly in the terminology used to describe personnel authorized to pronounce death.

Blood transfer on the floor and refrigerator from stabbing after victim sat down. Note the passive drips on cupboards and floor and an expired stain on the back wall. Courtesy of Scott Collings, Hamilton Police Service.

Blood at a Crime Scene

There is unlimited variation in the appearance and extent of crime scenes. Some are barely recognizable as crime scenes, lacking either a body or any indication of violence. In stark contrast, other scenes may present a bewildering array of blood in many forms—pools, wipes, impression transfers, droplets, and spatter, all of which convey crucial information to a trained bloodstain pattern analyst.

The presence of blood at a crime scene may reveal to investigators any or all of the following:

- the movement and direction of persons or objects when shedding blood.
- the position of persons or objects during bloodshed.
- the mechanism or object used to create a specific pattern.
- the direction a stain was traveling when it was deposited.
- the area of origin of an impact bloodstain pattern.
- the minimum number of impacts during an occurrence.
- the sequence of events.

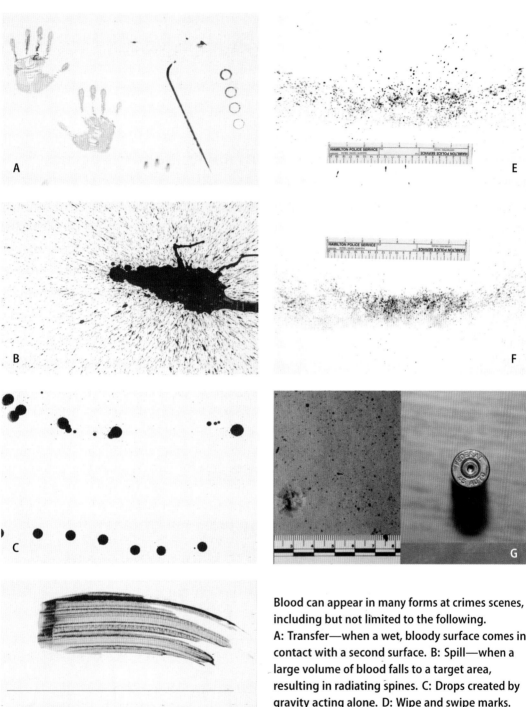

Blood can appear in many forms at crimes scenes, including but not limited to the following.
A: Transfer—when a wet, bloody surface comes in contact with a second surface. B: Spill—when a large volume of blood falls to a target area, resulting in radiating spines. C: Drops created by gravity acting alone. D: Wipe and swipe marks. E: Low-velocity impact. F: Medium-velocity impact. G: High-velocity impact.
Images courtesy of Scott Collings, Hamilton Police Service. All rights reserved.

Although MacDonell (MacDonell and Bialousz 1971) is recognized as a pioneer in the discipline of blood pattern interpretation, there was considerable interest in the field prior to his contributions (see Bevel and Gardner 2002). Nevertheless, MacDonell (MacDonell and Bialousz 1982) may have been the first to create a modern ordered system of gathering, classifying, and interpreting bloodstains.

Bloodstain Pattern Analysis and Properties

Bloodstains have specific properties that are characteristic of whatever action caused them. *Passive* stains are a result of blood falling naturally due to gravity. *Transfer* stains are caused when an object or person bearing blood comes in contact with another object, like a wall or a floor. Finally, *spatter* stains are found when blood drops are propelled onto a surface by a force or energy. This type of stain may be encountered when a victim is shot or beaten and a mist of small blood droplets are projected onto a surface (Sibley, personal communication 2009).

The shape of the blood drops also indicates the angle at which the blood struck the surface. Blood striking a floor at or near 90 degrees leaves stains that have a markedly different appearance from blood striking a wall at 45 degrees.

Bloodstain pattern analysts must conduct their duties with an awareness of the biohazards associated with their discipline. Other forensic technicians may encounter this type of danger sporadically, but it is a constant reality for those who record, gather, and interpret bloodstain evidence.

Specific equipment is required for blood examination, including personal safety equipment (protective suit, gloves, and mask) measuring

Analysts assessing and measuring areas of bloodstain. Image courtesy of Scott Collings, Hamilton Police Service.

aids, such as scales and calipers, not to mention chemistry required for blood enhancement and the photographic equipment required for recording the bloodstains. It should be noted that accuracy in measurement and photography are essential to the accuracy of conclusions they engender.

Assessing Bloodstains

As with all forensic procedures, the steps go in order from least invasive to most invasive. It is critical at the beginning to determine how many separate scenes exist that are relevant to the investigation, the names of all personnel that have had access and contact with the scene, and (as much as possible) the history of the event, including the number of persons involved and the manner of death.

Next the analyst will do a careful walk-through of the scene to determine the exact location(s) of the bloodstain evidence, taking overall photographs and in some cases video recordings. When the evidence has been located and appraised, a range of close-up photographs (bearing scales) is taken.

The areas of interest in the scene are broken down separately by the analyst and marked accordingly, for example, Area A, Area B, and so on. Each bloodstain in the area is described, and the mechanism that may have caused the stains is determined if possible (Collings, personal communication 2009). Sometimes a sketch of the scene is done, showing the interrelationship of the stains and the location of significant objects.

The point of origin of an impact can sometimes be determined in several ways. *String reconstruction* uses angular estimates based on the length/width ratio calculation and pieces of string to link the stains to a common origin (see Wonder 2007). The *tangent method* requires calculation of the incident angle and determination of the area of origin through trigonometry. Finally, the computation of point of impact can be achieved through the use of a 3D computer program such as Back-Track™ or HemoSpat™. These programs are very accurate, efficient, and effective for determining point of origin, and their exclusive use (rather than stringing) has been suggested (Bevel and Gardner 2002). Though any of the three methods will give a similar result, the software option is a rapid extension of the same mathematics used in the string and tangent processes.

In addition to the evidence previously described, a bloodstain pattern analyst occasionally encounters scenes that have been altered or cleaned, a finding that may also be significant to the investigation. Blood wipes, invisible in white light but located through the use of luminol or Blue Star™, can offer evidence of clean-up as well as sites for collecting DNA samples.

Bloodstain pattern evidence frequently supplies investigators with answers to vital questions about what actually happened at a crime scene. The information gleaned through the precise measuring of the presence

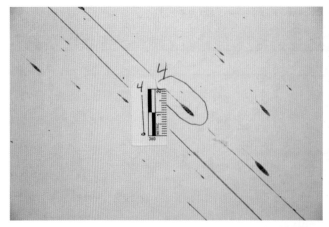

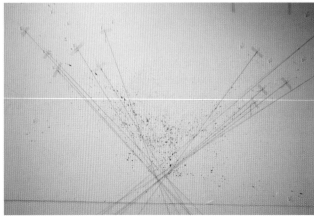

String reconstruction uses angular estimates based on the length/width ratio calculation and pieces of string to link the stains to a common origin.
Images courtesy of Scott Collings, Hamilton Police Service. All rights reserved.

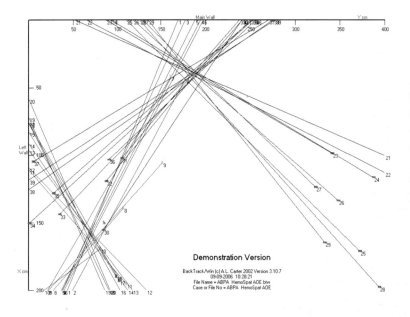

An image generated by the 3D computer program HemoSpat to compute the point and direction of impact.
Image courtesy of Scott Collings, Hamilton Police Service. All rights reserved.

 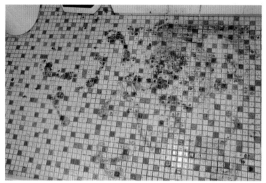

Left: **Floor that has been cleaned of blood.** Right: **Same floor that has been treated with LCV-luminol reveals evidence of blood at the scene.** Images courtesy of Scott Collings, Hamilton Police Service. All rights reserved.

and position of blood can clarify events that otherwise might remain un-decipherable, for example, the number of blows and the position of the victim, if a person was struck repeatedly and while standing or in a kneeling position. This information may well speak to the motive of the subject, and serve to corroborate or disprove other evidence and determine which charges should be laid. Due to major advances in the field, bloodstain pattern analysis is now routinely accepted in courts throughout the world (Sibley, personal communication 2009).

Bloodletting and arterial spurting from stab wounds. Image courtesy of Scott Collings, Hamilton Police Service. All rights reserved.

Victim was shot in the leg, damaging the femoral artery and supplying his left shoe with a continuous supply of blood. Blood is transferred to the sidewalk as a single-angled transfer pattern each time his foot landed as he continued running from the perpetrator. The longer pattern that runs through the transfer is a cast-off from his left leg swinging forward to take the stride. Images courtesy of Scott Collings, Hamilton Police Service.

Coroners versus Medical Examiners

The terms *coroner* and *medical examiner* have often been confused by the general public and used synonymously, usually because their activities are not clearly defined by the media. Indeed, they are both involved with deaths and legal inquiry, but they have very different roles and a different history with the legal investigative process.

The term *coroner* comes from the Latin word *corona*, meaning crown. The position was established in England by the twelfth century and originally had to do with safeguarding the king's monetary interests. The coroner was also in charge of handling the relinquished property of felons, murderers, and suicides, hence, the early association with death and crime. Eventually, the responsibility for recording these deaths and keeping track of all criminal matters in the county led to an official position. By the nineteenth century, the English coroner's function and chief duty was to inquire into the sudden or violent deaths of individuals and conduct an *inquest* (a legal inquiry) to determine the probable cause of such deaths. Early colonists brought this tradition with them to North America.

ZarPro™, a promising new product for recovery and enhancement of blood impressions, will become available very shortly. This product consists of lifting strips with a proprietary coating that bond quickly and efficiently with proteinaceous materials present in blood and other body fluids.

The strips are activated by spraying with a 50 percent solution of methanol and then pressed to the substrate, ensuring total continuous contact. This can be achieved with a fingerprint roller. When completely dried, the lift may be examined under laser (532 nm) or forensic light source (505 nm). Transferred impressions exhibit strong fluorescence.

The process appears to be user and environmentally friendly and inexpensive, as well as effective on older and faint blood impressions. Operational use will determine its true value.

Blood impression six months old on cotton cloth.

Impression transfer on ZarPro strip in ambient light.

Impression transfer on ZarPro strip in fluorescent mode under forensic light source 505 nm.

Images courtesy of Jessica Zarate, Michigan State Police.

In modern times, the coroner is an elected or appointed official involved in the investigation of the sudden and/or unattended death of any citizen, and whenever there is suspicion of *foul play* (suspicion that the death occurred by the actions of another or others). In the United States, some state laws do not require that coroners be medical doctors if they are not responsible for directly handling or examining the deceased. In this case, coroner's duties are chiefly administrative and focus on consolidating information provided by investigators, police, and witnesses.

The coroner is also empowered by the state to seek out the assistance of any specialist, when necessary, to determine the *cause* and *manner* of death (see following discussion) and to assess whether foul play was involved. In cases where death is unexplained, sudden, and/or accidental, especially in work-related areas and public spaces, an inquest may be held by the coroner to further investigate the death. A coroner's report is issued out of this inquest, which often highlights safety issues and recommends changes aimed at preventing further deaths in such circumstances.

The *medical examiner* is a legally appointed medical doctor, usually one specializing in forensic pathology, who reviews deaths occurring as a result of accident, homicide, and suicide. Any death that is suspicious becomes a case for the medical examiner who then becomes the central figure in the forensic investigation. The medical examiner visits crime scenes, examines medical and laboratory evidence, and is chiefly responsible for the *autopsy*, the medico-legal examination of the deceased (see later discussion).

In the United States, both the coroner and medical examiner system are in effect, depending on the region. Since there is no federal law requiring that coroners be licensed physicians, certain states give the coroner the right to empower a medical examiner to carry out a medical investigation and conduct autopsies. In other states, the coroner has been entirely replaced by the medical examiner, who is appointed to carry out the same form of investigation.

There is no national system requiring medical examiners to be certified as pathologists. Thus, in rural communities and in more remote areas, physicians can act as local medical examiners. In either system, the point of such administrative duties is to provide judicial authorities with details of cases involving a death. In short, whenever and wherever a death has occurred, the manner and cause must be accounted for either by the coroner, the medical examiner, or both.

Cause and Manner of Death

When investigating the death of an individual, there is an important distinction made between the *manner* and the *cause* of death. In a legal investigation there are several categories that define the manner in which a person has died. This includes how the death occurred, where and when it occurred, and whether death could have been brought about by *accident*, *suicide*, *homicide*, *natural causes*, or *undetermined circumstances*.

The cause of death is the actual trauma, event, disease, or illness that triggers the physiological processes resulting in death. An example of cause of death would be *asphyxia* (lack of oxygen), and whether it was self-imposed (suicide), accidental, or done by another (homicide) describe the manner of death.

Pathologists conducting an *autopsy* (see following section) examine the soft tissue of the body in an attempt to determine the manner and cause of an individual's death. The standard procedure involves examining the exterior body, noting any abnormalities, and then dissecting the body to expose and examine the internal organs.

There is often sufficient information in the soft tissue to establish a good picture of what took place just prior to and during the individual's death. Vital organs, by their position in the body and their size, shape, and/or contents can reveal, for example, whether an individual drowned, suffocated, was asphyxiated, poisoned, shot, stabbed, strangled, or struck by a vehicle.

The Autopsy

Autopsies are performed for both medical and forensic purposes, and the overall procedures are the same in both arenas. However, the reason and focus for either type of autopsy differ substantially.

Medical autopsies are performed by pathologists in hospitals for the purpose of understanding the course and extent of an illness, disease, or injury. The individual's identity and the cause of death are known prior to a medical autopsy. If these were not known, the death would then have to be referred to the coroner, thereby changing the nature of the autopsy and the personnel involved. Permission to perform a medical autopsy must be given by individuals with legal control of the body, as in the next-of-kin or a religious leader entrusted by the family (see Nafte 2000).

Generally, the medical autopsy is a learning procedure that provides doctors and medical students an opportunity to observe pathologies and collect biological material (tissue samples, cells, and fluids). In the case where they are performed on the bodies of soldiers returned from war zones and battles, autopsies serve to not only assess the extent of wounds and injuries but also establish recommendations in changes to protective clothing, gear, and equipment.

Establishing Identity

Forensic autopsies are performed by pathologists in conjunction with or by the medical examiner as part of the legal investigative process. Permission is not required by the next-of-kin and can be performed on the request of the coroner. Often the request is received in the form of a coroner's warrant to seize the body and conduct the autopsy. The primary purpose of the forensic autopsy is to establish the events leading to a death (manner of death) as well as the immediate physical cause (cause of death). Special emphasis is placed on establishing the identity of the deceased when possible, determining the approximate place and time of death, and collecting trace evidence. The medical examiner acts in support of criminal investigations by providing this information in the form of a medico-legal report submitted to a judicial body.

The autopsy follows a routine procedure in which the body is systematically examined externally and internally. The entire process is thor-

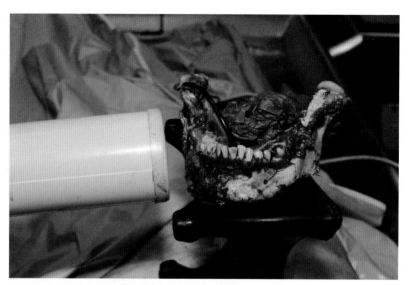

Dental remains are x-rayed for identification purposes. Image courtesy of Scott Collings, Hamilton Police Service. All rights reserved.

oughly documented in note form and through dictation, photography, and sometimes videotape.

Forensic investigators and homicide detectives may be present at the autopsy, providing the pathologist with a verbal and photographic tour of the scene of death. They may also photograph the procedure for their own files, and during the autopsy they may be required to seize personal items and/or clothing for storage or further analysis.

Before external examination begins, radiographs of the body may be taken, blood tests are administered to check the body for any infectious diseases, and fingerprints are recorded if the fingers are intact. Invaluable medical and dental records of missing individuals are evaluated and compared, as they confirm and establish the identity of the deceased. However, for these records to narrow the range of possibilities or yield any results, a tentative identity of the victim must be obtained.

In cases where the body is in an advanced state of decomposition and identification by next-of-kin or witnesses is not possible, fingerprint recovery may be still be an option. The friction skin on the fingers, palms, and soles is thicker than the epidermis elsewhere on the body and can be recomposed for identification. Fingertips (*distal phalanges*) may be amputated by the pathologist and placed in a jar of tissue-building solution, which rehydrates *friction ridges* (see chapter 7). The forensic identification officer can then recover a legible fingerprint impression. Alternatively, a syringe of air or tissue-building solution can be injected right into the fingertips of the deceased. The skin temporarily swells the friction ridges, making them impressionable enough for recovery.

In other conditions the body may be mummified, with the fingers hard and wrinkled. The writer has experienced success in using liquid

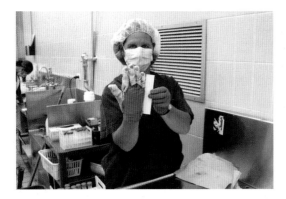
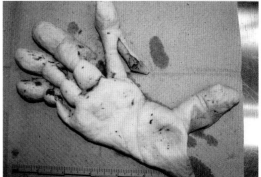
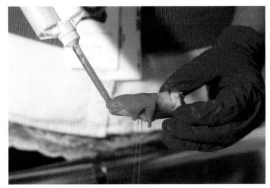
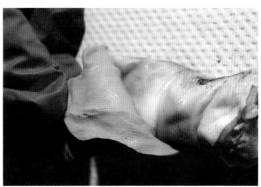

Top: **Victim's hand is degloved for identification.**

Center: **The use of vinyl polysiloxan creates a thin high-resolution copy of the friction skin from a detached distal phalange.**

Bottom: **Fingerprint powder is used to enhance contrast for printing fingertip.**

latex and dental impression materials like vinyl polysiloxan to create a thin high-resolution copy of the friction skin.

In cases where bodies have been submerged in water for a lengthy period of time (see chapter 6) the skin of the hands and feet can often be peeled right off in a process called *degloving*. Palm prints and fingerprints can be taken for comparison from these remains, photographed directly or dusted with black powder to enhance contrast (see Modeste and Anderson 2009).

Efforts to positively identify the victim may include news releases, a facial reconstruction from remains (see chapter 7), the questioning of witnesses, and the sought-out premortem medical and dental records.

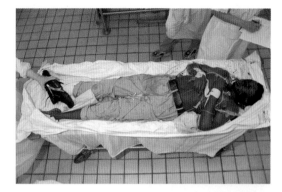
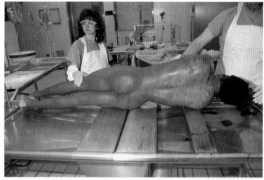
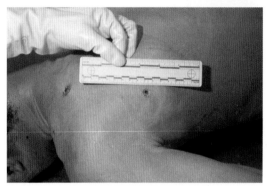

External examination of a shooting victim. Images courtesy of Toronto Police Forensic Identification Services.

Former surgeries, artificial limbs, any hospital visits, and dental work are all compared with those observed in and on the victim. The autopsy continues when the pathologist is satisfied that law enforcement has exhausted all means to make a positive identification.

External Examination

During the external examination, a description of the deceased is recorded along with any items of clothing, jewelry, or wrappings. All items removed from the body are documented, packaged, and carefully transferred for further evidence analysis. Labeling and logging all materials removed from the body are essential in beginning and maintaining the chain of custody. Superficial marks on the body as well as any injuries, tattoos, previous medical treatments, and wounds are assessed and documented.

Great care is taken when handling the body, especially one in an advanced state of decomposition. Tissue is vulnerable to further damage, and body parts, hair, and external cavities may bear trace evidence of considerable importance, such as insect larvae, bodily fluids from a different individual, or fibers from a suspect's clothing.

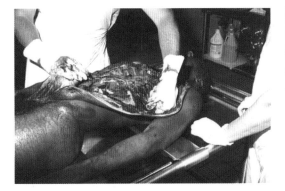
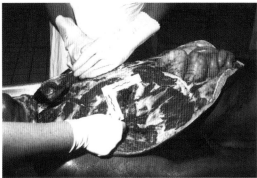
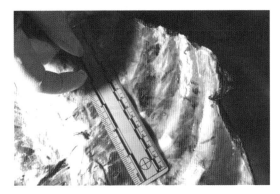

Internal examination allows the pathologist to observe any evidence of trauma and cause of death.

Internal Examination

When the external examination is complete, the body is opened up for an internal inspection. If the body is relatively intact, the regions that are given the most attention are the head, chest, and abdominal area, where the major organs are located. Observing this area involves sawing open the skull to expose the brain and making a deep Y-incision from the top of both shoulders down the center of the chest to expose the internal organs. A small power saw is used to cut the ribs, which are removed for access to the heart and lungs. This method of cutting and removing is known as the Rokitansky procedure, after the late 1800s pathologist (Carl von Rokitansky) who developed this form of autopsy.

An overall visual inspection of the position of the organs within the body cavities is referred to as macroscopic. This is where the walls of the body cavities and the hard and soft tissues (muscle and bones) are examined for evidence of disease, injury, and trauma. Tissue samples are taken from some of these organs for microscopic examination. Organs are then removed from the body, examined, weighed, and measured. Blood or fluids present are measured and documented, and any abnormalities are noted. Tissue samples are sent to the appropriate forensic laboratory departments (such as toxicology and biology) for further analysis.

 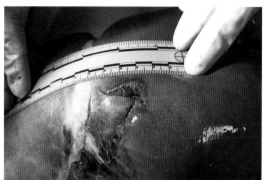

Measuring trauma in the vital organs, heart and liver.

The length, procedure, and goal of the forensic autopsy depend entirely on the condition of the remains. The process described is standard, performed when the body is relatively intact and not in an advanced state of decomposition. However, if the body is burned, severely decomposed, in pieces, or skeletonized, then the overall examination is modified and taken over by a forensic anthropologist assisted by an odontologist, thus precluding an internal examination.

Chapter 5

Evidence of Trauma

The Mortems

In all death investigations, pathologists, forensic anthropologists, and odontologists refer to three periods of time to distinguish when an injury took place: *antemortem* (before death), *perimortem* (around the time of or during death), and *postmortem* (after death).

The point of placing an injury into such periods is to understand its relevance to the case and its association (if any) with the individual's death. For example, a skull fracture that occurred years before a person's death may not be relevant to a current homicide investigation other than to help establish an identification. However, if it occurred at or around the time of death, it can provide crucial evidence.

In associating an injury with the time in which it was likely to have been sustained, the pathologist or specialist can sometimes determine the manner and/or cause of death, or at least reconstruct the likely events that occurred during any of these three periods.

Antemortem Injuries

Antemortem injuries rarely give any clues to the manner or cause of death, but evidence of them can make identification of the individual more possible. Premortem medical and/or dental records of a known individual must exist to compare with the postmortem x-rays taken of the unidentified remains. If the premortem injuries and/or past surgical procedures are the same in both x-rays, it is most likely the known individual and the unidentified remains are of the same person.

The reason for this important comparison is due to the distinctive characteristics of healed wounds and injuries. When tissue and/or bone heal, there is evidence of this in the scarring on the tissue and the remodeling of bone.

In the event that healing has taken place, it can logically be concluded that the injury was sustained before an individual's death. For example, when the hard, outer layer or inner spongy layer of bone is traumatized by a fracture, puncture, and/or break, a series of physiological events take place to repair the damage. Initially, the area in and around the le-

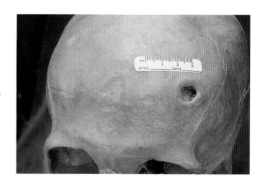

Evidence of an antemortem wound to the left part of the frontal bone of skull that has healed. Image courtesy of Dr. A. Keenleyside.

sion swells up and fills with blood generated by the injured blood vessels of the bone marrow, adjacent muscles, or the *periosteum* (the tissue covering the bone). This localized swelling is referred to as a *hematoma.* Its size depends on the nature and extent of the damage—the more serious the injury, the larger the hematoma (Nafte 2000, 126–9).

Plasma, the watery substance of the blood, contains proteins that eventually cause blood in the area of the lesion to clot, usually six to eight hours after the injury. Within a week, a fibrous matrix is formed within the blood clot. The fibrous matrix or *callus* forms the initial site where new bone cells are laid down to replace the ones that were damaged in the injury. The final result is remodeled bone, most of which retains a unique deformity because it is unlike the original form it has replaced.

The nature and extent of the injury, the age and health of the individual, and the location of the injury ultimately determine the length of time for tissue or bone to heal and remodel. In young children, for instance, lesions and fractures heal quite rapidly with visible signs of remodeling (apparent in radiographs) as early as two weeks and bone consolidation within four to six weeks after the injury. In adults, the process is much slower, with bone taking anywhere from three to five months to consolidate depending on age, health, and body weight (Merbs 1989, 163).

Bone that has healed and remodeled has a distinctive look. Therefore, any visible evidence of healing indicates that the individual survived the injury. Healed lesions, for example, originally caused by puncture wounds or an amputation, often have rounded edges. Their surfaces are smooth, and any depression marks are filled in. Lesions caused by fractures have marked areas where the edges united. The union may be complete, indicating that the healing process was uninterrupted.

Healing may continue up to the point of a person's death but not beyond it. Though it is impossible to date an actual injury simply by observing the lesion, in the event of bone remodeling it can only be presumed that the individual was alive when it occurred. Hence, if a skeletal or tissue wound is apparent, the more extensive the repair, the older the injury.

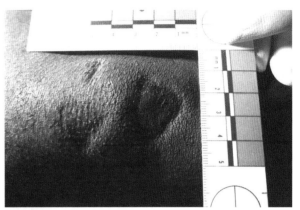

Highlighting an antemortem injury during an autopsy. Toronto Police Forensic Identification Services. All rights reserved.

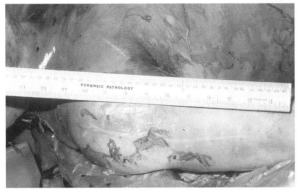

Identifying a premortem scar during the external examination. Image courtesy of The Office of the Chief Coroner, Ontario. All rights reserved.

Perimortem Injuries

Tissue and skeletal lesions with no evidence of healing usually indicate that an injury was sustained close to the time of or just after an individual's death. Distinguishing between these two periods, however, is difficult and can be even more ambiguous if the injury was sustained before the healing process became evident. When unhealed lesions and wounds are apparent, their pattern and nature become the focus of an investigation. They are defined as *perimortem* injuries and may be associated with the manner and/or cause of death.

When pathologists and forensic anthropologists assess perimortem tissue and skeletal lesions, two important factors are considered: the nature and cause of the lesion. The *nature* of the lesion refers to the type of injury incurred, such as a fracture, amputation, or puncture wound. The *cause* of the lesion refers to the implement or the event that caused the wound, such as a knife, an axe, or a stress injury. Determining the nature and cause of perimortem lesions along with the context in which the remains have been found help a team of investigators establish whether a further investigation is required.

Injuries to bodies and fresh bone caused by bullets, blunt objects, and sharp instruments often leave characteristic patterns that are identifiable

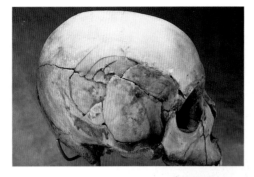

Perimortem head injury evident in blunt force trauma to the right temporal side. Image courtesy of Dr. A. Keenleyside.

Perimortem blunt force trauma to the left side of the head. Note fracture of the zygomatic arch (cheekbone) and lower jaw (mandibular body) as well as perforation through the posterior wall of the maxillary (upper jaw) sinus (background). Image courtesy of Dr. R. Lazenby.

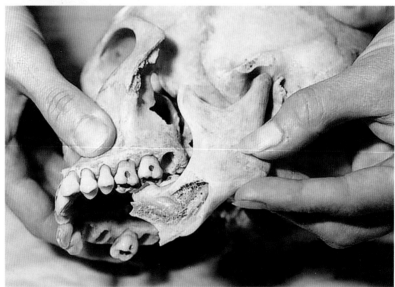

by forensic investigators. Most can be identified with the naked eye, whereas others require the use of a microscope, especially when the direction and angle of an injury are being examined. Following are a few examples of the nature and cause of perimortem lesions common to forensic investigators.

Bullet Wounds

A bullet is a relatively small object propelled at a very high velocity. The pattern of the wound it creates depends entirely on the type of tissue and bone it hits and the ballistic properties of the projectile; these include the temperature, volume, and pressure of the gases resulting from combustion, gravity, and air resistance, as well as the weight, shape, and caliber of the projectile (Spitz 1993, 311–412).

A gunshot wound to the skull leaves a pattern of penetration and fracture. The entrance hole is usually circular, beveled internally, and sharply edged, while the exit hole is more ragged and beveled externally (Di Maio

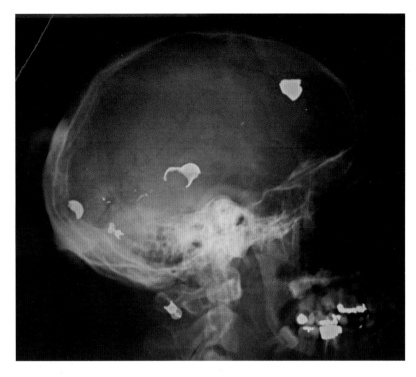

Radiograph of bullets and fragments lodged in the skull of the victim. Image courtesy of Her Majesty the Queen in Right of Canada as represented by the Royal Canadian Mounted Police. © 2009.

1993). Higher velocity projectiles cause greater and more rapid fracturing than lower velocity projectiles, and there may be radiating fractures to both the entry and exit wounds (Harkness et al. 1984).

A lower velocity projectile may incur a smaller entry wound with little to no fracturing and no exit wound if the bullet remains lodged in the skull. The patterns produced by radiating fractures are important to observe, as they help in establishing the direction of the bullet as well as the entry and/or exit wounds when either or both are missing.

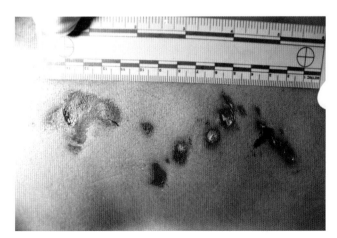

Shrapnel scars on the skin of a shooting victim. Image courtesy of Toronto Police Forensic Identification Services.

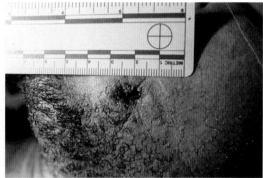
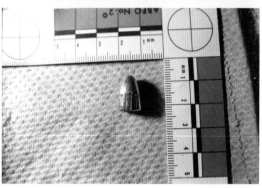
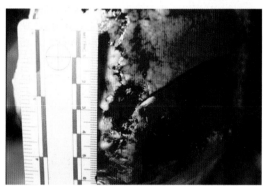

Clockwise from top left:

Entrance wound on head.

The larger exit wound.

Bullet extracted during autopsy.

Entrance wound causing fracture of the right parietal bone of skull.

Tracing the trajectory of a bullet through the victim's head.

Images courtesy of Toronto Police Forensic Identification Services. All rights reserved.

Gunshots to other parts of the body and skeleton do not leave the same pattern of fracturing as in the skull. Unless a bullet is lodged in the actual bone, there is seldom a complete bullet evident, and the marks left are often in the form of nicks and small depressions caused by the metal pellets or fragments. Bullet fragments can be dispersed throughout the body, and in decomposed or skeletal remains these are not evident unless the remains are x-rayed.

Sharp Force Injury

Any pointed and/or sharp implement including knives, picks, axes, and hatchets, can cause sharp force injuries. These leave identifiable

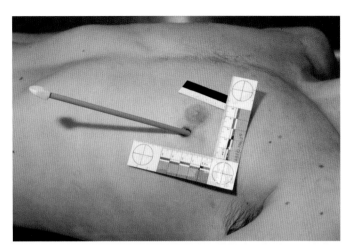

Inserting trajectory implement to measure the direction and velocity of a bullet wound. Image courtesy of Scott Collings, Hamilton Police Service. All rights reserved.

marks on tissue, muscle, and bone. Sharp-pointed instruments leave deeper and smoother holes than flat-bladed objects, which produce longer, v-shaped notches (Stewart 1979, 78). The sharp edges of a knife can often splinter and cut bone, creating clean or curled edges much like whittled wood. A dull edge can dent or gouge tissue and bone, leaving uneven edges.

Determining the direction of the injury and the instrument used often requires the use of a scanning electron microscope. This instrument highlights the fine details, such as the nicks from a blade, the scarring from the serrated edges of knives, or the sequence of the cut mark on bone not visible to the naked eye. Microscopic analysis helps identify the instrument and sometimes the intent of the perpetrator.

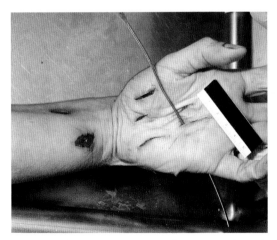
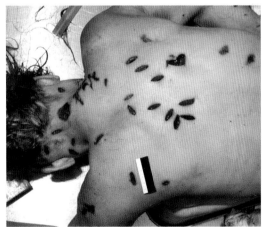

Left: **Sharp force penetrating defense wounds to the hands of victim.** Right: **Multiple stab wounds.** Image courtesy of Scott Collings, Hamilton Police Service. All rights reserved.

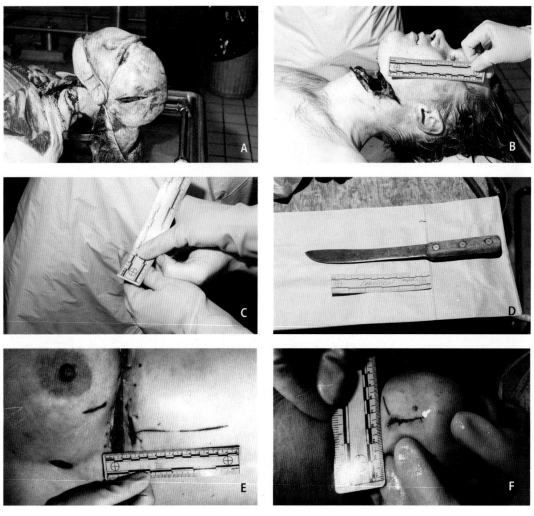

A. Sharp force trauma to left temporal-parietal area of skull penetrating the temporalis muscle.

B. Severe sharp force injury across the neck.

C. Sharp force trauma, defensive wounds on victim's fingers.

D. Knife used in slashing of victim's throat.

E. Deep-penetrating wounds of sharp force trauma.

F. Stab wound identified on the underside of the victim's chin.

Blunt Force Injury

A blow to the head from a blunt object (such as a club) can produce a depressed fracture. The site of impact is usually caved in, showing what is referred to as *inbending*, the size of which depends on the size of the object and the force behind it. The larger the object and the harder the blow, the wider and more caved in the depression will be. The area

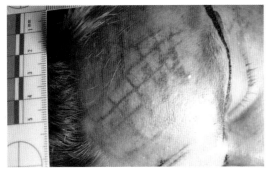

Above: **Blunt force trauma to head. Imprint of footwear marks victim's forehead.**

Below: **Depressed fracture to the occipital region of the head caused by a hammer.** Image courtesy of the Office of the Chief Coroner, Ontario.

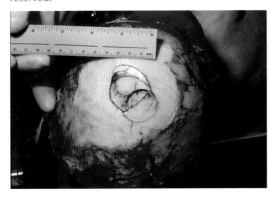

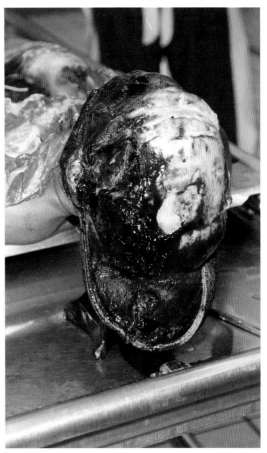

Above: **Blunt force trauma to the head causing the depressed fracture of the left temporal-parietal region of the skull.**

surrounding the site of impact will often have fracture lines that radiate away from the depression, called *outbending* (Gurdjian et al. 1950). The length and direction of the fracture lines depends on the site of impact and the force behind the blow, since a fracture will take the path of least resistance and spread until its energy is dissipated (Berryman and Symes 1998, 337).

Postmortem Trauma

Any injuries and/or modifications to the body occurring after an individual has died are considered *postmortem*. However, if injuries have been sustained at the time of and just after death, distinguishing between

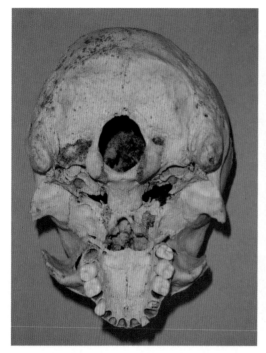

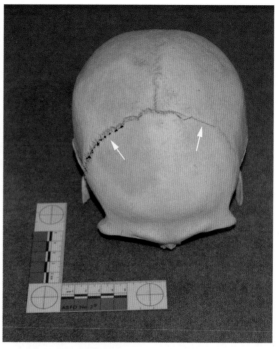

Basilar view of human cranium showing signs of animal scavenging. Note that both cheekbones are missing.

Part of a human skull (calotte) recovered during excavation by backhoe. Arrows point to separation of the coronal suture caused by the equipment, and not associated with perimortem trauma. Images courtesy of Dr. R. Lazenby. All rights reserved.

the two periods is nearly impossible. Hence, these sorts of injuries are considered *peri*mortem, even though the individual may have been dead at the time they were sustained.

↪ Postmortem injuries or modifications are categorized as *intentional* versus *unintentional*. Intentional postmortem injuries refer to the intent and acts of a perpetrator when dealing with the remains. An example of this would be dismemberment. Unintentional postmortem injuries refer to a variety of factors that may modify or damage remains, such as animal scavenging, weather conditions, a body submerged in water, or poor recovery methods.

Intentional Dismemberment

Remains that have been intentionally dismembered often represent an attempt by the perpetrator to hide the remains, make their identification impossible, or make their transport more manageable. Since it is necessary to cut through bone to take apart the human body, identifying marks are often found as remnants of this act. Knives, saws, axes,

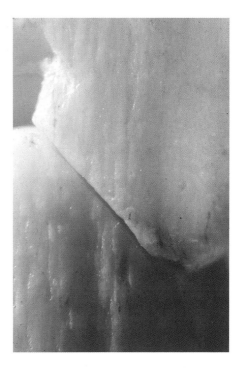

The even striations of saw marks left on bone after intentional dismemberment. Image courtesy of the Office of the Chief Coroner, Ontario. All rights reserved.

and hatchets all leave characteristic patterns, but to differentiate these patterns the marks must be viewed with a microscope. Therefore, body parts that are recovered by investigators are defleshed for a thorough skeletal analysis.

Microscopic analysis reveals that both serrated and straight-edged knife blades cutting against bone leave narrow marks with v-shaped and smooth striations. If applied to fresh bone, which is more elastic than dried bone, the wound closes on withdrawal of the knife. This leaves a cut mark with less of a width than the blade that caused it (Reichs 1998, 358).

Dismembered human remains, intentionally cut and ripped apart. Image courtesy of the Office of the Chief Coroner, Ontario. All rights reserved.

The marks left by saw blades tend to be more square in cross-section and wider than the blade itself. The striations are more visible and can be seen without a microscope since the saw blade is composed of rows of teeth with an extensive cutting edge. Axes and hatchets require extensive, repetitive force and chopping action to cut through bone. As a result, there may be a lot of chipping, splintering, or fracturing of bone, also known as *wastage* (Reichs 1998, 359).

Upon inspection, cut marks are smooth and v-shaped like a knife's but much wider. Under a microscope, striations are visible.

Unintentional Dismemberment

When a body is left exposed outdoors, it invariably attracts a variety of scavengers. First on the scene are dead-flesh-eating insects that burrow into orifices and open wounds, feeding exclusively on flesh. Their cycle of feeding and reproductive activity does not damage bone and is often important in assessing the *postmortem interval*, the amount of time that has elapsed since death.

Birds and small animals pick at the softer exposed fleshy parts like the area around the cheeks, lips, eyes, and ears. Carnivores including dogs, wolves, coyotes, and bears eat the available soft tissue as well as chew or gnaw on the remaining bones. Noncarnivores such as rodents, raccoons, and porcupines often arrive to gnaw on defleshed bone, deriving minerals and keeping their teeth sharp.

Dismemberment due to animal activity has a very different look and pattern. Bones that have been chewed bear impressions of teeth; the edges are generally more ragged with deep grooves, scratches, and fragmentation. The ends of long bones are often chewed first because these are areas rich in marrow. Without these distinctive articular surfaces, the remaining shafts that are fragmented are difficult to identify and can be

Maggot infestation on a cadaver.

Left: **Bone that has been gnawed by rodents. Note the uneven striations.**

Below: **Femoral diaphysis (the shaft of the femur bone) showing classic carnivore gnawing resulting in destruction of the epiphyses (bone ends), as well as rodent damage along the length of the center (linea aspera).** Image courtesy of Dr. R. Lazenby.

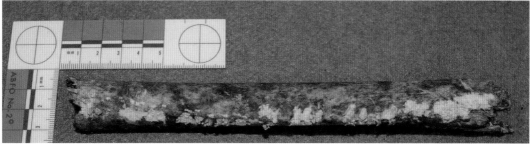

confused with other species. This is especially the case when they are dragged into animal lairs or dens, where they are commingled with other animal bones.

If an animal killed the individual, then any damage to the skeleton is considered perimortem. Most cases of animal scavenging are postmortem, but an individual's body does not have to be outdoors for this to occur. For example, there are many reported cases of animal scavenging by domestic house pets after a pet owner has died. Dogs and cats have been known to eat their deceased owners when confined with their bodies and no other food source is available.

Damage to the skeleton that occurs long after the individual's death is often recognizable due to the differences between fresh and old bone. Fresh bone is softer, moist, and more elastic. This makes it more pliable, so when fractured it splinters and has more irregular edges that remain attached. Old bone is dry and brittle and therefore shatters more readily, with cleaner edges and regular fragments. New surfaces that are exposed in old bone as a result of breaking or cracking will often be lighter in color, indicating that the break was postmortem.

Animal scavenging of human remains. In this case a dog has eaten and chewed the remains of its owner.

Site where human remains are scattered and skeletonized. Intentional dismemberment is evident along with animal scavenging. Image courtesy of Dr. R. Lazenby. All rights reserved.

Burned Bodies

The bodies of individuals who have been trapped in burning structures or vehicles, set themselves on fire, or were intentionally burned to dispose of their remains can still be identified in many instances. In short-duration fires, like those occurring in small structures and vehicles, a good portion of the skeleton can survive the firing process, and the burned skeletal remains will still be good indicators for determining the person's age, sex, and race.

In cases where the skeleton has been reduced to very small fragments and ash, as in cremation, identification is next to impossible unless fragments of the skeleton are recognizable. In both scenarios, identification is made more possible with antemortem dental and medical records that can be compared with the remains or items that have survived with the remains, such as dental appliances, surgical implements, and orthopedic devices.

Though the skeleton is not entirely destroyed in short-duration fires, it is considerably reduced in size to many bits and pieces. Prolonged firing of bone that contains flesh causes the intact bone marrow to heat and quickly expand, eventually causing the bone to shatter. Within a skull, the dense tissue and the brain matter expand, creating enough internal pressure to cause the skull to explode, pieces of which may be scattered some distance from their original site. Limb bones are reduced to less than half their original length, and ribs usually burn down to small stubs protruding from the vertebral column. The longer the fire and more intense the heat, the more reduced the skeleton will be (Maples and Browning 1995).

Fleshed or living bone burns differently from dry bone due to the difference in moisture and fat content. When bone with flesh attached is burned, deep transverse fracture lines appear on the bone because of the expansion and pressure caused by the heating of intact flesh. There is also considerable warping, and blackened tissue on or within the bone may still be visible. Conversely, dry bone that has been burned has very little warping with longitudinal fracture lines and some superficial cracking (Binford 1972, 376; see also Holck 1997, Schmidt and Symes 2008).

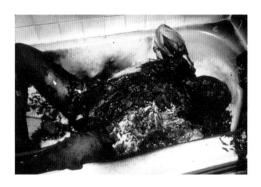

Burned remains from a short-duration fire.
Image courtesy of the Office of the Chief Coroner, Ontario. All rights reserved.

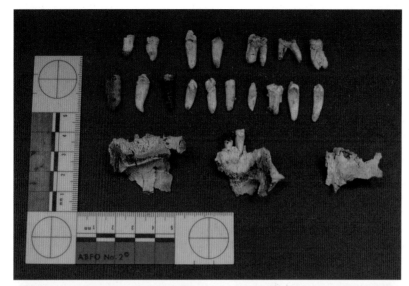

Dental remains recovered from a cremation, including portions of the upper jaw (maxilla). Image courtesy of Dr. R. Lazenby.

Debris from fire scene being sorted in the lab. The base of the forceps points to a human molar. Image courtesy of Dr. R. Lazenby.

Burned human skeletal remains are assembled according to size and shape. Note the blackened remnants of skin are evident on some bone. Images courtesy of the Office of the Chief Coroner, Ontario.

Burned human remains in situ. The fragility and fire-related destruction of tissue makes location and recovery a challenging task.

Scene of burned human remains now with a 2 x 2 meter grid divided into 20 x 20 cm units. The grid is employed to facilitate maximum controlled recovery. Image courtesy of Dr. R. Lazenby. All rights reserved.

Body undergoing cremation in high-intensity fire.
Image courtesy of Toronto Police Forensic Identification Services. All rights reserved.

Burned bone must be sorted through with all of the bits and pieces organized by size and shape. Ideally, some of the pieces can be fitted and glued together to the point where they can be measured and examined more completely.

Flat bones and irregularly shaped bones are placed together as they are normally associated with bones from the axial skeleton, originating from the skull, scapula, sternum, ribs, vertebral column, and pelvis. Bones with a remaining shaft and a small or large diameter represent the appendicular skeleton, those bones originating from the upper and lower limbs.

Chapter 6

Sudden and Not-So-Sudden Death

Defining Death

From a biological perspective, death does not occur as a singular event. Death can be said to unfold as a continuous process that occurs over a period of time, the length of which depends on the condition of the body and the environment it is in.

Somatic death is the first stage (see Table 6.1), when cardiac activity stops and respiration, movement, reflexes, and brain activity cease. Muscles, organs, tissues, and cells begin to break down and die at different intervals, which can vary from three minutes to a few hours. Complex chemical reactions take place, and certain enzymes are activated. The blood becomes acidic and begins to clot.

Cellular death (*autolysis*) is the final stage when metabolism ceases and all the cells in the body are dead. The time frame within which autolysis occurs is largely dependent on environmental factors. The higher the temperature, the faster cellular death occurs because the chemical changes taking place are accelerated by heat. During and after the stages of cellular death, the biochemical process of decomposition begins and, if uninterrupted, will continue until the body is completely skeletonized.

Table 6.1. The Process of Death

Somatic Death	• cardiac activity stops
	• no respiration or movement
Cellular Death (Autolysis)	• metabolism ceases
	• all cells are dead

Estimating the Time of Death

The Mortises

When the process of cellular death begins, late postmortem stages set in. The enzymatic changes and biochemical reactions taking place in the human body give rise to three conditions known as *algor, livor*, and *rigor mortis*. These conditions usually occur simultaneously, beginning in the first two to four hours after death and continuing until approximately forty-eight hours (see Table 6.2).

Algor mortis (*algor* is Latin for cold and *mortis* means deadly) is the stage where the body loses heat and its core temperature of about 98.6°F (37°C) falls to that of the surrounding or ambient environment. If death occurs in a hotter environment, however, the core body temperature rises and late postmortem changes are accelerated. The amount of heat loss or gain is highly variable and depends on factors such as:

- the temperature of the body before death,
- the temperature of the surrounding environment,
- the type of clothing on the individual,
- the size and age of the body, and
- how the body is contained.

The time of death, based on the development of algor mortis, can be estimated by measuring the core body temperature, since it falls theoretically at a predictable rate (approximately 1.5°F per hour), and comparing it to the ambient temperature. However, the factors just listed limit the estimates of time of death to approximations only. In other words, the time it takes for a core body temperature to reach that of its surrounding environment varies from almost no time to just over two hours depending on the individual and the environment.

While the core body temperature is falling, blood that is high in acidity begins to pool and clot in areas that are free of any pressure. Gravity pulls heavy red blood cells downward, and with no heart pumping circulation, these cells begins to sink and clot. This clotting produces a dark, bruise-like coloring. The parts of the body that are restricted by pressure from items, such as tight clothing, belts, or contact with hard surfaces, are often lighter or blanched as the capillaries are compressed and blood cannot settle in these areas. The patterns of bruising and blanching on the body as a result of blood clotting is a condition referred to as livor mortis (*livor* is Latin for "bluish color").

The trained professional can detect livor mortis soon after blood begins to settle approximately fifteen to twenty minutes after death. However, it is usually not evident until at least two hours after somatic death. Livor mortis advances further with clotted areas darkening and eventually becomes *fixed* approximately four to six hours after death.

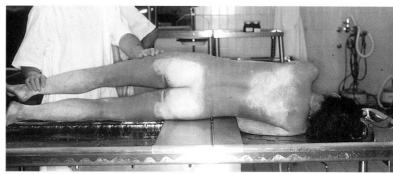

Livor mortis apparent and fixed on the body.
Image courtesy of the Office of the Chief Coroner, Ontario. All rights reserved.

The onset of livor mortis is used to assess the amount of time that has elapsed since death, referred to as the *postmortem interval.* It is also useful for determining the position of the body at the time of death. If the patterning of the blanch marks do not correspond with the position the body was found, for example, there is blanching across the individual's stomach and upper legs, but the body was found face up, it can be assumed that the body had been moved from its original position some time after death occurred.

While blood is clotting and settling, muscle cells cease aerobic functioning. Since oxygen is not available, ATP (adenosine triphosphate) is no longer produced and muscle cells must function anaerobically (without oxygen). As a result there is a build-up of lactic acid in the muscle tissue, which in turn causes a chemical reaction. The proteins (actin and myosin) in the muscle begin to fuse, and where they would have come apart with the presence of ATP, they now form a gel-like substance and maintain the contraction of the muscle. The presence of this gel in contracted muscle tissue creates stiffness throughout the body. This state is referred to as rigor mortis (*rigor* is Latin for "stiff").

Initially rigor mortis invades small muscle groups, like the face and hands, within two to four hours after death. Within a twenty-four hour period, it gradually works its way into larger muscles, after which the entire body will be in a state of rigor and remain so for at least twenty-four to forty-eight hours. Within the forty-eight-hour period, chemicals in the muscle cells are consumed, coagulated blood reliquefies, and rigor mortis dissipates, leaving the body flaccid once again.

The amount of time it takes for rigor mortis to permeate the body is determined by several factors. The onset of the rigor will be faster and last for a shorter period of time in a hot environment, in the very young, in the very old, or when an individual has an increased body temperature due to a fever. Heavier and more sedentary individuals with normal body temperatures have a slower rate of onset and a longer period of duration. Conversely, physical activity like running or vigorous exercise just prior to death increases lactic acid levels, which leads to a faster onset of rigor in shorter duration.

Table 6.2. Late Postmortem Changes

Postmortem State	Time Elapsed Since Death	Characteristics
Algor mortis	0–2 hours	• body loses heat • core body temperature falls to that of the surrounding environment
Livor mortis	1–4 hours	• blood clotting • bruising/blanching become evident • blood coagulates • livor mortis becomes fixed approx. 4–6 hours after death
Rigor mortis	2–4 hours	• lactic acid build-up in muscle tissue • proteins in muscle begin to fuse • muscle groups stiffen • stiffening dissipates after 24–48 hours

Though algor, livor, and rigor mortis occur simultaneously, they are independent of one another. Environmental and physical factors will interfere with their onset and length, delaying or prolonging them in an unpredictable way. Estimating the time of death within a forty-eight-hour period (during late postmortem changes) is fairly reliable because of the relatively short period of time that has elapsed since death. As decomposition advances however, estimates beyond the forty-eight-hour time frame vary in accuracy and are less reliable.

Also important to consider is the legal versus the physiological time of death. The legal time of death is the time recorded when the death certificate is signed, that is when death is pronounced at the scene, even though the body may have been discovered hours earlier. The legal time of death is recorded by the coroner or medical examiner appointed to pronounce death. The physiological time is the moment when all vital functions ceased and is an estimate of the postmortem interval. This could only be assessed by the pathologist or medical examiner based on the condition of the remains. As well, the legal and physiological times of death may differ in terms of days, weeks, months, and years depending on when the body was discovered and the extent to which it has decomposed.

"Death cannot be experienced by the individual; it can only be observed in the other."

Immanuel Kant (1724–1804)

The Decomposing Body

To fully understand the postmortem interval and the nature of the internal and external changes taking place, decomposition is organized into stages. The sequence of these changes is somewhat consistent if the body is left undisturbed and within the same environmental conditions. However, the rate at which these changes take place is directly related to the size, age, and condition of the body at death and the quality and time of the body's exposure to factors such as insect activity, climate, animal scavenging, water, and soil composition (see Tables 6.3, 6.4, and 6.5). Extensive decomposition can take a matter of days in hot, humid climates, but can persist for many years in cold, dry climates. Understanding the stages of decomposition for the purpose of estimating the postmortem interval is based on a consideration of these factors, their interplay, and how they differ throughout various geographic and climatic regions.

The early stages of decomposition begin internally, caused by microorganisms already present in the body. Although the body's external appearance may seem fresh, organisms like bacteria and protozoa become active and multiply rapidly throughout the intestinal tract. Gases and

Table 6.3. The Stages of Decomposition

Stage	State of the Remains
Initial decay	• microorganisms active internally • extensive gases produced • body intact and fresh in appearance
Putrefaction	• intensified microbial activity • internal gas causes rapid bloating • purge fluid builds up and leaks • strong odor of decay
Black putrefaction	• body collapses with increased pressure, gases and purge fluid drain • very strong odor of decay • mottled and blackening of exposed flesh • internal organs and tissues break down into a creamy consistency
Butyric fermentation	• biochemical fermenting of exposed flesh • tissue begins to dry slowly • flesh becomes a firm, cheesy consistency
Dry decay	• flesh dries and hardens into a papery or leathery texture
Skeletonization	• soft tissue slowly disintegrates • bone becomes more exposed • tendons, ligaments, and/or cartilage break down slowly and some may be intact • environmental factors determine the level and process of decay in bone

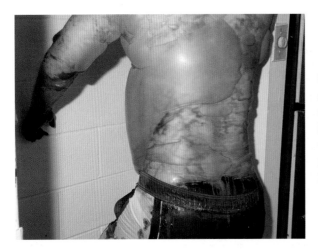

Suicide victim found in mid- to late stages of putrefaction. The marbled green, red, and yellow discoloration, and extensive blistering of the skin indicate at least a week has passed since the time of death. Image courtesy of Scott Collings, Hamilton Police Service.

acids produced as by-products of this activity create rapid swelling and bloating due to increased volatile organic compounds (VOCs). The intestinal tract swells and ruptures, spreading these compounds and pushing out fluids and waste. The body is thus in a state of *putrefaction*. Bacteria *hemolyzes* blood (ruptures red blood cells), creating the green and red marbleizing most notable around the thighs, back, and shoulders. Often there is blistering evident around exposed skin that is filled with fluid. If removed, the skin below is bright pink.

During the later stages of putrefaction, the entire body becomes bloated with the pressure of this internal gas and eventually collapses, leaking what is referred to as *purge fluid*. At this point, the body gives off very strong and distinct odors, caused by VOCs like cadaverine, methane, and putrescene (odors caused by the breakdown of amino acids and intensive microbial activity). The exposed flesh blackens, and the internal organs

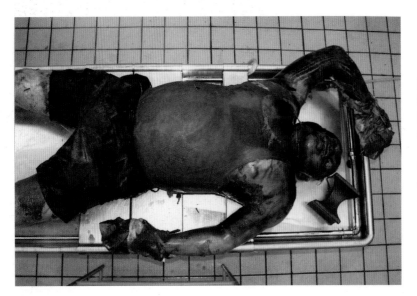

Body is bloated with increased internal gases heightened during mid-stages of putrefaction. Note the bagging of hands to preserve trace evidence. Image courtesy of Toronto Police Service.

Table 6.4. Physical Variables Affecting the Rate of Decomposition

Condition of Body	Decomposition Rate
Small vs. large body size	• Small bodies decompose at a faster rate than large bodies.
Whole vs. wounded/ dismembered	• Whole bodies decompose at a slower rate than wounded or dismembered parts. • There are more tissues and openings available for microbial and insect infestation in the wounded/dismembered body, accelerating decay.
Nude vs. clothed and/or wrapped	• Nude bodies decompose at a faster rate due to exposure to elements. • Heavy clothing or wrapping around body slows rate of decomposition.
Contained and buried vs. not contained and buried	• Contained and buried bodies decompose at a slower rate.

Source: Adapted from Mann et al. (1990).

and tissues take on a creamy consistency. This stage is known as *black putrefaction.* The body then hastens toward fermentation and molding, referred to as *butyric fermentation.* The remaining flesh at this stage is a cheesy consistency and is slowly hardening and drying. Eventually it *desiccates* (dries up) during the stage of *dry decay.*

If a body has been submerged in water (see later discussion) or contains water and a lot of fatty tissue, a layer of what is referred to as *adipocere* (*adipo* is Latin for fat and *cere* means "wax") forms over soft tissue and bone. During the decaying process, a soft, whitish substance then becomes evident on the body. This is caused by the formation of fatty acids

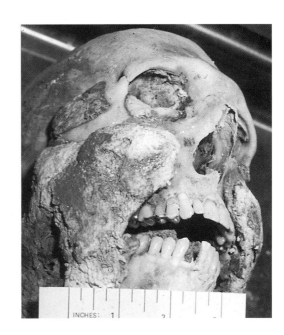

Adipocere covers the skull of an adult male. Image courtesy of Utah State Office of the Medical Examiner. All rights reserved.

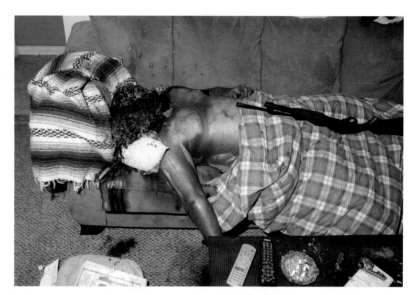

Body in stages of black putrefaction apparent in extensive mottling, the draining of purge fluid, and overall darkening of exposed wounds and flesh. Image courtesy of Scott Collings, Hamilton Police Service.

through the *hydrolysis* and *hydrogenation* of body fats (a chemical reaction involving water that essentially converts body fat to fatty acids).

Though adipocere formation can occur only a few days after death, it does not become visible for at least three months. Once formed, however, it is relatively permanent and may preserve surface features of the body for years if left undisturbed.

Skeletonization

The last stage of decomposition is known as skeletonization. This occurs when most of the soft tissue is gone, exposing the bone. Ligaments, tendons, and cartilage are usually still intact after flesh and muscle decay. These may dry, crack, and eventually disintegrate, depending on environmental factors. Bones at this stage may have a greasy texture, indicating that there is still fatty tissue present. Greasy bones with a brown to dark yellow color represent remains that are months old. Over time, fatty tissue dries up and bones blanch (whiten) if exposed to sunlight and extremes in weather. Bones that have been exposed to the elements for many years often crack and chip (*exfoliate*). If bones are buried, they may absorb the soil contents and become stained. In acidic soils they may disintegrate altogether.

Like the postmortem changes and the initial stages of decomposition, many factors determine the rate at which skeletonization and bone decomposition take place. For instance, if a body is buried in acidic soil in a warm, humid climate, skeletonization of an adult body can take place within a two-week period. In a body that has been left exposed on the

Fully skeletonized human remains are recovered from a sewer. Images courtesy of Buffalo Police Archives/John Doucette. All rights reserved.

Body discovered in marshes, displaying advanced dry decay and skeletonization. Image courtesy of Toronto Police Forensic Identification Services. All rights reserved.

ground in a cold, dry environment, the process can take years. In an arid outdoor climate, it can take anywhere from five to eighteen months.

Insect Activity

Insect activity affects the rate and process of decay and modifies the condition of the remains. If the body is in an outdoor environment or is indoors with open windows, the odor of decaying flesh attracts a variety of *carrion* (dead flesh-eating) insects. These insects scavenge and reproduce in many of the soft tissues and natural body openings, as well as in areas of flesh exposed by cuts or wounds. Insect activity accelerates decomposition and in certain environments, notably hot and humid ones, can reduce a body to bones within a week. The variety and species of insects reproducing and feeding on fleshy remains depends entirely on the ecological area and the time of year. In warm climates where a body may be fully exposed, insect activity can begin before death even occurs, whereas in colder climates, there may be little to no insect activity.

Blow flies (*Calliphoridae*) and flesh flies (*Sarcophagidae*) are generally the most common type of insects at a death scene. The females lay their eggs or deposit larvae (maggots) in open wounds and body orifices. During their developmental stages they feed voraciously on the tissue. In doing so, they can skeletonize a full-grown adult anywhere from four days in a hot, humid climate to weeks in a dry, cold environment.

Observing the level and stages of insect activity is most useful in estimating the time of death. Forensic entomologists collect samples of the insects at the death scene to assess the time in which they or their eggs arrived. Because a variety of insects arrive on the body in succession dur-

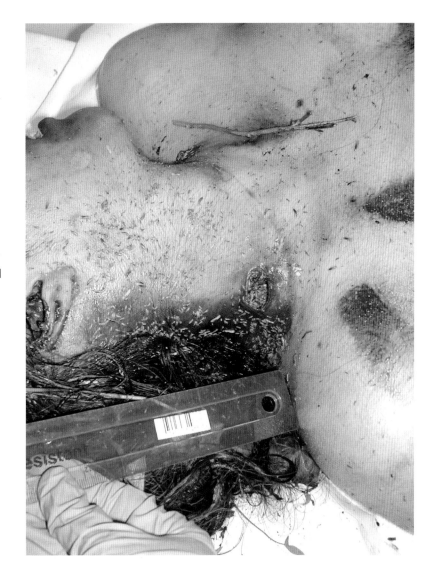

Larvae exiting stab wound. Image courtesy of Dr. Helene LeBlanc.

ing the process of decomposition and begin a predictable pattern of feeding and reproduction, entomologists assess the type and age of the insect and can associate this with the postmortem interval.

Bodies in Water

Corpses found in water present a challenge in determining an accurate time of death. The season and water temperature and whether it is salt or fresh water have an effect on the rate of decomposition. Likewise, factors such as the local tides, the level of injury to the body, and the amount of animal and aquatic scavenging determine the condition of the remains.

A body found floating in water would have been in the water long enough for tissue decomposition. This will highly depend on water temperature as well as the factors already discussed. As in the stage of algor mortis where the core body temperature falls at a predictable rate of 1.5°F per hour, in water it is about 5°F per hour with the body reaching the ambient water temperature within five to six hours. Drowning victims or bodies thrown into water just after death will usually sink due to gravity and remain there until the gases from putrefaction create buoyancy and cause them to rise to the surface (see Davis 1986, 291–97, also Spitz 1973).

The stage of putrefaction occurs at a slower rate in cold and salt water, so bodies will tend to rise after two to three weeks. However, in very cold and very deep water as in the Great Lakes in North America and in the ocean, the body may never resurface. In warm and shallower waters, bodies decompose at a much faster rate and will generally rise after eight to ten days. Though heavy clothing, weights, or rocks may keep the body submerged, they often do not prevent it or parts of it from rising once bloating occurs.

Under water, there are common patterns of swelling during putrefaction where hands and feet and the outer layer of skin separates from

Body found in water in an early stage of putrefaction with extensive wrinkling of feet and hands. Image courtesy of Toronto Police, Forensic Identification Services. All rights reserved.

Table 6.5. Environmental Variables Affecting the Decomposition Rate

Environmental Variable	Decomposition Rate
Cold climate	• Decomposition rate slowed, can be completely prevented if body is frozen. • Frozen bodies that are thawed decompose rapidly. • In cold, dry climate decay is slower than in cold, humid climate. • Decay is slower in cool, shaded areas.
Hot climate	• Hot, humid weather accelerates decomposition. • Decomposition is slow in hot, dry climate. • Dry heat desiccates flesh, preserving skin and hair (mummification). • In direct sunlight, dry decay is accelerated.
Moist and/or acidic soil	• Decomposition rapid if body buried in these types of soil.
Sand, clay, and gravel soils with high pH (alkaline) levels	• Decomposition is slower if body buried in these soil types.
Presence of water	• Bodies submerged in water will decompose slower than bodies on land, unless scavenged by aquatic organisms (fish, turtles, crustaceans). • Decomposition is delayed in bodies submerged in very cold to freezing water.
Insect activity	• Accelerates decomposition.
Animal/bird scavenging	• Promotes and accelerates decomposition.

Source: Adapted from Mann et al. (1990) and Galloway et al. (1989).

the underlying tissues after approximately five to six days in temperate water. There is also extensive wrinkling of the palms of the hands and feet referred to as the washerwoman stage. The outer layers of hands and feet, including the nails, can be peeled off like gloves. Fingerprints can be taken from these (see chapter 5). As such, body tissues are very fragile at this stage and most often when fished out of the water sustain extensive damage through the use of hooks and ropes.

Since bodies always float head down in the water, the presentation of livor mortis is often irregular and will be most apparent in the face, neck, and chest. If there is a lot of movement in the water, *lividity* may appear lighter in some areas and is quite blotchy throughout. Signs of instantaneous rigor may also be present in bodies found early enough. If the individual had been struggling and grasping to hold on, indicating they were alive and conscious at the time, items like weeds, sticks, grasses, and branches may be clutched in his or her hands.

There is often a wide range of postmortem injuries sustained by the body that is left to drift and be carried by currents. Rocks along seabeds or banks, passing watercraft with propellers, and the scavenging by a variety of sea life all contribute to cuts, abrasions, tearing, and dismemberment (Davis 1986; Spitz 1973).

Aquatic scavenging apparent on body pulled from the water in a state of advanced putrefaction.
Image courtesy of the Office of the Chief Coroner, Ontario.

Part III

Positive Identification

Chapter 7

Positive Identification

This chapter looks at some of the methods of biological identification in forensic science, primarily in the field of DNA analysis, fingerprinting, and facial reconstruction, three areas that are intimately involved with uncovering the identities of both victim and perpetrator. Although these investigative methods have been controversial in the past, they continue to draw from an array of scientific research, advances in imaging techniques, and evolving computer technology. Ending the chapter is a special section on biometrics, which encompasses a much wider array of identification techniques, based on individuation.

I: DNA Fingerprints

Accompanied with highly innovative computer technology and sophisticated imaging techniques, research on molecular genetics has seen a dramatic rise over the past twenty years. Creating an individual's genetic profile, as in the DNA "fingerprint," is now an established method of analysis used in rape and homicide investigations worldwide. As well, DNA analysis has been portrayed as a highly effective means of assessing ancient remains, understanding biological relationships, and examining the genetic basis of disease.

DNA fingerprinting has had a major impact on the way criminals are pursued and convicted. In the hands of biologists, trace samples of bodily fluids, hair, skin, and bone can be processed to reveal a genetic identity in the form of a mysterious collection of bands on a computer screen. The power of such evidence has led to the conviction of thousands, at the same time enabling hundreds of others to be exonerated and released from life imprisonment or death sentences.

The following section discusses the fundamentals of this highly charged area of analysis, beginning with a brief description of what DNA is and the methods used by forensic scientists to create the so-called fingerprint.

DNA Structure and Function

Deoxyribonucleic acid (DNA) is the genetic information that dictates the form and development of an organism—the fundamental blueprint

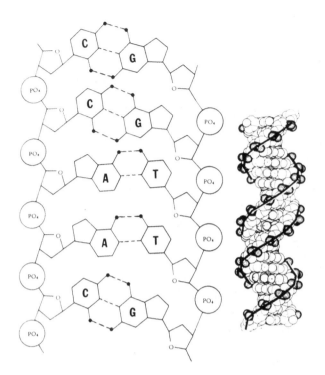

The DNA double helix is composed of a phosphate group, a type of sugar called deoxyribose, and one of four nitrogen-containing bases. The bases are adenine (A), thymine (T), guanine (G), and cytosine (C). Hydrogen bonds between the bases of each strand hold the double helix together in a regular and specific pattern.

of all living matter. Structurally, it is a two-stranded molecule composed of chemical compounds that contain an enormous amount of information. As such, the strands of a DNA molecule are arranged as a double helix, twisted like a spiral staircase, and efficiently packed into the nucleus of each cell.

Each strand of the helix is comprised of long chains of *nucleotides* composed of a phosphate group, a type of sugar called *deoxyribose*, and one of four nitrogen-containing bases. The bases are *adenine* (abbreviated as A), *thymine* (T), *guanine* (G), and *cytosine* (C). Hydrogen bonds between the bases of each strand hold the double helix together in a regular and specific pattern: for example adenine (A) will only bond with nucleotides containing thymine (T), and guanine (G) will only bond with nucleotides containing cytosine (C). These subunits form what are called *base pairs* (bp).

Strands of DNA form codes for proteins (genes) that provide genetic information in the organism, like eye color, height, hair texture, and skin color. Most human genes appear to be made up of 5 to 10,000 AT or CG base pairs, but some may be made up of several hundred thousand. A total of approximately 3 billion chemical base pairs make up human DNA.

DNA strands also contain noncoding sections, or the code is unknown at this time. These parts of the strands were long referred to as *junk DNA* because scientists didn't understand their function. However, current research in the field has proven that various segments of noncoding DNA

A buccal swab to gather cells from the inner cheek for DNA extraction.

are vitally important for the proper regulation and translation of genes and for reshaping the genome through the modification and reshuffling of existing genes (see HGP 2008). In humans, at least 10 percent of our DNA represents actual genetic information and approximately 50 percent is made up of this noncoding junk (HGP 2008).

If it were stretched out as a long, continuous series of base pair sequences (at ten base pairs per inch) a DNA molecule would extend 9,400 miles in length (though it is actually measured in *angstroms*, which is a hundred-millionths of a centimeter). The structures carrying these molecular strands are known as *chromosomes*. There is one molecule of DNA in each chromosome (chromosomes range in size from 50 million to 250 million bases), and every species has a characteristic set of chromosomes. One cell's collection of chromosomes is known as a *genome*. Humans inherit a genome of twenty-three chromosomes from each parent for a total of forty-six.

The chemical structure of DNA is the same for all cellular organisms, but the length and sequence of the base pairs along the DNA strands differ within and between species. For example, the base pair sequences that code for traits such as ten fingers and ten toes are identical in all primates including humans, but the base pair sequences that code for the size, shape, and color of those fingers and toes are unique in each individual. One can think of DNA as a type of genetic phone number. Each species has an area code, and each individual has their own telephone number made up of millions of digits.

The length of DNA is measured by the amount of base pairs in its strand, and this varies depending on the organism. One thousand base pairs are abbreviated as *kb*, and *Mb* represents one million base pairs.

The DNA Fingerprint: The First Case

In the small English village of Narborough, police were in the midst of investigating the rape and murder of two fifteen-year-old girls between 1983 and 1986. Though the murders were three years apart, based on the patterns displayed at both crime scenes, police suspected the same individual committed the two murders.

A tip led the police to arrest a seventeen-year-old shortly after the second murder in 1986. He confessed to only one of the murders, denying any involvement with the other.

At this time, a genetics professor at Leicester University, England, Dr. Alec Jeffreys, had been studying DNA variation and the evolution of gene families. He was interested in detecting inherited variation within genes between different individuals. Jeffreys's goal was to develop *markers* (a type of identification tag) to track the position of these genes.

Earlier in 1980, Jeffreys's lab had produced one of the first descriptions of what are termed *restriction fragment length polymorphisms* (RFLPs). RFLPs are DNA restriction fragments (sections of DNA on a particular chromosome that have been cut into fragments by an enzyme) that vary in length between individuals within the same species. The cause of the length difference was found to be the result of a variation in base pair sequences. It was also found that some of these sequences were repeated in particular patterns inherited from one or both parents. Subsequently, Jeffreys and his colleagues described a general method for processing large numbers of these highly variable regions of human DNA from bodily substances for observation and comparison (Jeffreys et al. 1985a).

By 1984, Jeffreys successfully tested the use of DNA analysis for identification purposes. When the DNA of several individuals was processed (see later discussion for the methods used) different banding patterns were seen for different individuals. The image produced by this banding pattern of DNA was dubbed a "fingerprint" because of its ability to differentiate between individuals (Jeffreys et al. 1985b).

As a result of his published findings, police in Narborough sent Jeffreys a blood sample from the seventeen-year-old person who had confessed along with samples of the semen found on both victims. The DNA banding patterns showed that the semen samples were indeed from the same individual; however, they did not match the DNA extracted from the blood sample. The police realized that the confession from the seventeen-

Dr. Alec Jeffreys.

year-old had been a false one and released the suspect from custody. This was the first case in which DNA analysis eliminated a suspect.

Following Jeffreys's conclusive analysis of the semen samples, police had the true assailant's genetic identity. With this information for comparison, they began collecting blood samples from males in the vicinity between the ages of thirteen and thirty-five. Launching the world's first genetic manhunt, police in Narborough submitted 5,000 blood samples for forensic analysis.

A sudden break in the case came several months into the processing of the samples. Someone tipped police that they had overheard a man in a local pub boasting that he had paid someone to submit a blood sample in his place. When approached by police and confronted with the murder accusations, the individual quickly confessed, convinced that his blood would "give him away" (Proctor et al. 1998).

In 1987, the twenty-seven-year-old assailant was arrested, his blood was tested, and his DNA matched the DNA extracted from the semen samples taken from the two murdered girls. He was convicted and is currently serving two life sentences.

DNA Fingerprinting, Typing, and Profiling

DNA fingerprinting has become one of the most popular areas of forensic science since the crucial Narborough case. Different methods of extracting and analyzing DNA from human, animal, plant, bacterial, and viral samples have rapidly evolved throughout Europe and North America alongside major advances in genetics research and technology. Its application ranges from gene therapy and genetic engineering to studies of ancient bone, plant, and animal life.

Over the past twenty years, the terminology defining various DNA extraction, processing, and analytic methods has also changed, leading to some confusion outside of the field. Terms such as DNA *fingerprinting*, DNA *typing*, and DNA *profiling* have been used interchangeably to refer to the act of processing DNA as physical evidence. Each term however, denotes a specific process that is substantially different from the next.

DNA *fingerprinting* is a first-generation typing system (the original method) developed by Dr. Jeffreys and his colleagues in the mid-1980s (Jeffreys et al. 1985b). This method looks at sections of DNA located in different regions on different chromosomes, also referred to as a *multi-locus* typing system. Fingerprinting produces patterns that are entirely unique to an individual, except identical twins. The process is quite lengthy and expensive, and the results are usually rendered as a sequence resembling a bar code.

DNA *typing* describes the system of assessing variation in sections of DNA for analysis. Hence, one can use the term "DNA typing" or "DNA typing systems" to refer to a variety of methods that isolate and extract

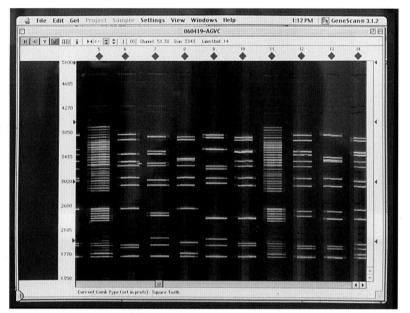

The bar code-like analysis of extracted DNA fragments referred to as an electropherogram.

sections of DNA (plant, animal, viral, and/or bacterial) for observation and comparison.

DNA *profiling* is a second-generation typing system (a more recent development) that looks at one area—a single locus—on a specific chromosome. This is now the method in use for forensic analysis. Profiling produces patterns that unrelated people are unlikely to share. The probability of individuals matching varies considerably and depends entirely on the section of DNA examined; the more loci tested, the more discriminatory the profile. However, close relatives, especially siblings, are likely to share patterns produced by this form of DNA typing, hence the traits are not entirely unique in a population, and so they are not considered fingerprints.

DNA Extraction

In human populations, DNA shows little variation between individuals. Despite what appears to be a whole range of differences in physical traits and appearances, 99.9 percent of our DNA is identical (Blake 1999). The small percentage that is different between individuals is the basis for the fingerprinting and profiling used in medical research, genetics, and forensic science.

DNA can be extracted from bodily substances that contain any cell with a nucleus such as sperm, saliva, blood, vaginal secretions, hair with roots, perspiration, organs, bones, teeth, and skin. The DNA processed

Extracting DNA under sterile conditions for PCR amplification.

for fingerprinting is not of the genetic sort associated with observable characteristics, such as eye color and height. Sections of this type of protein-coding DNA do not distinguish individuals from one another like noncoding DNA does. The only exception to this is the observation of sex determined by the presence of XX chromosomes in females and XY chromosomes in males.

In regions of DNA found to contain repeated sequences of base pairs (identified as junk DNA) there is a great deal of variability between individuals. There are, in fact, hundreds of thousands of these repeated sequences distributed on all chromosomes, but the number of repeated sequences and the pattern of their distribution on each chromosome are unique in every individual except for identical twins. It must be noted that even identical twins do not have perfectly identical DNA due to *epigenomic* variations, which are changes triggered largely by environmental and chemical modifications during embryonic development. Sections of this noncoding DNA (referred to as *polymorphisms*) are extracted for examination and processed into an image, producing a fingerprint or profile.

The Use of DNA: Standards and Protocols

In 1988, the sudden introduction of DNA analysis into U.S. courts provoked debate and controversy in both the legal and scientific arenas. Biotech start-up companies with no experience in forensic science flawed early DNA typing with inadequately defined procedures while scientists argued over its practical applications and statistical calculations (Lander and Budowle 1994). An early criminal case involving DNA analysis was thrown out in 1989 after a joint statement was issued by scientists for both the prosecution and the defense. The evidence, they claimed, was

STR Analysis

The tandemly repeated sequences of DNA are typically classified into different groups based on the size of the repeat region. Regions with repeats of nine to eighty base pairs are referred to as *variable number tandem repeats* (VNTRs, also known as mini-satellites), while regions that contain two to five base pair repeats are called *short tandem repeats* (STRs, also known as micro-satellites).

STR analysis is currently a popular method of DNA typing in forensic science and is the technique illustrated here. It examines smaller regions of repeated sequences and therefore does not require large quantities of DNA. It can also use DNA that has degraded. Combined with a technique called *polymerase chain reaction* (PCR), STR analysis has made DNA typing less time-consuming and more reliable, and has added a higher degree of discrimination.

1. DNA is extracted chemically from the sample by breaking down the components of the rest of the cell to isolate the DNA from the nucleus.

2–3. Copies of the DNA are made using the PCR technique (often referred to as PCR amplification). PCR is a fast technique that uses an enzyme for making an unlimited number of copies of DNA from different samples. This enables a lab to generate enough DNA from minute or degraded samples, such as saliva from old chewing gum or a bloodstain found on an article of clothing. PCR amplification is highly sensitive and must be done under sterile conditions, since the DNA being copied can easily be contaminated by foreign DNA, for example, from a technician's sneeze.

4–5. Steps 4 and 5 analyze the extracted DNA fragments of interest taken from the same regions on a particular chromosome in different individuals. The most common method for analyzing these fragments is through what is called electrophoretic analysis.

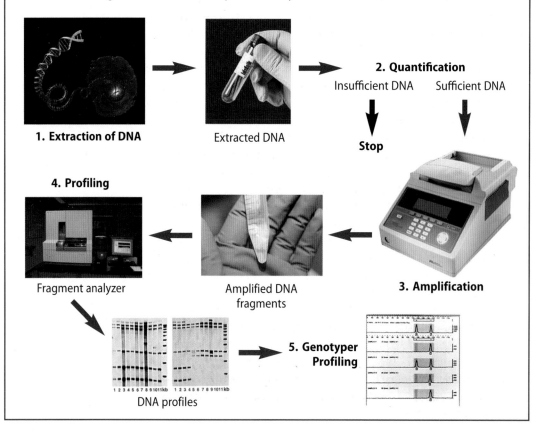

1. Extraction of DNA   Extracted DNA

2. Quantification

Insufficient DNA   Sufficient DNA

Stop

4. Profiling

Fragment analyzer   Amplified DNA fragments   **3. Amplification**

DNA profiles   **5. Genotyper Profiling**

unacceptable due to poor processing (see Lander 1998). However, despite the initial inconsistencies and controversies, DNA typing was recognized as a spectacular new technology that promised to redefine the field of genetics research and criminalistics.

Prior to the introduction of DNA typing as a forensic tool in the late 1980s, there were no laboratory standards established which could apply to its processing. Furthermore, the policy governing its use in a court of law was highly ambiguous. Expert testimony only allowed for the witness to state the mathematical *probability* of an individual matching a sample and whether the suspect could be excluded. Concluding that an individual's DNA profile *positively* matched a sample was not permitted. The technology was still very new, and scientists were using a variety of methods with different *matching rules* (how and whether two samples matched) as well as different protocol standards.

By the early 1990s, the use of forensic DNA typing increased at a rapid pace. Private laboratories began providing DNA typing services to law enforcement officials with their own expert witnesses to translate laboratory results and consultants for attorneys. High-profile criminal cases detailed the intricacies of DNA typing with lengthy descriptions of the statistical probabilities of various matches. Yet a standard protocol regarding the use of such highly personal and sensitive information was still not in place, and the scientific and legal communities raised many of the same questions regarding reliability, interpretation, and validity.

In response to these issues, the National Research Council Committee from the National Academy of Sciences published a comprehensive report in 1992 on the use of DNA technology in forensic science. The report addressed the need to develop standards for collecting, analyzing, and presenting data and called for DNA typing procedures to have built-in measures that would ensure stringent procedures, confidentiality, and consistency in the field (see NRC Report 1992, and NRC 1996). Because of the possibilities for its misuse and/or misinterpretation, laboratories would also be required to provide a detailed description of their typing method with a precise and objective matching rule, and to undergo regular, mandatory proficiency tests. In fact, DNA typing methods would be tested internally to ensure that they were being done properly. Because DNA evidence can now outweigh all other evidence in a trial, it became essential that high standards and a strict protocol governing its use be enacted.

DNA typing was firmly established for use in forensic investigation by 1994. Research in the field accelerated from a few papers in the late 1980s to more than 400 by the middle of 1994, combined with over 100 scientific conferences (Lander 1998). Newer and quicker methods were continually being introduced, prompting three sets of laboratory guidelines to be released from the Technical Working Group on DNA Analysis Methods (TWGDAM).

A robotic workstation where scientists can implement different stages of DNA analysis with more speed and accuracy. Image courtesy of the Centre of Forensic Sciences. All rights reserved.

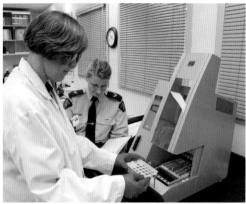

DNA extraction using the DNA EZ1 Bio-Robot (Qiagen). Image courtesy of Her Majesty the Queen in Right of Canada as represented by the Royal Canadian Mounted Police. © 2009. All rights reserved.

The FBI took more of a definitive stance toward developing procedures, and initiated public discussion on the use of computer databases containing DNA profiles (see later discussion). By 1997, a new FBI policy went into effect as a result of advances in testing that narrowed the odds from a 1 in 1,000 chance to a 1 in 260 billion chance that another person besides the suspect had the same DNA profile. This in turn allowed expert witnesses to testify that a DNA sample positively matched a suspect's, as opposed to stating it obliquely through statistical probability. Consequently, DNA testimony became more definitive and clearer to juries.

Rapid technological advances in the field of molecular genetics further affected the debate surrounding the use of forensic DNA typing, bringing an end to questions of its reliability. Highly sensitive testing methods can now process smaller and more degraded samples of DNA, enabling scientists to analyze a wider range of materials and thereby increase the array of admissible evidence. Previously, items such as a sweaty T-shirt, a stamp on an envelope, hair on a comb, or a chewed-up piece of gum could not have been biologically linked to an individual.

Due to such rapid breakthroughs in a very short period of time, DNA was no longer considered a controversial method of analysis but one of the greatest advances in forensic science since the development of fingerprinting in 1892.

CODIS: The DNA Database

In the late 1980s, the FBI initiated talks surrounding the establishment of a database that would store and access the DNA profiles of con-

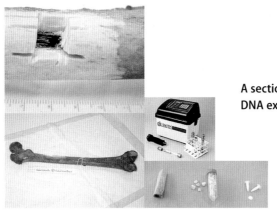

A section of bone from the human femur is prepared for DNA extraction.

victed individuals when needed. The underlying philosophy guiding the project was based on the premise that a criminal could change looks, address, and name but could never change his or her genetic profile. Thus, if evidence containing genetic material were present and if that material was available on a computer file, a match would be guaranteed.

A software program called the Combined DNA Index Systems (CODIS) was developed and piloted by the FBI in 1990. CODIS is a double indexing system of DNA profiles; the Convicted Offender Index contains genetic profiles of sex offenders and other violent crimes, and the Forensic Index contains profiles developed from crime scene evidence such as blood and semen. There is also information on the laboratory's identifier and the names of those responsible for processing the DNA profile. Information such as an individual's criminal history, Social Security number, or details of criminal cases is not stored. CODIS is designed to automatically search both the Convicted Offender Index and the Forensic Index for matching DNA profiles.

Initially the FBI provided the software, installation, training, and technical support free of charge to fourteen state and local DNA laboratories, permitting them to compare and exchange data and link serial crimes with known offenders. Within four years of its release, CODIS generated more than 400 hits (matches) that often led to the release of individuals for crimes not committed (see NIJ Report 1996). The success with the program allowed further research into the use of such databases worldwide.

In October 1998, the FBI introduced the National DNA Index System (NDIS) the final and highest level of CODIS that was coupled with a State DNA Index System (SDIS) and a Local DNA Index System (LDIS), all of which enabled federal, state, and local laboratories to compare DNA on a national level (see U.S. Department of Justice, DNA Database Press Release 1998; CODIS Program Overview 1998).

DNA profiles are entered into CODIS by participating laboratories across the United States and directed to the state and national levels to determine any links in crime scenes, convicted persons, arrestees, and missing or unidentified individuals. By November 2005, almost 3 million DNA profiles had been uploaded to the NDIS with over 175 national laboratories participating (see U.S. Department of Justice, Audit Report 2006).

At the present time, all fifty states have passed legislation requiring convicted offenders to actively and retroactively provide blood samples for entering into the database. The Federal DNA Identification Act of 1994 limited the database to DNA from convicted felons for violent crimes such as assault, murder, and sexual offenses. The passing of the DNA Fingerprint Act in January 2006, however, allows all states to collect DNA from any persons arrested, detained, or facing charges, including all persons who are non-U.S. citizens.

As stated, the controversy over the use of DNA in the 1980s focused primarily on testing methods and the interpretation of results. Currently, the debate is centered on the implications of collecting DNA from any individual who has been arrested. Like physical fingerprinting, either with ink or a computer scan, DNA collection is now part of standard booking procedures in the United States (and the United Kingdom). Because DNA can provide more than just information on sequences of base pairs, such as physical traits, medical issues, and relatedness, some fear that this information carries the risks of proportionality, stigmatization, and discrimination.

Civil libertarians and civil rights groups throughout North America and Europe are challenging the practice of storing the genetic information of millions of individuals, both innocent and guilty, among them illegal and legal immigrants who may have been unlawfully detained. They not only have raised issues relating to the right of genetic privacy but whether and how quickly DNA information can be removed from the database when innocence is established.

Proponents of national and international DNA databases have countered that the ultimate motivation behind the DNA Fingerprint Act and consistent DNA collection is the prevention of future rapes, homicides, and child abductions. Several research papers and reports advocate early and timely DNA collection and analysis, citing brutal crimes that were solved as a result of the database and crimes that could have been prevented had the DNA been originally collected from all arrestees. Many report that the collection of DNA at minor crime scenes has led to matches from other major crimes (see NIJ DNA *Field Experiment* 2008, NIJ DNA *Initiative* 2009).

Any and all access to database information is restricted to law enforcement officials, and a court order is required to use this information in all judicial proceedings. The location of the databank is kept secret for security purposes and when any hits are made, laboratories responsible for the profiles are required to contact each other to verify the information exchanged. DNA analysts must then confirm the match again before contacting the related law enforcement agency. CODIS also maintains a population file, which is a database of anonymous DNA profiles that are used to determine the statistical significance of a match (see FBI CODIS Program Overview 1998; 2006).

The success of the DNA database has been consistent despite a controversial beginning and the ongoing debate surrounding its storage. There are well over 4 million offender profiles currently in the U.S. system, making it the largest databank in the world next to the United Kingdom. To date, there have been over 50,000 matches that have exonerated and convicted many individuals for the most heinous crimes. Success in the form of these direct hits is detailed in reports put out by the FBI and the National Institute of Justice (see FBI CODIS Program Overview 2006; Promega.com 2007; Hadlow 2008; NIJ Report 2009).

II: Fingerprinting

The science of fingerprints was first referred to as *dermatoglyphics* in the late 1800s (from the Greek *derma* meaning "skin" and *glyphics* meaning "carving") (see Cummins and Midlo 1943; Campbell 1998). It is arguably the most valuable weapon in the arsenal of police investigators and has solved more crimes than any other process.

For over 300 years the discrete and impressionable patterns left behind on countless objects and fixtures were the source of close scrutiny among only a handful of individuals. These few believed a person's identity was directly linked to the patterns made by the tips of their fingers. It took many years of painstaking research, public ridicule, and a serious flaw in another identification system before the adoption of fingerprinting as the world standard it is today.

The following section outlines a brief history of the use of fingerprinting, its genetic origins, and the current trends and changes in the field. It concludes with a comprehensive overview of fingerprinting tools and techniques, the methods of analysis, and the use of fingerprints as evidence.

A Brief History

Dr. Nehemiah Grew (1641–1712) wrote one of the earliest known European publications dealing with fingerprint observation in 1684 (see Grew 1684). This British scientist had completed an intense study of the skin and described the pores and friction ridges found on the tips of fingers, palms, and soles of the feet. Two years later, Italian scientist Marcello Malpighi (1628–1694) used the newly invented microscope to study fingerprints. He observed the elevated ridges on the finger ends, the spirals formed by these ridges, and the pore openings of sweat glands on the surface of the ridges. Malpighi was probably the first to examine friction skin microscopically. To this day, one of the layers of skin cells bears his name, the *Malpighian layer*.

By 1788, a German physician named Andreas Mayer (1747–1801) was the first person to publicly recognize that fingerprints are not duplicated by nature (see Mayer 1788). Sometime later, a young Czech university student, Evangelist Purkinje (1787–1869), supplemented Mayer's work. Using the improved version of the compound microscope in 1823, he made a series of paper thin slides of the skin to examine the complexity and configuration of ridge detail on fingertips. Out of this series he classified nine major groups of fingerprints based on size and shape variations. These major groups have not changed and are currently used as guidelines in the field (see following discussion).

A few decades later two British men, Sir William Herschel and Sir Francis Galton, agreed on the premise that a person's fingerprints do not change their patterns during a lifetime. As proof, they demonstrated the lack of change in their own fingerprints over a period of thirty years. Sir Herschel brought fingerprinting to the attention of the English public, and through the work of Galton from the years 1890 to 1895 the use of fingerprinting became a scientific pursuit (see Crow 1993). Although the public accepted their research, the judiciary chose not to take notice.

Undaunted, Sir Francis kept up his studies and in 1892 published a book titled *Finger Prints*. He stressed that though the gross features of fingertips were useful for classification purposes, real identification was

Sir Francis Galton, 1822–1911. The use of fingerprinting became his scientific pursuit.

Juan Vucetich, an Argentine police commissioner and an ardent follower of Galton's research and ideas, is credited with being the first to solve a murder through the use of fingerprints. He used his own funds to independently create a fingerprint classification system and initiate a file of criminal fingerprints.

In 1892, two children were brutally murdered. The mother claimed that a jilted lover had committed the crime, but he repeatedly denied any involvement and subsequently proved to have an alibi. The police inspector assigned to the case applied Vucetich's methods and training to identify the bloody fingerprint of the mother at the scene. She confessed when confronted with the fingerprint evidence.

accomplished only through the attention to the *islets, forks,* and *ridges* that form the patterns (see Galton 1892).

As did many measuring systems attempted during this historical period of the late 1800s, Galton's fingerprinting scheme set out to differentiate individuals for identification. Counting and measuring, comparing and sizing led Galton to conclude that an individual's prints were persistent over time and unique to an individual, at least sufficiently for use as evidence. Furthermore, he proposed that a classification scheme be created that would permit efficient filing and easy retrieval of such vital information (Galton 1892).

Sir Edward Henry, who was the inspector general of the lower provinces of India, read Galton's book. The two men corresponded throughout 1894, and Henry was inspired to expand on Galton's classification system. In 1896, Henry ordered the Bengali police to begin collecting fingerprints of inmates and felons, along with the Bertillonage measurements on filing cards. Within the year, Henry refined Galton's classification system and published a monograph titled *The Classification and Uses of Fin-*

Thomas Bewick was a British author and naturalist with a love of engraving. He created highly accurate and detailed engravings of fingerprints, true even to the shape of the ridges and the pores opening on them. Portrait courtesy of the Natural History Society of Northumbria. All right reserved. Fingerprint engraving courtesy of Christine Farmer.

Sir Henry Faulds. It seems that with any pivotal development in history, the goal is to record and acknowledge the contributions of those persons responsible. All too frequently, however, history is written with a broad and imperfect brush, leaving some of the pioneers unsung, or at least undersung. Such a man was Scottish physician Henry Faulds (1843–1930).

Sir Francis Galton is credited with recognizing the persistence of fingerprint detail through one's lifetime and published the landmark book *Finger Prints* in 1892. Ridge characteristics have been named "Galton details" in his honor. Yet twelve years earlier, Faulds's letter to *Nature Magazine* (October 1880) revealed his conviction that fingerprints or "skin furrows of the hand" would become an important tool in criminal identification, as well as the knowledge that fingerprints did not change in life. Furthermore, six years before the publication of *Finger Prints*, Faulds's efforts to have fingerprint identification recognized by Scotland Yard were ignored.

The actual course of events may never be known, but Henry Faulds was indisputably a fingerprint visionary whose contribution to the science should be recognized.

gerprints. It was a system based largely on assigning a numeric value to each finger. Patterns were then identified by a number and added to a base value. The ease with which individuals could be classified made this a more popular system of identification. It eventually replaced the Bertillon method of classifying criminals.

The Henry Fingerprint Classification System gained official acceptance in the British Empire by 1899 and remains the universally accepted method of classifying and identifying fingerprints.

The Genetics of Fingerprints

All primates have ridged toe and fingertips as well as palm and sole creases primarily for traction and gripping. In human primates, fingerprints are formed while an unborn child is still in the womb, specifically during development of the skin (*ectoderm*) of the embryo from the fourth to thirteenth weeks. The ectoderm at this stage of development (four weeks) is only a single layer of skin cells and the fetus has little bumps or *volar* pads for finger and toe tips.

The ridges that ultimately form fingerprints are created by a genetic pattern that is written into the connective tissue of the more complex layer of skin called the *dermis* formed by *mesoderm* and *neural crest* cells from the sixth to the eleventh week. However, ridge patterns and creases have to be established within a particular time frame based on chemical cues,

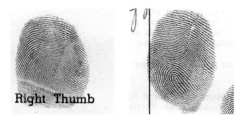

Scarred fingerprints twenty-one years apart. Damage to the dermal layer results in a scar as permanent and immutable as the original ridge structure.

thus after the skin is formed, the pattern is hard-wired into the dermis (Meier et al. 1987; Kimura et al. 2001, Wertheim and Maceo 2002).

Delays in ridge pattern formations, as well as any environmental modifications during this phase of fetal development, occur in tandem with chromosomal abnormalities and variations within individuals, even between twins. This explains why the fingerprints of twins are similar but not identical (see discussion on identical twins). Also, the ridge patterns are hard-wired into the dermis so any cuts or abrasions to the fingers during a person's life results in the skin using this pattern to reform the print (see Meier et al. 1987, Wertheim and Maceo 2002).

However, if there is any direct trauma to the dermis, like a deep cut or serious burn, the original pattern will be altered. When the skin heals, a deformed or reformed print will emerge. This is not controlled by genetic disposition but by the original pattern established in the dermis and modified by environmental factors (Ashbaugh 1999).

Thus, the process of altering or removing fingerprints is possible by deep burns or cuts to the dermis layer. Many perpetrators have attempted this to avoid identification. However, if they continue to leave modified prints behind, it only makes them more distinct.

Though human genetics determine the positions in which these ridge characteristics are formed, and the level and intensity of their secretion, environment, culture, and biodynamics modify their ultimate appearance. Hence, no print is ever the same, and this certainty is what remains the hallmark of the use of fingerprints as a positive means of identification.

Identical Twins

Monozygotic twins (or identical twins, as they are sometimes incorrectly labeled) are arguably the most alike of any living beings on the planet. They are the result of a single fertilized egg (zygote) that divides to form two separate entities. Up to that point, they have undergone identical and concurrent development. They share the same DNA. From the point of division on, however, their environmental experiences may be similar but are a little different. They occupy different positions in

Left and right thumbs, respectively, of mirror-image monozygotic twins. The left thumbs are both double loops, but the right thumbs are not the same pattern type. There is no agreement between the minutiae of the right and left thumbs.

the womb and similar but different currents of amniotic fluid pass across their skin. The twins receive different amounts of nutrition from the mother. Indeed, the extreme case of this is called *twin-to-twin transfusion syndrome* (TTTS), in which the circulation systems of the two fetuses become linked. Blood is transferred disproportionately from one twin, "the donor," to the other twin, "the recipient," posing a serious threat to both (see Berger et al. 2000, Johnson and Moise 2006).

Anyone who has examined monozygotic twins closely knows that the adjective *identical* is not accurate. They were never identical from their inception, and their different environmental experiences only serve to widen the gap. While the similarities may be striking, the differences are also readily apparent. One instance in which the differences may not be so apparent is that of mirror image twins.

Mirror image twins are the result of the egg splitting late (more than a week) after fertilization. One twin facing the other will have the effect of looking in a mirror—and in some cases, certain parts of the body may be mirrored. If one twin has a hair swirl on the left side, the other may have it on the right—and in the opposite direction. If one is right-handed, the other may be left-handed. In very rare cases, the actual position of organs in one twin may be opposite (mirror-imaged) to normal, with the location of the appendix, for example, being in the lower left of the abdomen.

If monozygotic twins can be said to be the most alike of living beings, mirror image twins possess the highest degree of similarity in that group. On one occasion, the writer had the privilege of fingerprinting a pair of mirror image twins, ten-year-old boys. They were eerily similar, to the smallest detail, when standing side by side. Their mother was asked if she had difficulty knowing which was which, and she replied that if they stood still and didn't speak, she could not tell them apart.

However, comparison of their fingerprints revealed that in spite of striking similarities in overall ridge flow, not all of their fingers bore the same pattern types. There was no correlation whatever in the second-level detail—the minutiae.

Fingerprint Composition

The hands are the primary tactile connection with the world. To do this well, the skin on the palms and the soles of the feet must have certain attributes.

- *Sensitivity.* There are many more times the number of nerve endings in friction skin than are present in skin from other parts of the body. These ensure that highly accurate messages regarding items touched are sent to the brain for processing.
- *Thickness.* The skin on the palms and soles must be thick and tough to withstand a heavy daily workload of touching, gripping, lifting, and twisting. If this skin were not so thick, the high concentration of nerve endings would be sending constant messages of pain, just from routine contact with objects. Anyone who has had a blister on a finger and has removed the skin on the blister to reveal the dermal layer below knows that pain can be felt by simply blowing on that skin.
- *Purchase.* We need skin on our hands that facilitates grasping and manipulating tools. The ridged skin on the palms and soles resembles corduroy, and gives us the necessary purchase.

Along with ridge patterns and padded tips, the fingers and hands have a substantial number of sweat glands and pores. In fact, there is a much higher concentration of sweat pores on the hands and feet than on any other part of the body. This constant exudation of perspiration enhances the gripping efficiency of our hands and fingers. Occasionally we use up this natural assistance faster than it can be replenished, and we must supply it artificially, as when we lick a finger to more easily turn the page of a book.

Contrary to popular belief, there are no oil glands present on the palms and soles. Imagine having oil on your hands while trying to twist the lid open on a stubborn jar. It is easy to see this difference in friction skin when a body is submerged in water. Hands and feet will swell and wrinkle as water is absorbed, because there is no oil secreted to resist it. The rest of the body is protected by sebaceous oil, and this swelling does not happen.

Friction skin on the fingers and palms allows for the secure gripping of objects.

The potential composition of fingerprint deposit is virtually unlimited. Common ingredients may include:

- amino acids
- uric acid
- urea
- lipids
- contaminants picked up
  from other surfaces

- organic salts
- inorganic salts
- water
- sebaceous oil
- vitamins

The composition and relative amounts of each of these compounds can vary from day to day, even in the fingerprints of the same person (after Coltman et al. 1966).

So what is left behind when individuals touch, hold, and grab? The nature of fingerprint examination is only possible due to its secretions. When a person touches a surface with a finger, palm, or the sole of a bare foot, these secretions remain behind. Whether enough is transferred to be forensically useful is another question. The amount, composition, continuity, and clarity of the transfer are dependent on several factors:

- metabolic rate
- diet
- condition of skin (clean/dirty)
- condition of surface (clean/dirty)
- temperature/humidity
- sympathetic nervous system (fight or flight)
- nature of substrate (the surface below the print)
- pressure and duration of contact

When people are calm and relaxed, the normal metabolic rate can vary considerably. Some individuals have very dry hands, whereas others have hands that are perpetually damp. The sympathetic nervous system activates when stimulated by fear, anger, or excitement. The rate of perspiration increases, and therefore a larger deposit is available for transfer.

Each fingerprint detection technique targets a different component or components of the fingerprint. It stands to reason that if the technique targets ingredients A and B and the fingerprint has only C and D, the fingerprint will not be detected by that method. Thus, any detection technique has the potential to detect a fingerprint missed by any other technique. This is a sound reason for using *sequential processing* whenever possible.

Sequential processing is defined as the use of as many development techniques as necessary to process a latent print. By applying the least invasive to the most invasive techniques in a proven sequence, investigators can target many variations of ingredients in fingerprint secretions. The sequence, however, has to be established as having a cumulative effect, and one technique must not eliminate the ability to use another technique effectively.

Fingerprint Classification

The inner surfaces of the finger and palms and the soles of the feet are referred to as the *thenar* and *plantar* surfaces, respectively. Raised skin, or ridges, form intricate patterns across these surfaces, which are the basis of fingerprint classification.

The following are terms of classification and will be helpful in understanding the definitions of the general pattern types.

- *Delta or tri-radius:* Consists of a point at which ridges converge from three directions. An essential landmark in the classification process.
- *Core:* The inner or central portion of a fingerprint pattern. It includes the ridges, which determine the pattern type.
- *Recurving ridge:* A recurve is any ridge that retraces its course, including the 180° recurving ridges of a loop, and the spiral and oval recurving ridges of a whorl pattern.

Pattern Types

Experts agree that there are as many as nine different fingerprint patterns that have been accepted as the world's standard (see Olsen 1978). Eight are easily recognizable, but as can be seen in the example, there

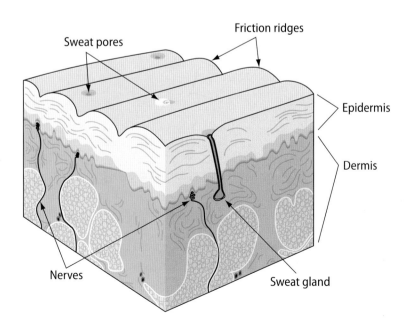

An illustrated cross-section of friction skin.

Arch

Tented Arch

Loop (Ulnar and Radial)

Whorl

are two that are composed of two different types of patterns: a *composite* and a nonspecific pattern type referred to as *accidental*.

These are the inherent and various types of patterns evident on individual fingertips. They are designated as follows.

Fingerprint Patterns

- **Arch:** Composed of ridges lying one above the other in general arching formation.

- **Tented Arch:** Consists of at least one up-thrusting ridge, which tends to bisect superior ridges at right angles.

- **Ulnar and Radial Loops:** Consists of free recurving ridges and one point of delta. In *ulnar loops*, the ridge enters the pattern area, recurves 180° and exits on the little finger side (nearest the ulna bone in the forearm). In *radial loops*, the ridge enters the pattern area, recurves 180° and exits on the thumb side.

- **Whorl:** Consists of one or more free recurving ridges and two points of delta. A straight line between the two points of delta will bisect at least one of the ridges recurving around the core.

- **Double Loop:** Consists of two loop formations, separate and apart, each with a point of delta.

- **Central Pocket Loop:** Consists of one or more free recurving ridges and two points of delta. A straight line between the two points of delta will not bisect any of the ridges recurving around the core.

- **Composite:** Consists of at least two of the preceding basic patterns, excluding the arch.

- **Accidental:** Consists of two deltas, one related to a recurve, and the other related to an upthrust. An *upthrust* is a ridge that does not conform to the general ridge flow, but whose course is in an upward direction and if continued, would bisect superior ridges at approximately right angles.

Double Loop

Central Pocket Loop

Composite

Accidental

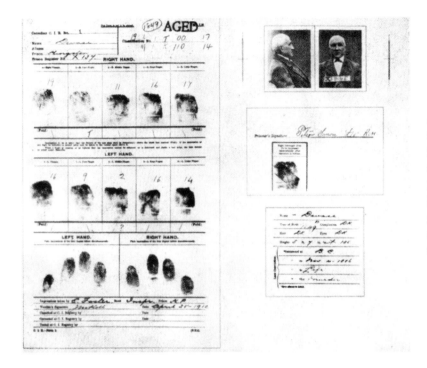

A traditional classification card with inked impressions and mug shots. Image courtesy of Her Majesty the Queen in Right of Canada as represented by the Royal Canadian Mounted Police. © 2009. All rights reserved.

For decades, fingerprint examiners have relied on these accepted standards to classify and identify fingerprints. Every time a person was arrested for a criminal offense, their fingerprints were recorded on a form specific to individual police departments. Even today, these are known as *inked impressions*. Once taken, the prints were sent to a fingerprint technician or examiner for further processing.

The classification of fingerprints was the basis for a filing system that allowed the fingerprint examiner to examine a print, determine its pattern, and manually retrieve similar prints from existing fingerprint files. These highly skilled examiners were also able to use the filing system to search for the identity of a criminal who may have left a fingerprint behind at a crime scene. They would determine the pattern type from the accepted standards and conduct a detailed search of prints in their files. Known criminal fingerprints of that same finger and pattern type were examined for a match. See the section on AFIS for an overview of more current methods.

Identification

Fingerprinting, or more accurately any friction skin identification, is based on the following three scientific axioms:

1. Friction ridge patterns begin to develop early in fetal life and are completed well before birth.

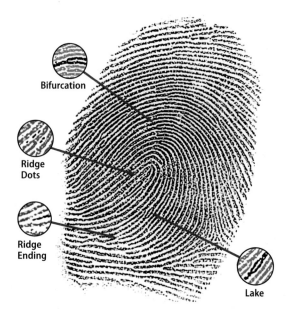

Different types of ridge characteristics.

2. These patterns do not change throughout the life of the individual except through injury or disease.
3. The patterns are unique
    a. From individual to individual,
    b. In an individual, from digit to digit,
    c. In ridge formation,
    d. In ridge characteristics, placement, thickness, and shape, and
    e. In pore structure and placement.

As stated previously, nature simply does not duplicate. Friction ridge identification is therefore based on the agreement of ridge information in a continuous unbroken sequence (see Ashbaugh 1999).

The analysis process begins with very general class characteristics and proceeds to increasingly finer and more specific attributes. It may be possible at level 1 scrutiny for example, to eliminate the impression as from the same source as the known, thereby making any further analysis unnecessary.

Levels of Detail

Level 1	Basic pattern type
Level 2	Path of the friction ridges
	Location, direction, type, and clarity of minutiae
Level 3	Shape and outline of individual ridges
	Location of pore openings
	Fine details

Fingerprints Defined

There are three types of fingerprints found at crime scenes. These are defined as: *latent*, *visible* and *plastic*. It is vital to distinguish between these three types.

Latent prints refer to any print that is hidden or concealed, existing but not yet developed. In the field of forensic identification, most of the work is involved in uncovering this type of evidence.

Visible fingerprints may be left in blood, dirt, grime, oil, or any other visible material. They may be suitable for comparison to known impressions with little or no work other than photography.

Plastic, or indented, fingerprints are located in materials or soft surfaces where a suspect has pressed into the item and left an identifiable print. Surfaces such as drying paint, mud, gum, putty, wax, or soft chocolate provide ideal areas for the deposition of these prints. Again, there is little or no work involved in seeing and capturing images of these prints. The only difficulty may come in maintaining the clarity of the ridges; especially in surfaces such as wax and chocolate, where heat quickly deforms or extinguishes the print.

Much of the research and development in the forensics field has been devoted to uncovering, developing, and identifying *latent* fingerprints. Scientists and law enforcement officers have made great progress in this field over the years and have developed processes ranging from brush and powders to chemicals, dyes and the use of alternate lights sources.

Identifying a latent print. Image courtesy of Her Majesty the Queen in Right of Canada as represented by the Royal Canadian Mounted Police. © 2009. All rights reserved.

A visible fingerprint in blood.

A three-dimensional fingerprint in clay.

Livescan

Historically, fingerprints have been recorded in ink on white finger-print cards, a system that continues to the present in many jurisdictions. Livescan however, is an electronic method of inkless fingerprint capture. The fingers are rolled onto a glass plate or *platen*, much as they would be if ink were used, but the fingerprint minutiae are read through the platen and converted to digital information, which can be added to or searched against a database.

The Livescan station informs the technician if any digit is not satisfac-torily recorded, and it can be retaken immediately. In addition to a grow-ing number of police agencies, Livescan is currently in use at border crossings and by state governments (including California) for criminal history back-ground checks that may be required as a condition of employment, li-censing, certification, foreign adoptions, or visa / immigration clearances.

Automated Fingerprint Identification System (AFIS)

When crime scene fingerprints have been developed (see "Develop-ment Techniques") there are two levels of initial comparison—persons

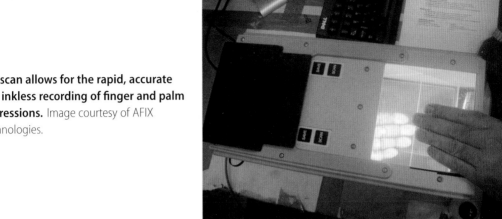

Livescan allows for the rapid, accurate and inkless recording of finger and palm impressions. Image courtesy of AFIX Technologies.

who may have legitimately touched evidence, and those from known suspects. Any impressions not identified should then (ideally) be compared to known criminals in a regional or national database and to fingerprints from other crime scenes of unknown origin.

The first single fingerprint databases were manually classified, filed, and searched. The system was imperfect, and the technicians classifying the fingerprint frequently saw it differently than the ones searching it—an easy thing to do when the prints are recorded at different times and may be only partially recorded, with critical details not present. It was vital to create a search system that removed the interpretive aspect from the process to the degree this was possible.

Computer technology lends itself beautifully to the storage and search of very large fingerprint databases at very high speed. The first AFIS system was conceptualized and developed in 1974 by Printrak, then a division of Rockwell International. The FBI adopted the system, with the first ten print card readers installed in 1975. Since that time, many companies large and small have supplied AFIS technology to every corner of the world.

Currently all AFIS systems:

- Scan and classify all ten fingers of each entrant at high speed;
- Store all vital and personal record information of each entrant, including name and date of birth;
- Maximize clarity of ridge detail to ensure optimum accuracy when searched;
- Compare an unknown fingerprint, classified in the same way, to a database of known impressions, and unknown impressions from other crime scenes;
- Ignore all of the fingerprints that could *not* be a match and generate a numerical score for each of the top possibilities, based on how closely the minutiae sets match the fingerprint being searched; and

An AFIS search of latent impressions gives rapid results. Courtesy of AFIX Technologies.

- Display a match report with scores for each of the top possibilities that *cannot be eliminated* on the basis of the information received.

The system should arguably be called the Automated Fingerprint Elimination System, because identification is not a function that computers currently have any part in. At very high speed they eliminate a huge volume of nonmatches and create a short list of possibilities for a qualified fingerprint technician to review. It should be noted that routinely there is no match among the featured possibilities for the fingerprint being searched. The user determines the number of possibilities displayed.

The software of an AFIS system conducts the search algorithm, and has a fundamentally different basis for classification and search than the one used in defunct manual single fingerprint systems.

When a trained technician individually classified fingerprints, the whole impression (including an entire core and all deltas) had to be present to arrive at an accurate designation, even at the primary pattern level, not to mention the subclassification that followed. This applied to both arrest prints making up the database and latent fingerprints searched. If any critical elements were missing in either impression, the match would not be made.

Plotting detail in AFIS is based on the number, location, and direction of *minutiae* (ridge endings and bifurcation). If part of the pattern detail

Both impressions were made by the same finger, but with one delta missing, a pattern-based search would not link the partial print to the database copy.

 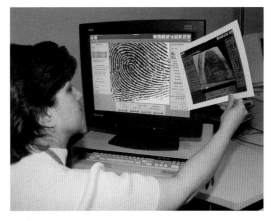

Fingerprint technician examining prints for classification.

Comparing prints in the database.

is missing in either impression, it does not affect the search. That said, any AFIS system is entirely dependent on the quantity, quality, and clarity of fingerprint detail entered (Caudle, personal communication 2009).

Within AFIS the following searches are possible:

- Latent to database: Crime scene impressions are searched against the database of known offenders.
- Latent to latent: Crime scene impressions are searched against unidentified prints from other crime scenes.
- Ten print: A known set of fingerprints can be searched against the database to determine if the subject is there under another name.
- Restricted: Searches may be limited to a specific part of the database—region, age, or gender, for example.

The efficiency and hit rate of the system is directly related to the quality of the database and the skill of the operator.

Palm Prints

On average, one-third of all impressions recovered from crime scenes and exhibits are palm prints. Until the last few years of the twentieth century, these were underexploited. There was no universal protocol for automatically recording palm prints for criminal charges; therefore, if a palm impression was developed at the crime scene, there may not be known samples to compare it to even if there were suspects.

Palm prints require more care to record properly and completely than fingerprints, and because of their size and flexibility, there is more opportunity for smearing and distortion. Consequently, one rarely finds a full palm print at a crime scene—fragmentary impressions are much more common. Unlike fingerprints, they can present a broad expanse of gently arching ridge detail, without useful features like deltas and loops. Also, it can be difficult to determine whether the print is from the right or left hand, or even which way is up.

An extremely valuable methodology was developed in 1990 by Ron Smith (Smith, personal communication, 1992) that enables examiners to analyze, locate, and compare partial palm prints quickly and accurately. Smith was also one of the practitioners involved in the development of automated palm print searches in the late 1990s—a capability now offered by most (if not all) AFIS systems.

Intensive research had been devoted in recent years to extending the AFIS plotting and search capability to include third-level detail—the placement of pores on the ridges. To date, no such system is operational.

Children's Fingerprints

The investigation of a 1995 child murder in Knoxville, Tennessee, left investigators with very few clues. Not only did they have to place the suspect at the scene of the crime, they also had to place the victim, a little girl, in the suspect's car.

Though she was seen entering the suspect's car by witnesses, forensic experts were unable to locate any latent fingerprint evidence of her presence. The alleged killer initially confessed, but later withdrew his confession, further frustrating the efforts of investigators. A trial followed, and he was subsequently convicted, but the question remained as to why there had been no visible or latent fingerprints of the little girl on or in the suspect's car.

The lead investigator, Art Bohanan, had speculated that the secretions left by the child's touch had somehow disappeared. The FBI had no current data on this phenomenon, nor did Scotland Yard, so he turned to the Oak Ridge National Laboratory (ORNL) in Oak Ridge, Tennessee, for some answers. As part of a network of the U.S. Department of Energy, the facility offers research in various areas of science, including chemical and analytic science. Bohanan asked for their assistance in understanding whether children's fingerprints were somehow different from those of adults (see Xiques 2006; also Kotz et al. 2008).

Taking on this scientific challenge, as is their mandate, a group of researchers from ORNL was quickly assembled. They collected samples of fingerprints and their chemical secretions from groups of children and adults by having different age groups shake vials of alcohol between their thumb and forefinger. Using gas chromatography and mass spectrometry, they set about analyzing the chemical composition of children's versus adult fingerprints (see ORNL 1995).

Independently, Bohanan devised his own very basic and telling experiment where he had children and adults handle cases of soda bottles. One sample he placed in a cold basement as a control, and the other he placed in his warm car to replicate normal conditions (see Xiques 2006).

Both ORNL's lab and Bohanan's home experiments came back with the same results; children's prints were very different from adult fingerprints. Children's prints, according to Michelle Buchanan, who headed the research team, "contained more volatile chemicals, such as free fatty acids, while adult prints displayed longer lasting compounds" (ORNL 1995). The child's latent deposits had evaporated, but the adult's prints that remained contained larger quantities of fatty acid *esters*, or salts. Once deposited, the esters remained while other secretions evaporated. The researchers commented that this was like the difference between footprints left after walking in gasoline and those left after walking in oil. They are composed of similar chemical compounds, but the gasoline evaporates while the oil traces remain.

Since dusting for fingerprints with standard equipment has proven to be ineffective in detecting the presence of a child at a crime scene, this pivotal research has created the need for new testing methods. Presently, researchers at ORNL have begun looking at a test for latent juvenile fingerprints as well as creating markers for the chemical composition of fingerprint secretions. In the meantime, DNA analysis, through simple swabbing techniques, can be applied in such cases until research in this area is complete. Since DNA is unique to the individual, areas that may have been touched by a child could be swabbed to better indicate their genetic presence.

Fingerprint Development

As stated in chapter 1, the goal for all forensic practitioners is the recovery of all physical evidence from crime scenes and exhibits, with particular attention to those items and impressions that exist at the threshold of perception. Experience has repeatedly revealed that the most overt and easily recovered impressions, for example fingerprints, are not always the most significant to the case.

Maximum evidence recovery will be most effective when a process of diagnosis and triage is followed, leading to the use of the *sequence* of techniques that are most likely to produce results. These decisions will be based on the type, condition and history (where known) of each substrate. For example, if it is known that a paper document has been immersed in water, amino acid-targeting techniques such as DFO and indanedione will not be effective and need not be used. Therefore, it is strongly recommended, wherever circumstances and finances allow, that examination by lasers and light sources for intrinsic fluorescence are conducted prior to chemical treatment.

There are literally dozens of fingerprint techniques targeting different components and properties of latent impressions, for use on a wide range of substrates. These have not only undergone research and development in different laboratories, but different degrees of scrutiny and testing. Even when the same techniques have been subjected to comprehensive and careful comparison in different parts of the world, the results can vary significantly. This speaks to the variables encountered in the processing of exhibits for fingerprints. These include but are not limited to diet, metabolism, emotional state, humidity, temperature, pH factor and substrate. In short, the identification professional is encouraged to examine carefully the history, research and performance record of any new technology before adopting it for operational use.

As mentioned previously, fingerprints detected at crime scenes that are designated as latent refer to the vast majority of fingerprints, crime scene or otherwise, that are hidden.

Latent prints are composed of a long list of components that the body has expelled through pores, including water, salt, amino acids, lipids, and urea, to name a few (Olsen 1978). These ingredients are not visible on most surfaces and require chemical, physical, or light development to make them useful for comparison.

The world is experienced through our sense of touch, and with acknowledgment to Locard, material is picked up and dropped off at every contact. This does not mean, however, that every transfer involves sufficient material to be forensically useful. Even a usable latent fingerprint will typically contain less than a nanogram (one billionth of a gram) of total material, with the component targeted by any detection method being only a fraction of that.

There are many inherent fingerprint ingredients, but there is also a virtually unlimited list of external compounds acquired during regular activity. The challenges faced by those who seek to find fingerprints are based on the fact that most fingerprints left on objects or at crime scenes are invisible, present on virtually any kind of surface. Also, fingerprint residue can be composed of almost any combination of many ingredients depending on:

- state of mind (anger, fear, nervousness)
- diet
- dry vs. damp skin, and
- temperature and humidity

The relevant detection technique must therefore target one or more specific ingredients or properties of the fingerprint. However, it is impossible to know what any given fingerprint is composed of, and a fingerprint may have a variety of ingredients, but not enough of the one targeted by the method used. As such, the print in these situations will not be rendered visible.

Currently, there exist dozens of techniques, chemical and physical, for the detection of fingerprints. Without knowing in advance the composition, age, or quality of the fingerprints they seek, forensic specialists improve the odds of successful discovery through an understanding of the strengths and weaknesses of their professional toolkit. Likewise, they must employ expert application of the techniques while conducting a triage of the *substrate*—the surface under which the fingerprint sits. Last, the application of *sequential processing* allows for the targeting of multiple fingerprint components, thereby increasing the chances of success.

The ensuing section does not purport to be a complete list of current technology, but the methods herein have all been used successfully in actual investigations, and can be viewed as mainstream and proven techniques. Included are different formulations of the same technique favored by specific agencies.

Development Techniques

Nonporous versus Porous

Developing a latent fingerprint means it is rendered visible and thus becomes physical evidence that can be documented, analyzed, and compared. Methods of development range from the use of traditional powder to the most current use of reagents, fluorescent dyes, and lasers. The technique used is primarily determined by the nature of the *substrate*, the material under which the print is found.

Forensic investigators divide the substrate into two distinctions: *nonporous* and *porous* exhibits. *Nonporous* exhibits refer to all materials that are impermeable, where the print and its development are captured on a surface level. Materials like plastic, vinyl, all painted surfaces, metal, and glass do not absorb fingerprint secretions, thus the development technique must adhere to these secretions and not be absorbed by the substrate.

Conversely, *porous* exhibits are defined as materials that absorb fingerprint secretions. These substrates must therefore use solutions, sprays, and dyes that create a chemical reaction and permeate the substrate to reveal the latent print. Although powder techniques have on occasion been used successfully on papers and card stocks, chemical reagents are more amenable to the development of older and more marginal impressions. Porous exhibits include paper, wet cardboard, cotton, silk, linen, other fabrics, unpainted wood, and drywall, for example.

The following section is a comprehensive outline of the most current and up-to-date methods of developing latent friction ridge patterns on both nonporous and porous exhibits. It must be stated, however, that many more techniques are currently in use but are too many to list here.

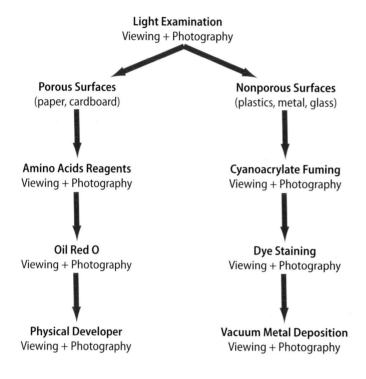

Laboratory Exhibit Processing

Light Examination
Viewing + Photography

Porous Surfaces
(paper, cardboard)

Nonporous Surfaces
(plastics, metal, glass)

Amino Acids Reagents
Viewing + Photography

Cyanoacrylate Fuming
Viewing + Photography

Oil Red O
Viewing + Photography

Dye Staining
Viewing + Photography

Physical Developer
Viewing + Photography

Vacuum Metal Deposition
Viewing + Photography

Suggested processing flowchart for commonly encountered surfaces. Atypical exhibits may require other methods described in this book. Application of some methods (including vacuum metal deposition) will be limited by the manpower and material resources of the agency.

Nonporous Exhibits

Fingerprint Powder

For three-quarters of a century, the choice was reasonably simple. The property first exploited by police in search of latent fingerprints was the relative stickiness of the deposit, due to the presence of sebaceous oil.

Extremely fine powder was developed and applied to a surface bearing fingerprints. The powder would adhere to the stickiness of the print, and not so much to the surface on which it appeared. It is easy to imagine this discovery made by accidental contact of some common material like coal or charcoal dust, and the seemingly magical appearance of fingerprints.

Improvements followed over time with the development of powders expressly for this purpose, with greater adherent qualities and colors to offer maximum contrast to the background. Soft brushes were designed for optimum application of the powder without causing damage to the impression.

Powder is the oldest of the fingerprint detection methods, and it is still a valuable tool. Success with powder depends on the stickiness of the impression versus that of the substrate. It is best applied to nonporous surfaces, and when properly used will make the impression vis-

Dusting for prints. Image courtesy of Her Majesty the Queen in Right of Canada as represented by the Royal Canadian Mounted Police. © 2009. All rights reserved.

ible by creating a contrast with the background. Powder, unlike other methods, allows the impression to be lifted from the substrate and retained for identification (see guide to follow).

That said, powder might not always be the best choice. It is certainly the quickest, cheapest, and most convenient choice, but in terms of sensitivity, there are frequently better options. Powder has no equal for crime scene processing of doorframes, windowsills, window glass, furniture, and other objects that cannot be moved. In major case investigations, however, it is the writer's opinion that every effort should be made to apply all of the most effective techniques in the prescribed sequence.

Guide: How to Powder and Lift Fingerprints

The following is a step-by-step guide to the use of fingerprint powders and the lifting of fingerprints from various substrates.

Powder Choice

The powder must be chosen on the basis of its ability to do three things:

- Adhere to the fingerprint ridges
- *Not* adhere to the substrate, and
- Provide maximum contrast between ridges and substrate

It is essential to select a powder color that provides maximum *contrast* with the background. If the surface is white or light-colored, a dark gray or black powder would be the best choice. Conversely, white or light gray powder would give better contrast on a black or dark surface.

No other fingerprint development technique has been in continuous use as long as powder and brush.

All impressions should be photographed in situ prior to lifting, for the following reasons:

- shows the location and direction of the impression,
- records what may be the best and most complete detail,
- impressions could be damaged or degraded during lifting,
- records the laterality of the impression, and
- eliminates suggestion of forgery or transfer.

Fluorescent Powders

Occasionally a situation arises in which fluorescent powder may be more appropriate than the more conventional ones. Powder is applied very sparingly with a feather duster. Overdusting and subsequent loss of

Fluorescent powder and feather duster.

Dusting for prints on dark glass with white powder for maximum contrast.

Magna Powder and Wand. If the wand makes direct contact with the surface under examination, any fingerprints may be degraded or destroyed.

ridge detail is a real possibility. In the writer's opinion, there are often better options than fluorescent powder.

Magna Powder

Magna powder contains finely subdivided magnetic particles that are introduced to the surface with a magnetic wand instead of a brush. It is not recommended for use on ferrous metals, but is effective on rough surfaces and has been used to reveal fingerprints on the skin of murder victims. Direct contact between the wand and the surface under scrutiny will almost certainly degrade or destroy the impression.

Brush Technique

A fiberglass brush is used to gently apply the powder to the surface of the exhibit. The powder will cling selectively to sebaceous oil, water, or possibly foreign material.

Zephyr brush over paper.

A squirrel hair brush is used to clean dusted impressions.

- The latent print is marked with the investigator's initials, impression number, and date, using a grease pencil.
- A squirrel or camel hair brush may be used to clean or touch up developed impressions. It may also be better suited than the fiberglass brush for dusting the identifying marks.

Lifting the Latent Print

Once the latent print has been developed, the forensic officer or crime scene technician is left with the task of removing it for examination by a technician.

The first step is to take several photographs of the print with a scale ruler included in the picture. The scale is used when the photograph is developed or printed and a technician can restore the photo to an exact life-size image using the ruler. The photograph is invaluable, especially in a case where a mistake is made by the examiner, and the print becomes smeared during the removal process.

The forensic officer or technician writes his or her initials and the date beside the print, brushes the writing with a bit more powder, and uses a special lifting tape pressed onto the latent print. Made especially for forensics, the tape is carefully pressed onto the latent print, air bubbles removed, and then it is slowly peeled off, bringing the developed latent print with it.

The taped print is then pressed onto a sheet of clear plastic acetate, which preserves the print for further examination. Several manufacturers offer a lifting system consisting of a piece of tape already attached to clear acetate.

Chemically developed latent prints on paper cannot be lifted because they form part of a chemical reaction, so they are photographed with a scale ruler to allow a life-size reproduction of the photograph. Photography plays a major role in the preservation of fingerprints. A simple slip of the hand or the fading of a chemical reaction can render the original print useless, but a photo will last indefinitely. Hence, whatever technique is used to reveal latent fingerprint impressions, a photograph of the evidence before it is handled is crucial.

The Knaap Process

Investigators have long been aware of limitations that fingerprint tape has when attempting to secure powder enhanced impressions from textured surfaces. All too frequently, when a latent fingerprint impression is developed on a textured surface, attempts to lift it using fingerprint tape fail, resulting in only the pattern of the surface being captured, and the fingerprint detail is lost.

In response to this problem, many forensic equipment suppliers now offer alternative lifting products. These include elastomers, gelatin lifters,

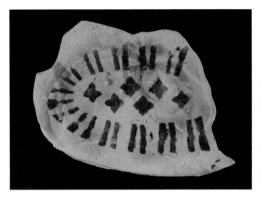

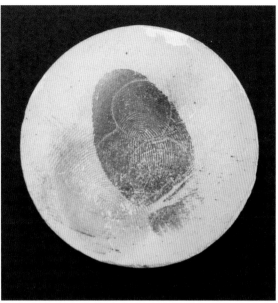

A dental stone cast with the captured two-dimensional fingerprint and footwear image.
Images courtesy of Toronto Police Forensic Identification Services. Photo credit: John Doucette.

stretch tapes, liquid gelled glues, polyvinylsiloxanes, and other rubber-like casting materials. Although these products may be effective options, most have a limited shelf life and can be cost prohibitive, especially where cluster fingerprint and palm impressions are to be lifted.

The *Knaap process* (first developed by forensic identification officer Wade Knaap in 2000) is an inexpensive alternative to these products. In lieu of other lifting materials, it uses dental stone to secure enhanced two-dimensional fingerprints or footwear impressions (see chapter 8). Dental stone is recognized throughout the forensic community as the preferred material for casting three-dimensional footwear and tire track impression evidence. It is an inexpensive dry mix gypsum product that yields excellent detail and is exceptionally strong and durable. Once cured, the cast is a true replication of the impression, with only a negligible amount of shrinkage. The shrinkage (approximately 0.08 percent) is so minute that it does not impede the ability to individualize.

Two-dimensional fingerprint and footwear impression evidence is developed or enhanced using black magnetic fingerprint powder with a magnetic wand. Magnetic powder is the best choice for most applications, as it provides excellent detail while reducing background development, which is more problematic when using granular powder on textured surfaces.

Once the impression is ready to be lifted, dental stone powder is combined with water to create a liquid mixture, which is then poured onto the impression and allowed to cure. Curing takes approximately thirty minutes. The hardened cast is then lifted from the surface, having indelibly secured the fingerprint powdered impression into the underside. As noted, this technique works for both 2D fingerprint and 2D footwear evidence where sufficient moisture content permits the powder to adhere to the impression. The quality of detail captured rivals the more expensive options, at a fraction of the cost.

Cyanoacrylate (CA) Fuming

CA or *superglue* has become the most common process for the development of fingerprints on plastics, glass, bare and painted metal, and even occasionally glossy cardboard.

Like many valuable inventions, superglue fuming was discovered by accident, apparently in different parts of the world at the same time (ca. 1978–80). In one such case, a police officer used a cyanoacrylate glue to repair a plastic Bakelite film-developing tank and was amazed to see white fingerprints appear magically on the surface of the tank. The superglue method was also used by the Criminal Identification Division of the Japanese National Police Agency in 1978, and introduced to North America by the U.S. Army Criminal Investigation Laboratory (German, personal communication, 1988). Word of the new technique spread rapidly in the police community, and the first version of it was simply an aquarium with a glass lid and a small amount of glue in a bottle cap.

A chemical called a *monomer*, CA is converted to vapor with gentle heating. It is intensely reactive and polymerizes (forms plastic) on contact

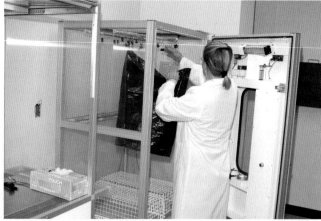

Above: **Technician places plastic exhibits in the cyanoacrylate chamber for processing.** Image courtesy of Her Majesty the Queen in Right of Canada as represented by the Royal Canadian Mounted Police. © 2009. All rights reserved.

Left: **Atmospheric cyanoacrylate chamber. These are available in different sizes and configurations.**

with certain components of fingerprint residue. Under magnification, the polymer has a spaghetti-like appearance. This structure has much to do with the ultimate visibility of glue-developed impressions immediately after processing. The polymer is reasonably robust and is not easily damaged on most surfaces by gentle abrasion.

Objects for treatment are placed in a sealable chamber, along with a quantity of liquid CA. All modern glue chambers have the ability to regulate the relative humidity and circulate the vapor evenly.

Depending on the amount of residue in the fingerprint, the nature of the background, and the method of viewing, the polymer-developed impression may or may not be visible in ambient light. Objects can be overfumed, resulting in too much polymer being formed and the polymer formation to flow from the ridge sites into the furrows, thus causing irreversible damage to ridge detail. Careful monitoring of the process circumvents this problem.

Surfaces that work best with CA fuming include:

- glass
- most plastics, including grocery and trash bags, wrap or bags similar to dime bags used in the illicit drug trade
- knives
- handguns and long guns (rifles)

Fingerprint detail developed by CA fuming in a vacuum has a dramatically different appearance from that developed atmospherically. The polymer lacks the spaghetti-like appearance and does not reflect light well. For this reason, dye staining afterward and viewing with a forensic light source is a necessity (see later discussion).

It is the writer's experience that impressions developed in the vacuum chamber are more fragile than those developed atmospherically. The

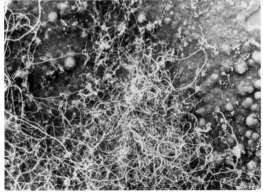

Microscopic image of fingerprint processed in ambient conditions.

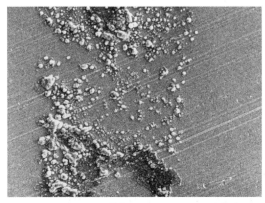

Microscopic image of fingerprint processed in vacuum chamber.

 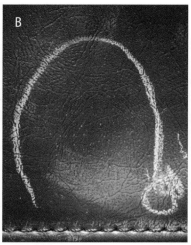 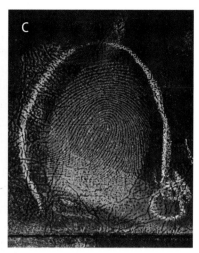

A: Fingerprint developed by cyanoacrylate alone, ambient conditions, on green garbage bag. The undyed polymer may be much less visible depending on several factors, including the amount and type of deposit components and the substrate.
B: Fingerprint developed with cyanoacrylate.
C: Stained with rhodamine 6G and revealed by Flare Plus 505 nm.

polymer seems to sit on top of the surface, much like a dusted fingerprint, without any firm bonding to the background material. Certainly, fingerprints developed in an atmospheric chamber can be damaged by abrasion, but not as easily as those created in vacuum conditions. The vacuum method has shown repeated success on otherwise difficult surfaces, including handguns.

Regardless of the fuming method chosen, it is now strongly recommended that post-cyanoacrylate treatment with *fluorescent dye* such as rhodamine 6G (see Menzel 1979, 1999) or brilliant yellow 40 (see following section) be standard procedure. The sensitivity of dye is much higher than CA fuming alone, and there can be no assurance that all im-

---

A young woman was attacked in her apartment building and forced back into her apartment, where she was raped and murdered. The suspect took her keys and fled in her car, which was parked underground.

The car, found abandoned on a major highway, was transported to Ontario Provincial Police Forensic Identification Services Laboratory in Toronto, where it was examined for physical evidence. The steering wheel, rear view mirror, and door handles were removed and treated with cyanoacrylate, followed by spraying with rhodamine 6G.

The steering wheel was a sport model composed of textured rubber, molded to appear as wrapped leather. No trace of ridge detail was visible in room light, but under laser a good-quality fingerprint was located and photographed. When the print was identified, it was the first time police were aware of the identity of the perpetrator, who was apprehended shortly afterward.

pressions developed by the CA will be revealed by scrutiny under ambient light. In any case, an effective dye must absorb specific wavelength(s) of light, fluoresce intensely, and adhere readily to the glue polymer but not to the substrate.

Prior to the introduction of cyanoacrylate fuming with dye staining, surfaces like textured vinyl were so unresponsive to powder treatment that they were largely regarded as unsuitable for fingerprint examination.

Vacuum Metal Deposition (VMD)

Vacuum metal deposition (VMD) is a technique used for the development of latent fingerprints on a range of polymer surfaces like plastic bags, as well as on fragile surfaces such as guns, bullets, semi-porous surfaces, or where traditional latent development has proven to be difficult (see Kent et al. 1976). It has a good record of revealing very old fingerprints on surfaces ranging from plastic bags and wrapping to smooth leather and glass. VMD is also capable of developing fingerprints on items that have been wetted.

Developed in England in 1936 (see Gaviola and Strong 1936) as a means of depositing thin layers of gold onto parts for the fledgling electrical industry, it was also used for coating reflective surfaces, the anti-reflection coating of camera lenses, and in the production of semiconductors. However, it was not until 1963 that someone saw VMD as a potential for developing latent fingerprints.

The process works by thinly coating pieces of fragile evidence with metal using a vacuum chamber. The conventional gold/zinc technique deposits two thin layers of gold and zinc onto the suspect material. Without oxygen (within a vacuum), metals can be heated and evaporated without burning. By reducing the number of air molecules, the evaporation cloud travels unobstructed from the source to the article and is deposited in very pure films.

The evidence is placed into the chamber and a small quantity of gold (4–5 mg) and several grams of zinc are loaded into separate evaporation dishes located under the exhibit. Pumps then reduce pressure to operating levels at approximately one millionth of an atmosphere (0.101325 pascals). Gold is evaporated and deposits uniformly over the surface and is absorbed by the ridges of the human sweat that form the invisible fingerprint pattern. Zinc generally condenses only onto another metal, so when the zinc layer is deposited by a second evaporation, it adheres only to the gold-coated areas that lie between the sweat ridges. In this way, a visible pattern is developed from the latent fingerprint image.

Recent experiments with VMD have shown that small pieces of aluminum wire evaporation may show better results than the gold/zinc process (see Gunaratne 2006).

The equipment, however, is expensive and is generally found only in the laboratories of large police agencies. Experience and expertise are re-

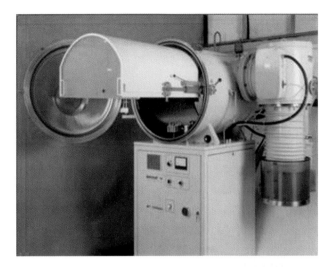

A vacuum metal deposition chamber.

VMD examination may result in either light or dark ridges against a contrasting background. In this impression developed on a black garbage bag from a homicide investigation, the ridges are black against the substrate coated with zinc.

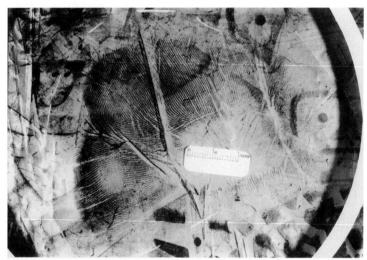

A fingerprint developed by vacuum metal deposition on an apple. VMD has frequently been successful in developing ridge detail on atypical surfaces that resist other methods.
Images courtesy of Her Majesty the Queen in Right of Canada as represented by the Royal Canadian Mounted Police. ©2009.

quired for successful implementation, and proper maintenance is crucial to the reliable operation of the vacuum chamber.

Iodine

Iodine is an infrequently used niche technique that can be used nondestructively before proceeding to a more invasive liquid or vapor method, particularly on nonporous, light-colored surfaces or human skin.

A preloaded iodine pipe is fitted with a squeeze bulb, similar to the one used in testing blood pressure. The heat of the hand causes the iodine crystals in the pipe to *sublimate* (change directly from a solid to a gas). Grasped in one hand, the iodine pipe forces iodine vapor through the pipe and onto the surface when the bulb is squeezed. In the best case, the iodine will be physically trapped by oil in the fingerprint. A yellow-brown discoloration usually (but not always) appears on the fumed area.

If ridge detail is rendered visible, it may be temporarily fixed and darkened by *huffing*, that is, breathing warm moist breath onto the surface.

The second phase of this technique is the application of a silver plate to the fumed area (Hinds, personal communication 1972, 2009). This

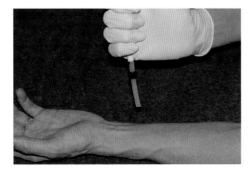

Iodine vapor is forced onto the skin surface and preferentially trapped within the structure of sebaceous oil, commonly found in a fingerprint deposit.

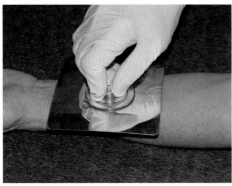

The silver plate is pressed firmly to the fumed area for approximately twenty seconds.

Fingerprint developed with iodine and transferred to a silver plate.

creates an instant photochemical reaction between the iodine and the silver. A high-resolution image is formed in silver chloride on the silver plate of whatever detail was present on the skin where the iodine adhered to the oil.

This extension of iodine fuming is currently almost exclusively relegated to the examination of murder victims, mostly because it targets oils. There are more sensitive procedures for oils on almost every surface, except skin. Hence, there is currently no one dominant technique for developing fingerprints on skin. Iodine/silver plate transfer has been responsible for two out of four cases in Canada in which a criminal has been identified by fingerprints on the skin of the victim.

Porous Exhibits

Silver Nitrate

Dr. Rene Forgeot, a colleague of Alphonse Bertillon, explored early chemical development of fingerprints in 1892 (see Fisher 1994). Forgeot invented a process using *silver nitrate*—a compound of silver salt. The solution is sprayed on porous surfaces like paper or wood and targets common salt (sodium chloride) a principal ingredient of sweat. The silver nitrate reacts with the sodium chloride to form silver chloride, a compound that becomes visible as a brown-black stain on exposure to light.

This technique was used by Dr. E. M. Hudson, a fingerprint expert who applied his skills in the famous Lindbergh kidnapping case of 1932. Fingerprints were actually developed on the wooden ladder found at the Lindbergh residence. Although no suspects were ever matched, one of these impressions was identified as made by one of the police investigators. Hudson also treated books and toys belonging to the Lindbergh baby, thinking that fingerprints might be crucial in any future identification. Thirteen useful fingerprints were found and photographed on these items.

Silver nitrate was such an effective fingerprint reagent (developer) that it was still the principal fingerprint reagent for paper exhibits in the 1970s, until the development of ninhydrin (see next section). One major drawback to silver nitrate is its dependence on the presence of salt in finger deposit. Sodium chloride is readily soluble in water, and humidity in the air quickly causes the salt in fingerprints to migrate, whereby crisp, sharp fingerprints are replaced by useless smudges.

Ninhydrin

Ninhydrin is a biological test for the presence of amino acids found in protein, peptones, and peptides (see Oden and von Hofsten 1954). It

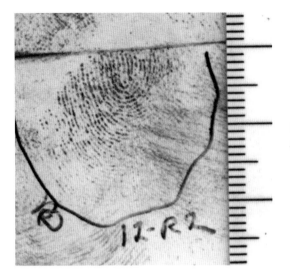

Ninhydrin was the first and for decades the best amino acid reagent for fingerprints on paper.

was the first technique to target amino acids in fingerprint residue, an important component because as many as twenty-one amino acids may be present in fingerprints (Coltman et al. 1966). In the early 1970s, it replaced silver nitrate as the method of choice for paper exhibits.

Ninhydrin is an excellent technique with a long history of success, both in terms of image quality and sensitivity to older impressions. Fingerprints known to be over ten years old have been visualized by ninhydrin.

In spite of its excellent record, ninhydrin has limitations. It is not effective on dark-colored or black paper exhibits because the Ruhemann's purple stain is not visible against such backgrounds. Also, there are types and colors of paper and cardboard that do not respond well to ninhydrin processing. Although a sequential process involving zinc chloride was developed that induced some ridge detail to fluoresce, the historic successes have been sporadic and infrequent.

The use of ninhydrin has been lessened with the advent of fluorescing methods like DFO and indanedione, but there continue to be niche applications for it, either in sequence with DFO or for exhibits diagnosed to possess intense substrate fluorescence.

A search began in the 1970s for a ninhydrin analog—a reagent with similar chemical structure and properties—that would prove to be more sensitive at revealing latent fingerprints. See below for the recommended stock and working solutions:

Ninhydrin Stock Solution:
- Dissolve 25 gm. ninhydrin in 225 ml Ethanol
- Slowly add 10 ml of Ethyl Acetate and 25 ml Acetic Acid while stirring
- Filter and store in dark with capped bottle

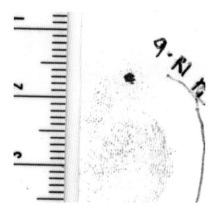
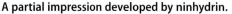
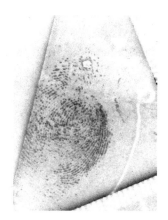

A partial impression developed by ninhydrin. The same impression after treatment with zinc chloride.

Ninhydrin Working Solution:
- Add 52 ml stock solution to 1 L HFE7100
- Immerse exhibits for 10–20 seconds
- Place in humidity chamber @ 50 deg. C and 80% rel. humidity

Zinc Chloride

Ninhydrin treatment occasionally reveals faint or indistinct "connect the dots" impressions that don't contain sufficient or clear detail for comparison purposes. In these situations, the power of luminescence can sometimes come to the rescue (see Herod and Menzel 1982).

A solution of zinc chloride is applied to ninhydrin-treated exhibits by spraying or dipping. Gentle humidity (steamer or kettle) will change the color of any developed detail from Ruhemann's purple to orange. The detail may luminesce under green light excitation (e.g., 505 nm Polight filter).

Zinc chloride is a hit-or-miss proposition. There is currently no ready explanation known to the writer as to why it works on some exhibits and not on others. It can certainly be a useful extension of ninhydrin when DFO or indanedione (see following section) is not available. For post-treatment of faint ninhydrin impressions with the use of zinc chloride, the following method is suggested:

- Mix 8 gm Zinc Chloride in 200 ml Absolute alcohol
- Mix thoroughly
- For treatment, using hand sprayer (mister) apply solution lightly with repeated sprayings
- Do not soak
- Expose to humidity in chamber, or with kettle or drapery steamer until the Ruhmann's Purple changes color to orange
- View under 505 nm FLS filter with orange goggles

This extension of ninhydrin treatment for paper exhibits was developed [Menzel] in the mid-1980s, before the introduction of fluorogenic methods like DFO and indanedione. However, it has proven to be infrequently successful, in the author's experience, and is not currently recommended.

Diazafluoronone (DFO)

The first and one of the best of the ninhydrin analogs has been DFO, introduced in 1990 (Pounds et al. 1990). This was the first single-step chemical reagent to exploit the sensitivity of luminescence operationally as a detection strategy. Although the visible color development may be weaker than ninhydrin, the fluorescence of the fingerprints more than compensates for it. To obtain the full sensitivity of DFO, one must excite the fluorescence with a laser or forensic light source (see section on forensic light sources). Technicians and researchers report finding on average as many as double the fingerprints with DFO as with ninhydrin.

It must be noted that a forensic light source is a necessity if one chooses to use DFO. Its power lies not in staining ridge detail but in its ability to induce fingerprints to luminesce. Some users also report additional fingerprint development with ninhydrin *after* DFO, indicating a different and complimentary reaction with amino acids.

The following is the recommended solution for 1,8 Diafluoren-9-One (DFO):

- To .25 g DFO, add 40 ml Methanol and 20 ml Acetic Acid. Cover and stir until dissolved.

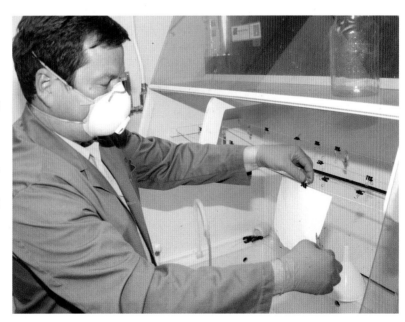

Forensic specialist drying a paper exhibit after DFO (diazafluoronone) development. Image courtesy of Her Majesty the Queen in Right of Canada as represented by the Royal Canadian Mounted Police. ©2009.

- Add to 940 ml HFE-7100.
- It is crucial that any oily deposit on the surface of the solution be removed with filter paper or molecular sieve prior to use.
- Dip exhibits in solution until saturated, allow to air dry and repeat dipping process.
- Place exhibits in a dry heat oven or dry mount press for 10 minutes at 200 degrees Celsius.
- View under green light using orange filter to view the yellow luminescence of the fingerprints.

The reaction produces reddish fingerprints in color mode, but the luminescence mode routinely produces considerably more fingerprints and enhanced detail. Paradoxically, DFO has been rated as two and a half times as sensitive as ninhydrin, but additional detail with post-DFO ninhydrin treatment has been reported.

1,2-Indanedione (ID)

One of the most dynamic and exciting developments in the detection of fingerprints on porous surfaces is 1,2-indanedione. Recent years have produced numerous studies comparing ID to DFO. There is no clear consensus at present, as respected researchers in different parts of the world report variations in their findings (see Almog et al. 1999; Almog et al. 2004; Stoilovic and Lennard 2006; Wilkinson 2000; Ramatowski et al. 1997; Alaoui et al. 2005; Wiesner et al. 2001; Roux et al. 2000). These differences may be attributable to a number of factors, including but not limited to the following:

- different chemical composition of papers, hence, better or worse response to the chemistry
- different climatic conditions (temperature, humidity)
- different diets and
- different formulae and processing procedures

Like DFO, indanedione produces a color mode, which has recently been named Joullie pink, in tribute to Madelaine Joullie, the principal

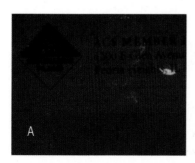
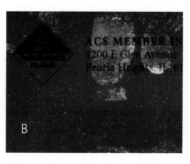

A: An envelope processed in DFO.

B: The same area after processing in indanedione.

Image Courtesy of R.S. Ramotowski, US Secret Service.

innovator of this technique (see Hark et al. 1994; Cantu et al. 1993). Emerging data indicates that ID-treated fingerprints fluoresce more intensely than those treated with DFO and may have a longer reach in revealing faint finger impressions. The writer's operational experiences are consistent with this finding.

ID is best illuminated with light in the 500–535 nm range. The fluorescence can be viewed with either orange or red goggles. This is a useful feature if the paper or ink fluorescence is obstructive. The fluorogenic properties of ID were extended significantly by the addition of zinc chloride to the formula. This is an interesting development, given Menzel's extension of the ninhydrin reaction with zinc chloride (see Kunkel et al. 2007).

Current and future studies may indicate the need to treat different types of paper with different reagents for optimum results. The following solutions for indanedione, referred to as the Australian Formulation, were provided by the Australian Federal Police:

Stock Solution
- Dissolve 4 gm Indanedione in 450 ml Ethyl Acetate
- Add 50 ml Glacial Acetic Acid
- Add 5 ml Zinc Chloride Stock Solution

Zinc Chloride Stock Solution
- Dissolve 8 gm Zinc Chloride in 200 ml absolute alcohol.

Indanedione-Zinc Chloride Working Solution
- Mix 50 ml stock solution with 450 ml HFE 7100

OR

0.8% formulation (received from R. Ramotowski 2013)
- 0.8 gm 1,2-indanedione
- 90 ml ethyl acetate
- 10 ml acetic acid (glacial)
- 80 ml zinc chloride stock (see below)
- 820 ml HFE 7100

Zinc Chloride Stock
- .4 gm zinc chloride
- 10 ml absolute alcohol
- 1 ml ethyl acetate
- 190 ml HFE 7100

Genipin

A most recent technique for amino acid reaction comes from work done at the Hebrew University of Jerusalem (see Levinton-Shamuilov et

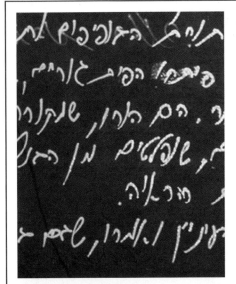

When this document is viewed under green excitation (suitable for DFO and ID), the writing presents a serious obstruction to any ridge detail that may be developed.

The document of a suspect bearing handwritten information was submitted for examination. Under green illumination (505–530 nm) the writing exhibited strong fluorescence, posing a significant obstruction to any fingerprint detail. This is the excitation choice for both DFO and ID.

Exciting research into a new class of amino acid reagents may increase the detection results on certain paper exhibits. Genipin, a derivative of the gardenia flower, reacts with amino acids to produce a blue-colored fingerprint. When excited by yellow light (590 nm) however, and viewed through a Kodak red filter no. 92, strong red fluorescence is seen.

The document was treated with genipin and illuminated with yellow light, as indi-

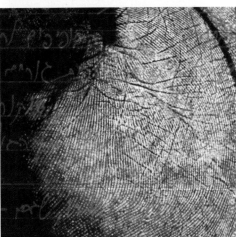

This palm print in genipin, as seen on the same document, is revealed by yellow light, which is less likely to excite obstructing background fluorescence. There is always the chance that yellow excitation will produce significantly less background fluorescence and hence less chance that critical fingerprint detail will be obstructed.

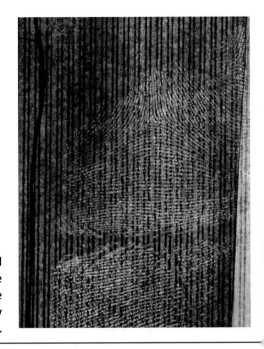

Palm print developed by DFO and excited by green light, on inside surface of envelope—strong ridge detail but partially obstructed by background fluorescence.

Color mode (blue pigment) of genipin revealed by white light—clear ridge detail partially obstructed by paper fibers.

cated. A palm print exhibiting strong red fluorescence was noted. Equally significant, the writing, a serious obstruction under green excitation, could barely be seen and did not obscure the ridge detail.

Even white light examination of genipin's color mode on some exhibits can produce unwanted background interference. Once again, genipin fluorescence, excited by yellow light, may reveal stronger clearer ridge detail unimpeded by background.

Note: This example underlines the need for careful assessment of exhibits prior to treatment. A niche reagent may produce results superior to those realized with the reagent normally used.

Courtesy of Dr. J. Almog,
Hebrew University of Jerusalem.

Fluorescent mode of same fingerprint excited by yellow light—stronger, more extensive ridge detail with reduced background interference.

Palm print developed by genipin and excited by yellow light on same envelope— strong ridge detail with little or no background fluorescence.

al. 2005; Almog et al. 2007). It is called *genipin* and is derived from the fruit of the gardenia plant. A natural product, it is the most environmentally friendly of the amino acid reagents.

Comparison to other amino acid reagents has not yet been reported, but initial testing offers hope that genipin may be used to advantage on certain types of paper that do not respond well to other amino acid reagents.

Genipin offers several interesting advantages. Fingerprints appear as bright blue impressions in white light, but they fluoresce under *yellow* illumination. The fluorescence occurs in the red region of the spectrum and is observed with a red cutoff filter Kodak #92 (see Almog et al. 2007). This may be a distinct advantage over DFO and ID in special situations because of less potential fluorescent obstruction from the substrate.

For use:

- Dissolve 1.7 gm Genipin in 57 ml Ethanol
- Add 86 ml Ethyl Acetate
- Add HFE 7100 to make 1 Liter of solution
- FLS 590 nm with Kodak #92 Wratten filter (no longer in production)
- Less effective substitute—505 nm with red goggles

Genipin must be viewed as an experimental technique at this time, producing somewhat inconsistent results. Although it has not yet displaced any of the mainstream methods for paper exhibits, it possesses remarkable properties. Requiring yellow light for excitation with red fluorescence, use of genipin has been shown on occasion to avoid obstructive substrate fluorescence. There are possible factors that, if resolved, may encourage operational use in specific situations. For example, the purity of genipin, the optimization of its formula, the optimization of excitation, and the identification of efficient filters as goggles and for photography.

The best source encountered by the author, for excitation of genipin is the Coherent Tracer laser (577nm). Effective filters and goggles are easily obtained for viewing and photography with this monochromatic source. When using a band of wavelengths (filtered lamp or LED source) however, a suitable replacement for the Kodak Wratten #92, which is out of production, has not been identified. Unless research can establish that genipin will outperform mainstream techniques in niche situations, it is unlikely that this will be pursued.

Lawsone

Lawsone is the most recent of a new group of amino acid detection reagents. Another natural plant product, it offers great promise and the same environmental advantages as genipin (see Jelly et al. 2008; Almog et al. 2009). It presents both a purple-brown color mode and yellow-excited luminescence on reaction with amino acids. Much more research will be required before the value of lawsone relative to other reagents can be assessed.

Physical Developer (PD)

Lipids are a group of fat-like substances including fatty acids, neutral fats, and waxes. Any or all of these may be found in finger residue. Sebaceous oil is consistently transferred from the face and neck to the hands. All of these components are insoluble in water.

Physical developer was introduced for police use in 1981 in the United Kingdom (see Hardwick 1981). A *maleic acid* prewash for filled papers was added in 1983 by Hardwick and Sears. Other researchers have modified and improved the formula (see Cantu 2001; Ramatowski 1996, 2000).

Paper exhibits that have been wetted or even soaked in water for extended periods of time are routinely encountered in criminal investigation, and the major weakness of amino acid reagents is revealed. The target compounds on which ninhydrin, DFO, and ID depend are water-soluble.

PD targets lipids in fingerprint residue, which do not dissolve in water. Also, a fingerprint may not be rich enough in amino acid residue to be visible after ninhydrin, DFO, or ID treatment, but may have enough lipid content for PD to be successful. Therefore, PD has the potential to reveal detail not detected by amino acid reagents. In water-affected exhibits, the lipid content of the fingerprint will be intact after the amino acids are dissolved away.

PD processing however, is time-consuming and more expensive than the amino acid treatments. There is perhaps no technique in the identification laboratory more unpredictable, unstable, and dependent on exacting standards of cleanliness and adherence to procedure. The chemistry has an extremely limited shelf life, and the working solution must be mixed fresh for each session. With these considerations in mind, some laboratories have adopted the policy of using PD only on major cases, or in specific cases where the exhibits have been wet.

It is also more cost-effective if the PD processing in a lab is done on a specific time rotation, such as the first Monday of each month, or as the volume of exhibits accumulates. This may be the best approach for obtaining the maximum benefit from the slow-moving process of mixing, dipping, and cleaning. Moreover, the component list is relatively extensive, and the preparation and processing times exceed those for almost any other fingerprint detection strategy.

The potential difficulties and time commitments aside, it is an extremely valuable and sensitive method for detecting lipid impressions on paper exhibits. There are two scenarios for using PD. The first is after amino acid treatment has been completed, and any impressions developed that have been photographed. In one case investigation, conducted by the author, a number of bank transfer envelopes were processed in ninhydrin, resulting only in fragments of ridge detail—evidence of touching. When the exhibits were subjected to PD treatment, multiple fingermarks were revealed, and ultimately identified two suspects.

The second application is for paper documents that have been wetted, either exposed to rain or immersed in water, thereby rendering them unsuitable for methods that target amino acids, which are readily soluble in water. PD targets the components of finger deposit that are not soluble in water and as such, requires the preparation of multiple solutions, three of which comprise the PD working solution. Ramotowski (2000) recommends the following formulas and procedures:

[*Please note that each chemical must be mixed in the order indicated, and each must be thoroughly dissolved before proceeding to the next. At each step, drain the solution, and add the next solution to the same tray:*]

Acid Pre-wash
- Mix 25 g Malic acid in 1000 ml RO–DI water
Shelf life indefinite

Redox Solution
- Ferric nitrate nonahydrate   30 g
- Ferris ammonium sulfate hexahydrate   80 g
- Citric acid monohydrate   20 g
- RO–DI water   900 ml
Shelf life approximately six months

Detergent Solution
- N-Dodecylamine acetate   3 g
- Tween 20   3 ml
- RO–DI water   1000 ml
Shelf life 6–12 months

Silver Nitrate Solution
- Silver Nitrate   10 g
- RO–DI water   50 ml
Shelf life indefinite if sealed and stored in the dark

PD Working Solution
- Redox Solution   900 ml
- Detergent Solution   40 ml
- Silver Nitrate Solution   50 ml

Treatment Procedure
1. Soak in RO–DI or distilled water bath for 10–15 minutes. Drain off solution.
2. Add the acid pre-wash to the same tray, and allow exhibits to stand for at least 10–15 minutes
3. Drain off malic acid

Above: **Fingerprint developed by oil red O.**

Left: **Oil red O processing of paper exhibits.**
Images courtesy of A. Beaudoin and M.E. Gagne, Sûreté du Québec.

4. Add the PD working solution to the same tray. Monitor development and drain off when sufficient gray-black ridge development has occurred.
5. Rinse thoroughly in tap water until rinse water is clear.
6. Gently place exhibits on absorbent material and allow to air dry. It is at this stage that accurate assessment of results can be made.

Oil Red O

Oil red O is a fat-soluble dye used to stain lipids. It has emerged as a relatively recent alternative (see Beaudoin 2004; Rawji and Beaudoin 2006) and even more recently, a complimentary process to PD for two types of exhibit situations:

• a search for additional fingerprints on exhibits that have already been treated with amino acid reagents, and
• exhibits that have been soaking or sitting in water

Current research indicates that Oil red O may be as sensitive for oil and lipid development on paper as PD in the short term. Oil red O reacts differently with lipids than PD, and if they are applied sequentially, additional detail may be revealed after each step, that is, Oil red O followed by PD (Beaudoin, personal communication 2009).

Suggested Solutions for Oil Red O

Stain Solution
- Dissolve 1.54 gm Oil Red O in 770 ml Methanol.
- Dissolve 9.2 gm Sodium Hydroxide in 230 ml distilled water.
- Add the Sodium Hydroxide solution to the Oil Red O solution.

Buffer Solution
- Dissolve 101gm Sodium Phosphate Monobasic Monohydrate in 1 L distilled water.
- Dissolve 338.79 gm Sodium Phosphate Dibasic Heptahydrate in 1 L distilled water.
- Shake both solutions until dissolved, then combine.
- Add distilled water to increase the combined buffer solution to 4 L.

Procedure
- Immerse the item in the stain solution, making sure that it is thoroughly wetted.
- Moderate to strong fingerprints should begin to appear within five minutes. Weaker impressions may take significantly longer.
- Remove and drain the exhibit. Place in the buffer solution.
- Remove and rinse in distilled water. Air dry.

Atypical Techniques

In the case where many exhibits cannot be neatly distinguished by their porous or nonporous substrates, a variety of chemicals and sprays are employed in an attempt to render prints visible. Friction skin patterns in blood and on sticky, or wet nonporous materials are examples of substrates that challenge the forensic investigator. The following section is an overview of these techniques that are deemed atypical.

Blood Reagents

Fingerprints, shoeprints, or even tool marks in blood may be distinct enough that they require nothing more than competent photography. All too frequently, however, only a fraction of the detail in the impression can be seen clearly in normal viewing, particularly if the impression is composed of very little blood and appears on a dark object like a black garbage bag. Many reagents are capable of increasing the visible detail in a blood impression to a surprising degree. They each have strengths and weaknesses. Once again, the skilled analyst must use knowledge and experience to match the best reagent to the task.

Left: **Knives from a brutal assault found in the victim's kitchen sink.**

Right: **Treatment with amido black renders a print visible on the blade of one of the knives, linked to the suspect.**

Images courtesy of Scott Collings, Hamilton Police Service.

Amido Black

Amido black is a highly sensitive stain that gives excellent contrast and detail on light to medium-colored surfaces. It is easy to use and has been a favorite of forensic analysts for decades. Other similar stains like Coomassie blue and Sudan black are equally effective. The stain and rinse solutions are as follows:

Stain Solution
- Mix 100 ml Acetic Acid with 900 ml of Methanol.
- Thoroughly dissolve 2 gm of Amido Black in this solution.

Rinse Solution
- Mix 100 ml Acetic Acid with 900 ml of Methanol.
  The methanol formulation is extremely flammable. Use appropriate safety precautions and provide adequate ventilation.
  OR
  Mix by stirring and combining the ingredients below in the following order:
- 500 ml distilled water
- 20 g 5-sulfosalicylic acid
- 3 g Amido 10B
- 3 g Sodium Carbonate
- 50 ml Formic Acid
- 50 ml Acetic Acid
- 12.5 ml Kodak Photo Flo 600 solution
  Dilute this mixture to one liter with distilled water. Rinse with tap water. The shelf life is unlimited.

No perceptible difference in sensitivity between the two formulas has been noticed by the author, and consequently, the less hazardous aqueous solution is recommended.

Leuco Crystal Violet (LCV)

Unlike amido black, LCV is not a stain but a colorless solution that reacts with blood to form a dark purple product. It has the advantage of reacting only with blood and not the background, usually resulting in

An attempted homicide took place in the room with much blood spilled. Perpetrator has tried to clean the walls and floors.

The use of LCV develops blood impressions.
Images courtesy of Scott Collings, Hamilton Police Service. All Rights Reserved.

crisp, well-developed blood impressions. LCV is also considerably cleaner to use than any of the stain techniques. It has the added advantage of exhibiting red fluorescence when excited by green light.

When using LCV, less is more. The preferred method of application is with a pressurized sprayer that delivers the solution as a fine mist. The following is the suggested solution:

- Dissolve 10 gm of 5-sulfosalicylic acid in 500 ml of 3% Hydrogen Peroxide.
- Add 3.7g Sodium Acetate.
- Add 1 gm LCV.
- Gently spray area of impression.
- Impression will be stained a dark violet.
- Photograph immediately to avoid overdevelopment of background.

Acid Yellow

Acid yellow was introduced in 2005 (see Sears et al. 2005) as a fluorogenic reagent for blood impressions on dark nonporous surfaces. It lacks a strong color mode, and finger or footwear impressions in blood on light-colored surfaces respond much better to other treatments like amido black. However, whenever faint blood impressions on dark nonporous objects require enhancement, acid yellow is a smart choice. Bloody finger or footwear impressions that are invisible in white light fluoresce vigorously under blue excitation (400–500 nm). The solutions are as follows:

Pre-wash
- Mix 46 gm 5-sulfosalicylic acid in 2 L distilled water.

A blood impression on green garbage bag is barely visible.

The same impression after treatment with acid yellow and illumination by Flare Plus 450 nm, viewed through orange goggles.

Working Solution
- Mix 2 gm Acid Yellow in 100 ml Acetic Acid.
- Add 500 ml Ethanol.
- Add 1400 ml distilled water.
- Mix with magnetic mixer for at least 30 minutes.

Rinse
- Add 500 ml Ethanol to 100 ml Acetic Acid.
- Add 1400 ml distilled water.

Procedure
- Place a paper towel over the blood impression. Gently spray the pre-wash on the impression through the paper towel, ensure that the entire impression is thoroughly wetted. Allow to stand for at least 60 seconds, or several minutes if the blood deposit is thick.
- Remove the paper towel and place a new dry one over the impression. Gently spray the impression through the paper towel with acid yellow, in the same manner as with the pre-wash. Allow to stand for the same amount of time as for the pre-wash.
- Rinse gently but thoroughly with the rinse solution, or with tap water.
- Dry by patting gently with paper towel and view under 450 nm light with orange goggles.

Luminol

Major crimes scenes frequently feature extensive blood evidence. In some cases, the perpetrator has taken considerable pains to conceal or clean up the crime scene. Luminol is a *chemiluminescent* reagent that reacts with iron found in hemoglobin. It is routinely sprayed on a scene, often in a broad search for blood. The application is done in total dark-

The location of a violent encounter reveals little or no sign of blood.

Luminol's chemiluminescence reveals extremely small traces of blood at the same location.

ness, and the slightest trace of blood, even highly diluted, will betray its presence by bursting into light. Fingerprints and footwear impressions are occasionally detected with luminol. Photography is also completed in darkness. The user should be aware that some substances, including bleach, may produce false positives. Nonetheless, luminol is invaluable for locating otherwise invisible traces of blood, particularly in cases where the perpetrator has endeavored to clean and remove bloodstains from a scene.

Adhesive Substrates

Self-adhesive labels, stamps, and all sorts of tape offer unique opportunities for fingerprint development—both in terms of quality and significance. When fingers come into contact with paper, a passive transfer of trace material occurs. When fingers come into contact with an adhesive surface like tape, the material is actively seized and retained in greater quantity than a normal transfer to a non-adhesive surface.

The adhesive grips the finger and prevents slipping and smudging. Impressions developed on adhesive surfaces have a characteristic crispness and clarity of detail.

Such impressions also carry a greater weight because they can imply guilty knowledge or participation in a criminal act. Consider an anonymous threatening letter. Depending on circumstances, a fingerprint on the envelope may or may not be significant. It may have been deposited before the envelope was delivered or even addressed. A fingerprint on the sticky side of the stamp or label, however, carries a far greater meaning. It points strongly to the donor taking an active role in the crime.

When tape or adhesive labels are removed from a surface, one may find a fingerprint on the sticky side in visible dirt transferred from the finger or by inherent fluorescence. More frequently, we must rely on chemical development.

Lightning/Liquinox

This is a simple, stable, and inexpensive solution that gives consistently good results on the adhesive side of light-colored tapes. A mixture of Liquinox liquid detergent, Kodak PhotoFlo, and Lightning Black fingerprint powder is blended to the consistency of shaving cream and brushed onto the adhesive side of tape.

After allowing the exhibit to stand for approximately ten seconds, the tape is gently rinsed under cold water. Repeat applications may improve development of the print (see *Minutiae* 1994).

This procedure requires careful handling of the exhibit. There must be minimal contact with the tweezers and the adhesive surface to avoid damaging ridge detail. Also, prolonged contact of the solution with the adhesive side may result in reduced contrast and/or loss of detail. Contact with the nonadhesive side should be avoided. Premixed products such as Wetwop and Sticky-side powder also give good results.

To use for light colored tapes and labels apply the following:

- Mix 20 ml Liquinox to 40 ml distilled water.
- Add 20 gm "Lightning Black" fingerprint powder.

Finger making contact in the act of placing a stamp on an envelope. The limiting factor is the area of contact, but the detail is frequently excellent.

A fingerprint developed by Lightning/Liquinox technique on the adhesive side of a postage stamp in a threatening letter investigation.

- Shake until mixture is the consistency of shaving cream.
- Apply with a camel hair brush and gently rinse under cold water.

Gentian Violet

Gentian Violet (see Kent 1980) and commercial products like TapeGlo and Photoflo perform well on the sticky side of black electrical tape. The writer has used it operationally with great success in the 1980s and 1990s, although a preference has developed for Lightning/Liquinox due to its increased contrast. For use apply the following:

- Dissolve 1.5 gm Gentian Violet in 100 ml distilled water.
- Immerse tape in solution for several minutes. Rinse gently under running water.

OR

- Dissolve 5 g Gentian Violet in 50 ml Ethanol.
- Add 500 ml distilled water.
- After mixing allow to stand in dark bottle for 24 hours.
- Immerse tape in solution for 5 seconds.
- Rinse gently under cool running water. If prints are weak, repeat the procedure.

For black electrical tape, a solution of titanium dioxide is recommended:
- Add equal portions of water and Photoflo (10 ml ea).
- Add Titanium Dioxide until mixture becomes the consistency of shaving cream.
- Apply with camel hair brush and rinse gently under cold water
- Process may be repeated.
- Allow to air dry.

Wet Cars and Vinyl

Small Particle Reagent (SPR)

SPR is a spray containing molybdenum disulphide. The active fingerprint adherent consists of small particles of powder suspended in a water/PhotoFlo mixture. It must be shaken frequently to keep the powder in suspension. The particles adhere preferentially to fatty, oily deposits common to fingerprint residue.

SPR can be viewed as a niche or special case technique because of the unique occasional advantages of applying fingerprint powder wet. The process consists of first spraying the suspension (after shaking vigorously) onto the exhibit. It is preferable that the surface under examination be vertical, so that the excess spray and rinse drop off quickly. After spraying, the exhibit is rinsed with water.

This technique has developed fingerprints on a wide range of surfaces, but it is best known and appreciated for fingerprint detection on vehicles, particularly those that have been exposed to rain, as well as textured vinyl. A treated surface must be examined very carefully because any ridge detail developed may be quite subtle.

SPR is also a good choice for cans and plastic bottles that are (or have been) wetted on the outside either with water or other liquids (see Almog and Frank 1993).

Dental stone powder has similar characteristics to pancake mix. Once water is added, it resembles pancake batter consistency. The following is a simple recipe mixture for use on single or cluster fingerprints. Palmar surfaces or footwear impression evidence require larger quantities. Bags containing the dry mix dental stone powder can be stored indefinitely, ready for use. When required, add water to the bag containing the powder and mix until a smooth consistency is obtained. Pour the mixture onto the developed impression and allow it to cure.

- 6-inch by 6-inch zip bag
- 38 grams dry dental stone powder
- 15 ml water (*Hint:* Swube brand swab tubes are 15 ml capacity)

Marking Impressions

It is important to have the identifying markings of the print clearly visible on the lift and in the photograph. If the exhibit is paper or paper-like, a pencil is used to mark impressions. Pens are less desirable for marking because inks may run and obscure fingerprint detail on immersion in the solvents used to carry the detection chemistry.

If the impression has been developed with powder, it is marked with a grease pencil and the markings are powdered. This will ensure that the

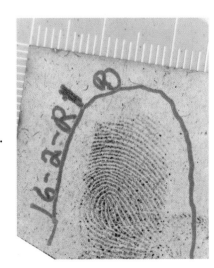

Print Marking with Scale.

Prints are marked with scale, digit number, and investigator's initials.

1. The impression is circled closely enough to isolate it, but well back from the outer limit of the ridge detail.
2. Markings are made along the outside of the line. A scale is always included. The letter R was selected because the correct laterality is easily verified.
3. Impressions are marked first with the exhibit number, followed by the impression number and investigator's initials, as close as possible to the impression without damaging it. This allows the impression to be photographed with the vital information included in the image.

identifying markings will appear on the lift with the fingerprint in the same gray level as the ridges.

Fingerprints developed by a fluorescence technique require a fine-tipped marker that fluoresces with an intensity similar to that of the ridges.

ACE-V: The Identification Protocol

The next step after photography is attempting to determine the donor of the fingerprint. This procedure is undertaken by a trained fingerprint technician. Depending on the agency, it may or may not be the same technician who developed and photographed the fingerprint.

The progression from first awareness that one fingerprint should be compared to another consists of four steps.

1. Analysis
- Note the substrate and impression composition.
- Assess the clarity of the detail.
- Note factors such as torque, pressure, and amount of recording medium.
- Note the details at levels 1, 2, and 3.
- Is the impression suitable for comparison?

2. Comparison
- Are the pattern type, ridge flow, and target points in agreement with the known?
- Are the minutiae in agreement as to location, shape, and direction?
- Is the pore structure visible in both, and is it in agreement?
- Are there structures in agreement—flexion ceases, scars, incipient ridges, and variation in ridge thickness or outline?

3. **Evaluation**
- Assess the value of the unique characteristics.
- Review differences in appearance.
- Form a conclusion.
- Individualization.
- Elimination.
- Insufficient clear detail for either conclusion.

4. **Verification**
- Peer review.
- Verify process and objectivity.
- Form a conclusion.

(After Ashbaugh 1999)

Fingerprints in Court

Since Juan Vucetich solved the first case through fingerprints in 1892, untold millions of criminal court cases have had a fingerprint component, with specialists stating their opinions under oath. Until recently, fingerprint evidence has enjoyed wide acceptance in courts around the world.

In 1993, a civil case initiated a threshold decision for the admissibility of scientific testimony and evidence. That case was *Daubert v. Merrell Dow Pharmaceuticals*. The Daubert outcome or opinion lists several factors regarding the nature of expert testimony and whether or not it constitutes admissible scientific knowledge (see Daubert v. Merrell Dow Pharmaceuticals 92–102, 1993). The term *Daubert* has come to represent court challenges to the concept of fingerprint identification as a science, but the real meaning is that any evidence or technique must meet the following requirements to be deemed admissible:

1. The method must be based on a testable hypothesis.
2. The known or potential error rate for this method is established.
3. Peer review is consistent.
4. There is general acceptance in the scientific community.

The courts recognize that any human endeavor is subject to error, and the rate of error is important in the admissibility process. There have been some recent errors in fingerprint identification, as revealed in the following cases.

The Mayfield Case

After the bombing of the commuter train system in Madrid in 2004, the Spanish police developed fingerprint evidence and sent it to the FBI for search in IAFIS (Integrated Automated Fingerprint Identification System). Of the candidates identified by the search, the FBI made a "positive" identification on Brandon Mayfield, a lawyer from Oregon. Subsequently, the Spanish police reported that they had identified the impression to a different individual. The error was acknowledged by the FBI, who attributed it to individuals not following standard protocols during the assessment process.

The Shirley McKie Case

In 1997, a thumbprint was developed in a house at a murder scene in Kilmarnock, Scotland. The impression was identified as made by Shirley McKie, a police officer. She denied ever being in the house and was charged with perjury, purely on the strength of the fingerprint identification. Other fingerprint experts refuted the identification, and she was found not guilty at trial.

Historically, the issues raised in the cross-examination of a fingerprint witness were related to the continuity and integrity of the evidence and the circumstances of the fingerprint deposition. In other words, the accused could easily have left a fingerprint at a time before the criminal occurrence, or he or she had legitimate access to the item or location where the fingerprint was found. Furthermore, inexpert or incomplete identification procedures could have resulted in the failure to detect the fingerprints of the real perpetrator.

The defense has also been known to ask hypothetical questions in an attempt to erode the certainty expressed by the witness: "Officer, if you were to see this impression with one less characteristic, what would your opinion be?"

In the writer's career, with more than fifty court appearances to tender fingerprint evidence, the validity of fingerprint science was never directly questioned or challenged.

Within the past fifteen years, however, the defense direction has changed radically. Today, a fingerprint expert in the witness box may or may not be confronted with the strategies previously mentioned, but he or she should be prepared to address the following:

- The *Daubert* ruling
- The Mayfield case
- The McKie case
- Confirmation bias—"Did you see what you wanted or expected to see?"
- Is fingerprint identification a science
- Do fingerprints really have the power to individualize
- What is the error rate of fingerprint identification

Why Do Criminals Continue to Touch Things?

It would be reasonable to assume that those who commit crimes are well aware, through books, film, television, and media accounts, that police can find fingerprints on many surfaces. Logically, one assumes that they would refrain from touching things when doing something illegal. There are equally good accounts in the same shows and movies of the forensic value of hairs, fibers, shoeprints, DNA, tool marks, tire marks, and trace chemicals.

Certainly, there are plenty of indications, routinely observed by police, of offenders doing exactly that—taking precautions to avoid leaving fingerprints, particularly when a crime has been premeditated and planned. Hence, not all of them get caught. However, for a number of reasons, avoiding the transference of fingerprints is not as easy as it seems.

We stay in contact with our environment largely through the use of our hands, both knowingly and reflexively. Anyone would be hard pressed to create a complete list of everything he or she touched with his or her hands in the previous hour, even in a state of emotional and physical rest. It becomes much more difficult to remember this (or to control it) when in a heightened state of emotional stress.

Some tasks are also difficult to execute while taking precautions like wearing gloves, not to mention how suspicious wearing gloves must look unless there is a legitimate reason for doing so in any given context. Even experienced forensic scientists and identification specialists must constantly remind themselves to take the appropriate precautions when handling exhibits, for the protection of themselves and the evidence.

When someone commits a premeditated crime, they are attempting through a combination of execution and illusion to obliterate all evidence of the actual chain of events while creating evidence of a false one. This increases in difficulty with the complexity of the events and the length of time involved. Someone once said that it's better to tell the truth because there is less to remember. Such a philosophy is perhaps more mildly cynical than altruistic, but it underscores the problem faced by plotting criminals—there is simply too much to remember. Many investigations over the course of history have revealed criminals going to almost unbelievable degrees of premeditation and precaution, only to be trapped by some piece of evidence forgotten, overlooked, or unknown. It is easier to be careful than to stay careful.

III: Facial Reconstruction

Facial reconstruction is a complex process that combines knowledge of human anatomy with artistic ability. A variety of methods have evolved over the years, demonstrating a progression from the purely artistic approach, with the emphasis on technique and skill, to the more scientific approach using revised data and sophisticated technology.

Scientists in the nineteenth century, primarily in Germany, gathered information on the size and shape of the skull together with the depths of the soft tissue of the face. To record the different levels of thickness of the face and head, they stuck things like knife blades (Welcker 1883), pins (Kollman 1898), and sewing needles (His 1895) into the flesh around the scalp, eyes, cheeks, forehead, and chins of cadavers. These measurements were standardized and ultimately formed the basis for the two-dimensional facial drawing as well as the plastic three-dimensional method of facial reconstruction.

The Police Sketch: Two-Dimensional Facial Reconstruction

The two-dimensional method of facial reconstruction is the drawing of a facial likeness from the skull or from witness accounts. It is often the primary technique of identification carried out by police artists and trained forensic anthropologists.

Referred to as the "artist's composite" or the "police sketch," the traditional two-dimensional reconstruction method uses a bank or kit (now computerized) containing a variety and range of eye, cheekbone, and jaw shapes collected over the years by forensic personnel. These features are assembled together by hand, or on a screen, according to victim and eyewitness accounts, and/or family descriptions, to form the composite or likeness drawing.

Alternatively, plotting the appropriate tissue-depths onto a photograph or x-ray of an unidentified skull and then tracing specific features on paper over the actual photograph or radiograph creates the compos-

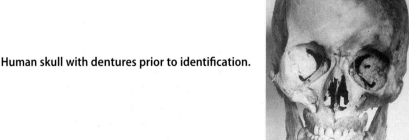

Human skull with dentures prior to identification.

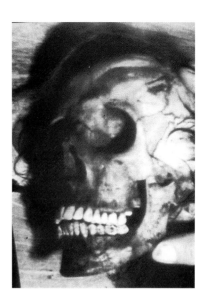

A two-dimensional facial reconstruction based on size and shape of the unidentified skull. Images courtesy of Toronto Police Forensic Identification Services. All rights reserved.

ite. The style and type of hair would be determined either by samples found on the scene or by estimation determined by the victim's age, race, and sex.

The use of the two-dimensional method for forensic casework in North America has been long and consistent throughout the last century. Manual methods are currently enhanced or replaced by software programs that substantially reduce the labor and time involved. Presently, most methods of two-dimensional reconstruction focus on identifying active perpetrators, whereas more advanced methods of three-dimensional facial reconstruction are applied to victim identification and cold case files.

Three-Dimensional Facial Reconstruction

The manual plastic three-dimensional method uses modeling clay or wax to reconstruct a face directly over a skull or a cast of the skull. A variety of sized pegs serve as tissue-depth markers and are glued onto specific landmarks of the skull where the flesh thickness varies. The malleable material fills the spaces in between the pegs as muscle and skin, and are built up in layers to further sculpt the face. Artificial eyes are placed into the orbits, and accessories such as wigs, glasses, and jewelry may be added to enhance the final reconstruction. Hairlines and facial hair as well as the length and shape of the nose are subject to guesswork for the most part.

Three-dimensional facial reconstruction was popular at the turn of the last century, when it was applied predominantly to archaeological remains and famous historic cases, as in the facial reconstructions of Bach (His 1895), Kant (Welcker 1883), Raphael (Welcker 1883), and Dante (Kollman 1898). The process, however, was highly subjective.

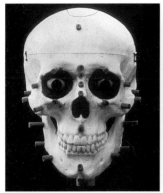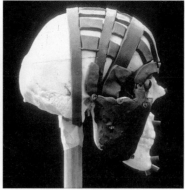

Three-dimensional facial reconstruction with modeling clay. Images courtesy of Dr. George Burgman. All rights reserved.

Methods were based largely on the artist's ability to re-create a famous face, and often they had visual references to work from, like portraits and early engravings.

In archaeological casework during the same period, facial reconstructions were made from casts of early hominid fossils. These were integral parts of museum displays that sought to re-create the distant past, fascinate the public, and bring them literally face to face with prehistory. Whether they were accurate re-creations was difficult to determine.

The forensic use of three-dimensional facial reconstruction was first introduced in Britain in the late 1920s. In North America it did not catch on until the 1940s (Krogman 1946). The goal of forensic facial reconstruction was to produce as close a likeness as possible of the deceased for identification purposes. However from the 1920s through to the 1960s its use was unpopular. Studies such as the one conducted by a scientist named Von Eggeling in the early 1900s (Gerasimov 1968) implied that the process rendered inaccurate results and was too subjective for use as an investigative method. Von Eggeling had sent the cast of a deceased individual's skull to two different artists for reconstruction. He received two different faces.

By the late 1960s forensic facial reconstruction experienced a revival in North America and Europe, as well as in Russia. Anthropologists with access to known and unidentified skulls began to test various methods and their validity, as more and more reconstructions were successfully identified (see Snow et al. 1970; Nafte 2009).

The technique of forensic facial reconstruction eventually gained full acceptance by the 1980s as a viable method of social identification. Artists, sculptors, and anthropologists shared samples and techniques and succeeded in broadening the discipline. However, it still employed the same measurements based on a small sample of cadavers from the last century, and thereby the method continued to raise questions of accuracy. Yet it was an exciting tool that seemed to draw tremendous support from the public, encouraging its own technological evolution (see following discussion).

Current Methods

With the advent of new diagnostic tools, scientists questioned the use of facial measurements drawn from cadavers. Since there are rapid changes in the human body after death, most notably the loss of fluids from the face, they argued that any measurements drawn from cadavers could not be accurate. It was noted that soft tissue depths taken from the head and face would result in faces that were "less fleshier" than perhaps they once were (Evison et al. 1998). As well, the sample of cadavers originally used was small and had no variation in age, sex, or race. Therefore, the measurement standards established could not accurately reflect the variety of size and shape differences among males and females within a multiracial, multiage population.

By the mid-1980s new soft-tissue data became available through techniques using ultrasound and images of craniographs. This allowed scientists to obtain data from samples of living individuals as well as developing new methods in taking cranial-facial measurements (Hodson et al., 1985; Dumont 1986; George 1987). The overall sample sizes were still admittedly small and not varied enough in age and race to merit substantial changes in the field. It was, however, a step away from sticking pins and needles into cadavers to measure the thickness of their facial tissue.

Consequently, the advances over the past twenty years in research and data for the three-dimensional plastic facial reconstruction have been minimal. It is still considered to be a highly subjective approach for identifying missing or deceased individuals.

Pragg and Neave (1997) state that because there are too many variables, a three-dimensional reconstruction based only on the skull cannot be completely accurate and should never be regarded as a portrait. Furthermore, the forensic community is careful to refer to the reconstructions as "approximations" rather than accurate reproductions. This is mostly due to the fact that unique traits such as hairlines, eyelids, lip shape and fullness, and skin folds have always been guesswork.

Facial approximations are designed to trigger recognition in the viewer, creating the possibility of a positive identification. However, the current success rates for identification resulting from facial reconstruction are roughly 50 percent (Archer 1998). Also, the process of making a cast from a skull, placing soft-tissue depth markers in place, and rebuilding the soft tissue from clay is labor-intensive. Making subsequent adjustments, adding accessories, or altering features is time-consuming and restrictive. As such, the three-dimensional plastic facial reconstructions are usually employed when other methods of identification are impossible or have failed to produce any results.

Computerized Facial Reconstruction

A whole new era in facial reconstruction has emerged with the advent of computerized methods. Over the past two decades the process of three-dimensional facial reconstruction has used computer software to increase time and accuracy. Tissue-thickness data are now derived from living individuals using ultrasound techniques and medical imaging.

Like its manual predecessor, facial tissue-depths in the form of pegs are glued onto the skull at their appropriate landmarks. An image of the skull with the pegs in place is then scanned onto the computer, which can then be stored and used as a template. Modeling clay is then applied to the skull, and the features are sculpted. The computer enhances these features further so the sculpting does not have to be as detailed and subtle changes can be made. With the use of a digitizing device, the image of the sculpted skull is then processed digitally (Vanezis et al. 1989; Ubelaker and O'Donnell 1992; Shahrom et al. 1996).

The use of the computer enhances the three-dimensional reconstruction by providing multiple variations of the same image and enabling fast alterations to features. It does not make the facial reproductions more accurate or exact. Hair color and style; the shape of the eyes, ears, or nose; the hairline and any facial hair can be altered or adjusted based on the evidence or information obtained. Also, accessories such as jewelry, eyeglasses, and items of clothing that may have been recovered along with the skeletal remains could be incorporated into the image.

Using the CARES for facial reconstruction.
Image courtesy of Toronto Police Forensic Identification Services. All rights reserved.

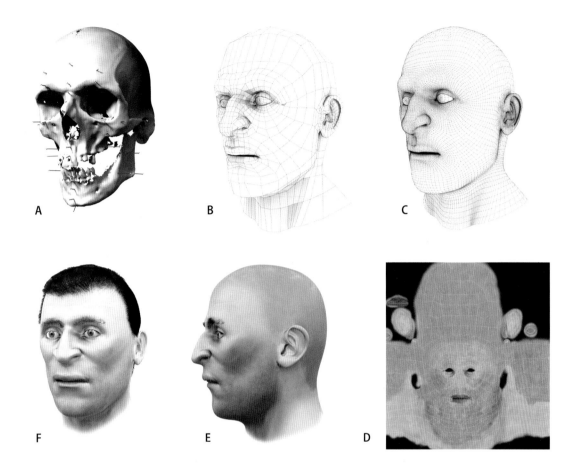

A: Laser-scanned digital 3D model of the skull. The tissue depth markers are added using 3D modeling software.
B: The completed low-resolution model of the reconstructed head and face.
C: The completed high-resolution model.
D: A 2D texture map of surface details that is digitally wrapped onto the model.
E: The completed model with skin texture and color.
F: The completed model with skin texture and color.

The computer has enabled the reconstruction process to be a fast, reproducible, and increasingly more precise method. Data can now be imported directly from images produced by hospital procedures, such as the computed tomography (CT) scan and magnetic resonance imaging (MRI). These high-resolution images from living individuals provide numerous accurate measurements of facial tissue depths. Software programs, such as CARES (Computer Assisted Reconstruction and Enhancement System), FACE, and another called Faces, use x-rays or photographs of faces or skulls. These are then digitized, and using banks of stored facial features, a face is electronically restored or reconstructed (Ubelaker and O'Donnell 1992; Archer 1998).

Despite the advances in computerized methods, practitioners in the field find that there are still inherent issues associated with facial reconstruction. There is still a shortage of up-to-date tissue depth information for different ages, namely children and various ethnic populations (Reichs and Craig 1998, 507). This is combined with a lack of standardization for approximating facial features such as the shape of eyelids, ears, nose, and lips. Also, there is still no method of predicting individual characteristics that are not apparent on the skull, such as hairstyle, excessive fat, facial hair, dimples, and superficial scars. Many of the current reconstructions avoid these subjective interpretations by leaving hairlines, hairstyles, facial hair, and skin color out of the final images (Cesarani et al. 2003).

With or without the aid of a computer, three-dimensional facial reconstruction should not be considered the only tool for positive identification. It is primarily a means of stimulating recognition or memory within a community and as stated earlier, often used as a last resort when other identification methods have failed.

Biometrics

Individuality

Nature does not duplicate; it does not simply run out of variations and manufacture repeats. An understanding of and confidence in individualized identification cannot be reached without knowledge of the degree to which all living things are different.

We group living things by general or *class* characteristics. For example, birds have two wings and two legs, but there are obvious and huge differences between an ostrich and a hummingbird. There are less overt but equally powerful differences between different hummingbirds, differences that require expert scrutiny and quantification.

People differ in countless ways from all other members of our species, although we all have the same general body configuration and the same number of fingers, toes, eyes, and ears. A scientific look reveals that iris, retina, lip flexion creases, teeth, ear configuration, and of course fingerprints (to name a few features) are distinctly different.

Methods developed for the *individualization* (identification) of people through intrinsic physical properties are called *biometrics*. The following is a brief overview.

Iris Scanning

- The iris is the circular contractile membrane behind the cornea that regulates the amount of light entering the eye. Systems have been developed, primarily in airport security and banking, that record database images of the iris for identity confirmation.

- Iris scanning is currently used at airports to identify passengers with precleared status. The Nexus program, a joint project between the United States and Canada, allows frequent travelers to acquire approved status through extensive security review. Identity is recorded through photographs, fingerprints, and iris scans. Identity is confirmed at the airport by iris scan, allowing the traveler to avoid long line-ups and wait times.

Ear Prints

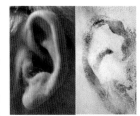

- Ear print identification has been researched in the Netherlands for many years, pioneered by Cor van der Lugt (Dutch College for Criminal Investigation and Crime Control). He collected ear impressions and tendered evidence in court (van der Lugt 1997, 2001) based on the wide variations of ear size and morphology. Such an impression has potentially high probative value, due to the unlikely scenario of someone innocently leaving an impression of his or her ear on a window or door of a crime scene.
- On the other hand, this type of comparison offers a great challenge due to the three-dimensional nature of the ear. Differing pressure results in significant differences in spatial relationship. Classification systems have been developed and used in Europe, although ear print identification has not yet attained wide peer acceptance in North America (Alberink and Ruifrok 2007).

Lip Prints (Cheiloscopy)

- Lip prints reveal a unique pattern of creases that have been used in court to positively identify victims of crime. Systems have been devised to record and classify lip prints in a manner similar to fingerprint classification (see Caldas et al. 2007).

Retinal Scanning

- The retina is the surface at the back of the eyeball that receives images through the lens. If one thinks of the eye as a camera, the retina is the film. A highly complex and minute network of small vessels supplies the retina with blood. As with fingerprints, the retinas of monozygotic twins are different. Retinal scanning devices have been in existence since the 1980s and have been employed by government agencies for personal identification. Although this process offers a high degree of accuracy and extremely high individualizing power, it is affected by certain diseases and is considered by many to be unacceptably invasive.

Facial Recognition

- Facial recognition is rather like a computerized extension of Bertillon measurements (he was arguably a man ahead of his time; his bio-

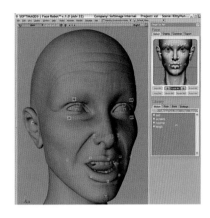

Digital facial recognition. Image courtesy of Autodesk Softimage.

metric system would have improved exponentially if computers had existed in his era). But like Bertillon's system (chapter 2), it has a major weakness. It does not have individualizing power equal to other biometric processes. The angle of view (between face on and full profile) can defeat the system, as can facial expressions, glasses, or facial hair. Applicants for a driver's license or passport are usually told not to smile when their photographs are taken.

- One significant advantage of facial recognition systems is that large crowds, at airports, casinos, or train stations, for example, can be scanned without the knowledge of the people present. If the mug shot of anyone in the crowd appears in a searchable database, he or she may be quickly isolated from the crowd and red-flagged for visual confirmation. This technology targets terrorists and high-profile wanted offenders. Facial recognition software was used in this context at the 2001 Super Bowl in Tampa, Florida, and was viewed as a success (see Bonner 2001).

- One facial recognition system, named BlueBear (by Vision Sphere) was a pilot project in 2003 undertaken by several Canadian police agencies including York Regional Police, involving the deployment and evaluation of facial recognition technology. Facial landmarks (called nodal points) are plotted and compared to known entries in a database. Approximately eighty nodal points appear on a human face, including:
  - distance between eyes
  - width of nose
  - cheekbones

- The cumulative measurements of these nodal points result in a numerical code called a faceprint that resides in a database. A faceprint may be generated from as few as fourteen nodal points. This project was viewed as successful, offering great promise for future operational deployment (Juck, personal communication 2010).

Friction Skin

- Friction skin is the oldest and most historically accepted biometric to have been used to identify persons. As previously stated, systems of classification and identification based on friction skin have been operational for over a century.
- Fingerprints are formed in the fourth fetal month and are completely developed long before birth. From this point on, ridge patterns do not change, except through injury or disease, throughout the person's life, and persist even after death.
- We use the term *fingerprints*, but the individualizing power applies to all of the body areas where friction skin appears—the inner surfaces of the fingers and hands and the soles of the feet and toes. Fingerprints, palm prints, bare footprints, and toe prints have all played significant roles in the identification of victims and criminals.

Chapter 8

Tracks, Treads, and Technology

This chapter examines an array of items ranging from bullets and firearms to computers and tire-track impressions. These items, much like fingerprints, often contain forensic evidence that is *latent* (hidden) in that they need to be processed further, examined at a microscopic level or with a particular type of software, to render them visible. For example, the striations on a bullet, the scratched-out serial number on a firearm, the hidden file in someone's computer; none of this latent evidence would be apparent at first glance or even with the naked eye. It is only with a variety of forensic techniques that such evidence can be collected, analyzed, interpreted, and presented in court. These are all discussed in the following sections.

Bullets and Firearms

Firearms as Evidence

The increasing use of firearms by criminals has meant that the science of collecting and analyzing the various forms of evidence found at such crimes has improved dramatically. Many investigations have been solved by expert interpretation of evidence when firearms were used. The potential findings include but are not limited to:

- Identifying a bullet as having been fired from a particular barrel—this depends on the condition of both the bullet and the barrel at the time of testing
- Identifying the type of firearm from which a bullet was fired and the caliber, in cases where no firearm was recovered
- Matching a cartridge case to a specific firearm by marks placed on the cartridge case during loading, firing, and chambering (depositing a round into the breech)
- Matching shotgun pellets and wadding to the manufacturer and/or gauge of the ammunition
- Determining the distance between the muzzle and the target by the dispersion pattern of firing residue around the entry hole

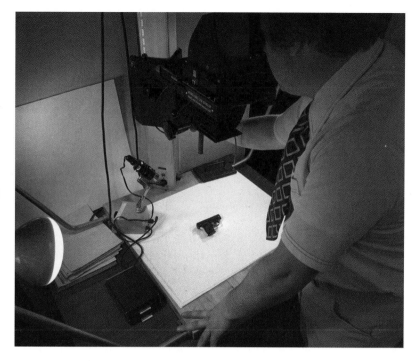

Photographing a handgun, 1978. Image courtesy of Buffalo Police Dept. Crime Scene Unit.

- Recovering multiple bullets and/or cartridge cases to indicate whether more than one firearm was involved
- Determining if a firearm is in active usable condition
- Determining if there is a tendency toward accidental discharge
- Restoring obliterated serial numbers and tracing the ownership history of a firearm
- Determining the direction and sequence of shots by examining bullet holes in glass

Spiral Grooves and Striations

Items that are manufactured to very exacting standards reveal unique characteristics and properties when examined with the right equipment, at the appropriate level of magnification, by someone who knows what to look for. Firearms are manufactured with a focus on uniformity because identical firing properties (accuracy) are crucial.

However, microscopic examination of two gun barrels leaving the production line consecutively bear similar but distinctly different striations—marks that in turn leave a signature on every projectile fired through that barrel. Forensic firearms analysis is based on this fact. The differences become even greater as the two barrels experience completely different "lifetimes"—for example, different frequency of firing, types of ammunition, storage, and cleaning methods. Simply put, the natural progression of events and effect are divergent, not convergent.

Spiral grooves are cut into the bore of a barrel during manufacture. These grooves are called *rifling*, and they grip and rotate the bullet as it travels down the barrel. The bullet is made to fit tightly inside the barrel and is pushed through by the gunpowder explosion. The grooves cause it to spin and prevent tumbling once it leaves the barrel. As a result, striations are cut into the soft metal of the bullet.

Since each gun barrel is made separately, each process leaves minute imperfections in the barrel from shavings or metal dust that is different from the barrel made before or the barrel made after.

In order to define these individual markings, bullet striations can be classed into two groups.

1. **Class characteristics:** All barrels of the same manufacturer, model, and caliber will leave these marks.
2. **Unique characteristics:** The manufacturing process cannot produce two barrels that are absolutely identical at the microscopic level. The marks cut into the bullet will not appear on bullets fired from any other barrel.

Whether or not these marks can be seen and compared will, of course, depend on the condition of both the barrel and the bullet. The critical parts of firearms are manufactured from different metals, each with its own properties. Many bullets are composed of lead, a very soft metal that is extremely vulnerable to damage—not only from the action of firing and the shock of striking an object but also from careless handling. Even a fingernail can make an impression in lead.

Hence, the careful recovery of bullets from a victim or a crime scene is vital in preserving these unique features. Plastic forceps that will not scratch the surface of the projectile are used for this purpose. To avoid superficially marking the surface of any bullet, careful removal must be exercised especially with bullets embedded in walls, trees, and other hard surfaces. No attempt should be made to dig out any embedded bullet. Rather, the section of the material containing the bullet should be dug out without disturbing it.

Bullet discovered during autopsy. Image courtesy of Toronto Police Forensic Identification Services. All rights reserved.

Using plastic tweezers to pick up a recovered bullet.
Image courtesy of Her Majesty the Queen in Right of
Canada as represented by the Royal Canadian Mounted
Police. © 2009.

During an autopsy the pathologist or medical examiner must retrieve
any bullets from a body by hand because sharp or hard tools may cause
damage. Forceps may be used for the recovery of shotgun pellets, and
any section of bone containing an embedded bullet should be removed
as a whole. Bullets are generally placed in a *druggist's fold* (a paper folded
to form a packet) and then in an envelope for transport.

Copper and brass are harder than lead but can still be easily marked
by contact with a steel firing pin or ejector. Careless handling can also
damage them, especially with a steel tool like pliers or forceps.

Steel, the material used to make barrels, firing mechanisms, and ejector pieces, is the hardest component of a firearm. Although not easily
damaged by inadvertent rubbing or contact, its greatest hazard is exposure to water. Rust can eat away the fine detail in the rifling, making it
impossible to compare the rifling marks left on a bullet.

Cartridge Cases

Often the term *cartridge* is mistakenly used interchangeably with the
word *bullet*. The cartridge is simply the casing or case that houses the

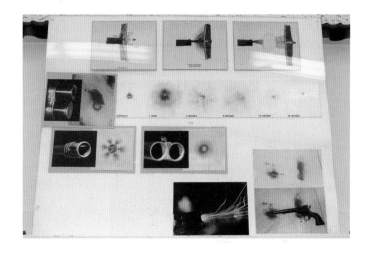

**A display of the ballistic properties
of various firearms.** Image courtesy
of Her Majesty the Queen in Right of
Canada as represented by the Royal
Canadian Mounted Police. ©2009.

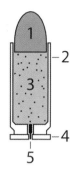

1. Bullet or projectile.
2. The casing that encloses the powder and bullet.
3. The powder that propels the bullet when fired.
4. The rim of the case that the extractor clutches when ejecting spent casings.
5. The primer that is struck by the firing pin, which then ignites the powder, causing combustion.

bullet, some gunpowder, and a primer (a small charge). Once a gun with a semiautomatic action is fired (the firing pin strikes the primer to fire the shot), the spent cartridge is pushed out by the hard metal surface of the gun's ejection mechanism. Other types of actions include lever, bolt, and single shot. In these actions the user ejects the cartridge case manually. A new bullet then drops into place, ready for firing.

Striations, gouges, and stamped impressions are left on cartridge cases by the actions of loading, firing, extracting, and ejecting. These markings are also microscopically unique and suitable for comparison by an examiner.

The position of spent cartridges can determine where the suspect was standing in relation to the victim and any other persons of interest. Forensic examiners must mark location and take measurements and photographs in relation to the position of the victim or target for any analysis to be feasible.

IBIS: Integrated Ballistics Identification System

A Canadian company called Forensic Technology developed an identification system called IBIS in 1991. It is a tool used to collect and analyze digital images of the unique microscopic markings found on spent bullets and cartridge cases from crime scenes. This information was stored on a server with access provided to law enforcement agencies through an accessible network.

9mm live round with latent fingerprint visible on casing.

Traditional method of testing and comparing firearms, ca. 1950s.

Comparing the marks on a fired bullet to the rifling of a suspect firearm has great similarity to a fingerprint expert comparing latent impressions to those of a suspect. Both operations rely on a known sample for comparison, analyzing crime scene evidence to known samples in a very large database, and both can connect unknown samples from different crime scenes. These crime scenes may be separated by many years or many miles. The power and reach of fingerprint comparison was greatly enhanced by the development of AFIS (Automated Fingerprint Identification System).

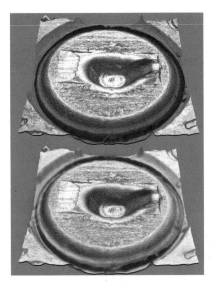

A 3-D rendering of a primer image.

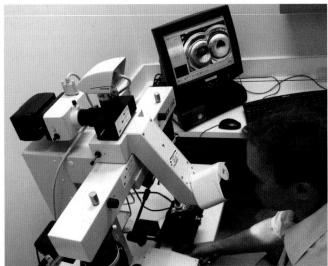

Examining the marks on a fired bullet. Image courtesy of Her Majesty the Queen in Right of Canada as represented by the Royal Canadian Mounted Police. ©2009.

The development of IBIS (Integrated Ballistics Identification System) gave an equally powerful and extended reach to firearm comparison.

Over the past fifteen years, IBIS technology has continually evolved and has been improved upon. Firearms examiners can see more detailed evidence and provide more timely information to investigators. The system is particularly effective in situations involving repetitive shootings and gang violence. IBIS networks can quickly link crimes, guns, and suspects across jurisdictions. These networks ultimately provide consistency, timely results and as such a significant public safety value.

Today IBIS includes new solutions such as Brasstrax-3D™, Bullettrax-3D™, and MatchPoint+™ (discussed shortly), which provide more automation and unique features that take firearms identification and crime solving to unprecedented levels.

IBIS systems are currently in use throughout the world by many law enforcement agencies since it is the only type of integrated identification system for firearms. It has the capability of being used to power a network of databases. For example, through its National Integrated Ballistic Information Network (NIBIN), the U.S. Bureau of Alcohol, Tobacco, Firearms and Explosives (ATF) deploys IBIS equipment into all state and local law enforcement agencies for their use in imaging and comparing gun crime evidence.

One of the chief benefits of IBIS is that it makes it possible to access and share intelligence across jurisdictional and international boundaries.

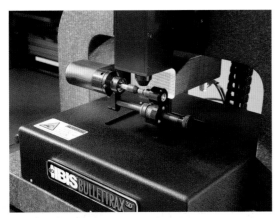

IBIS Bullettrax-3D. Courtesy of Forensic Technology. All rights reserved.

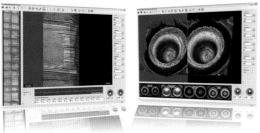

IBIS Bullettrax-3D comparing marks and striations. Courtesy of Forensic Technology. All rights reserved.

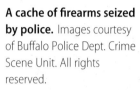

A cache of firearms seized by police. Images courtesy of Buffalo Police Dept. Crime Scene Unit.

More than 225 state and local law enforcement agencies are able to work together to analyze evidence and prevent recidivist gun crime. Since the International Police Agency (INTERPOL) signed an agreement with its member agencies, there is now worldwide access to IBIS information (see INTERPOL 2009).

Along with IBIS is another powerful reference tool called the digital FRT (Firearms Reference Table), a computer database put together by the Royal Canadian Mounted Police (RCMP) of firearm makes and models. The FRT is used in the accurate identification of firearms and is the most comprehensive, single-source firearms reference in existence, containing over 21,200 records of makes and models.

Computer Crime Scenes

Computer crimes and electronic evidence present a unique challenge to all law enforcement agencies. The range of crime is very broad and the network in which it takes place is overwhelming for law enforcement and criminal justice officials.

Crimes occurring in cyberspace are worldwide and include felonies like credit card and e-fraud, computer hacking, espionage, cyber-stalking, cyber-bullying, electronic embezzlement, and *phishing* (stealing personal information through e-mails or Web pages). Even more traditional crimes such as murder, kidnapping, fraud, and money laundering increasingly involve the use of a computer and other electronic devices.

Thus, electronic evidence can be best defined as any data or information of forensic value that has been transmitted and/or stored in an electronic device. Electronic devices can range from items such as cell phones, answering machines, iPods, digital cameras, and PDAs (per-

Electronic evidence can be gathered from a range of handheld-devices and computer systems.

sonal digital assistants) to laptops and a variety of computer systems. As a result of the type of information contained in these devices, the nature of such electronic evidence is considered latent because it is not visible prior to accessing it. Special handling procedures, software, and equipment are required to make such latent evidence visible and available for analysis and presentation in court.

As with all forms of technology, there is the constant and rapid changing nature of electronic evidence. Hence, a steady stream of technical experts and practitioners in the field must keep the information and investigative procedures up to date, specifically in areas such as recognition, documentation, collection, and packaging (see NIJ Report 2001).

Law enforcement response to electronic evidence also requires ongoing training with knowledge of the specific tools needed to properly disconnect, collect, package, and transport this type of evidence. For example, many commonly found electronic devices need a continuous power supply to maintain memory, and by simply unplugging or letting the batteries discharge, information is readily lost. As well, there must be consideration given to protecting stored data during its transport. Information

A forensic analyst examines digital media to enhance audio recordings. Image courtesy of the Centre of Forensic Sciences.

can be altered, erased, or damaged from electromagnetic fields such as through magnets, radio transmitters, and static electricity.

Last, there is a variety of nonelectronic evidence that is often closely associated or directly related to electronic evidence and must therefore be included as such. Crucial to all investigations in this area of electronic crime is the array of information such as passwords, printouts, calendars, notes, written statements, manuals, and literature. As with all forms of physical evidence, nonelectronic evidence must be handled, documented, and transported in a manner that best secures and preserves its forensic value.

Internet Child Exploitation

A more pressing and heinous computer crime confronting police agencies is Internet child exploitation. As of 2003 this area of computer crime has had a special unit to deal with the extent of abuse and images rampant in cyberspace. Internet child exploitation refers to the entire spectrum of sex-related offenses against children through use of Internet technology. The offenses include the sexual solicitation of children; cyberstalking; the online production, distribution, and trade of child abuse images; and sexual acting out against children.

The problem of Internet child exploitation has grown rapidly over the years in tandem with the change and ease of rapidly accessing and exchanging material online. What was once a hidden crime in outlying or dispersed regions is now a far more unified network of mutual support and encouragement. Perpetrators seek each other out, exchange files, and create venues to proliferate the abuse. Like all of the other computer crimes listed, these offenses are easy to commit, invisible, and extend over many national and international boundaries.

The initial response to the growing problem has for years been inadequate because Internet child exploitation is multijurisdictional and constant. The ability of offenders to offend is greater than the capacity of law enforcement to respond especially on an international level (see Butt 2009).

To increase the presence of police in cyberspace, law enforcement (as with any other branch of criminal investigation) is having to share intelligence, pool resources, and offer training to those who require it. Moreover, Internet technology advances quickly, and chat rooms that are closed down are up and running on other sites within minutes, forcing the police to maintain a constant chase. More challenging are issues surrounding privacy laws and legislation and the long wait for new laws to pass. Police are constantly "fighting this year's battle with last year's tools" (see Butt 2009).

CETS: Child Exploitation Tracking System

In 2003, Paul Gillespie, a Toronto Police detective sergeant sent a series of frustrated e-mails to several corporations and government agencies. Overwhelmed with the constant proliferation of child abuse images and computer data seized from suspected abusers, Gillespie requested technological assistance. With no effective tools to combat the increased production and distribution of such images, not to mention tracking the children in these horrific circumstances, the police were powerless. The accessibility and presence of personal computers had become the main tool for child pornography, therefore Gillespie had asked these agencies to help fight it.

Bill Gates from Microsoft, a recipient of one of these letters, took up the challenge and had his company's software engineers work closely with Canadian police. By the spring of 2005 they unveiled the Child Exploitation Tracking System (CETS), a high-level intelligence database that would enable police to follow hundreds of suspects at a time and identify the nonobvious connections leading to a child predator. The software tool would also allow police to sort, store, and share masses of information relevant to their investigations. They could then disseminate it locally and internationally enabling the identification (and ideally the rescue) of abused children (see Microsoft Public Sector 2006).

Since Internet crime is constant and borderless, the goal was to create a global network of investigators and experts. CETS has gone from being a Canadian law enforcement tool to a worldwide network. Adopted by countries such as the United Kingdom, Chile, Brazil, Spain, Indonesia, and Italy, the system has lead to hundreds of arrests and the rescue of many missing and abused children.

Footwear, Tire, and Tread Impressions

Footwear Evidence

Although footwear impressions of some description are present at almost all such scenes, the percentage of cases in which they are recovered and tendered as evidence is quite small (Bodziak 2000). The number and forensic significance of footwear impressions found at crimes scenes is commensurate with the skill, experience, and persistence of the person seeking them. In any case, no aspect of this physical evidence should be overlooked at a crime scene.

It is possible for a suspect to enter a location, commit a crime, and leave without leaving fingerprints or leaving anything inside that he or she has touched with bare fingers. It is infinitely more difficult to complete the same action without leaving some trace of footwear contact.

Footwear impressions photographed in situ.

Photographing footwear at a crime scene.

As with fingerprints, shoe impressions may be visible or latent, two-or three-dimensional, and require a variety of techniques for recovery and documentation.

Class vs. Accidental Characteristics

Two levels of detail may be present in a footwear impression; *class* and *accidental* characteristics. Class characteristics are common to all shoes of a specific manufacturer, a specific model, and a specific size. For example, all size ten sandals of a known model and make will have the same, or at least similar, class characteristics.

From the moment shoes are worn, however, they begin to acquire a life history (Cassidy 1980). Small cuts and gouges inflicted by glass, sand, rocks, and other surfaces create a combination of marks unique to that shoe. Even wear patterns will be specific to the weight and gait of the

These two leaves come from the same species of tree and consequently share common class characteristics. They are, however, individual on all other levels of scrutiny.

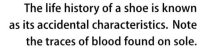

The elements of the sole configuration are referred to as class characteristics because they are common to all shoes of that size, brand, and model.

The life history of a shoe is known as its accidental characteristics. Note the traces of blood found on sole.

wearer. The general wear of a shoe and the specific wear and tear to the outsole also add distinctive characteristics (see Hammer and Kennedy 2009). In fingerprint science, class characteristics alone have little application beyond eliminating a subject. (If the crime scene impression is a whorl and the subject's prints are all loops, he or she can be eliminated as the source.) Beyond that, with few possible exceptions, the pattern type alone is simply too general to be of much evidential value. Class characteristics found in footwear impressions, however, have considerably more value. The tread pattern can limit the possible source shoes to only those of a specific manufacture. If the investigator can establish that relatively small numbers of a subject shoe were manufactured and that they were confined to a specific geographic area, even the agreement of the shoe model can be forensically significant. Determining the size can make the list even shorter and add to the weight of the evidence.

Evidential Value

Like any physical evidence, the individual circumstances of the footwear impression will determine the weight or level of *association* or *disassociation* (Hammer, personal communication 2009) that an examiner can attach to it, and consequently any one of the following conclusions may apply (see Bodziak 2000):

- The impression was *made* by the subject shoe
- The impression was *probably made* by the subject shoe
- The impression was *possibly made* by the subject shoe

- The impression was *not made* by the subject shoe
- The impression *lacked sufficient clear detail* for any significant conclusion

It is noted that there are other conclusion scales in effect for the reporting of footwear impression comparison conclusions (SWGTREAD, ENSFI Marks Group, etc.) (see Hammer and Kennedy 2009). Even when a conclusion of positive certainty is reached, the evidential value will depend on other factors.

As with fingerprints, there exists no method for dating footwear impressions. Furthermore, there may be no value whatever if the impression is located in an area to which the subject has legitimate and continuous access. However, if this factor cannot be explained in regard to the impression, and/or the impression can be placed in the same time frame as the occurrence, it takes on far greater meaning. For example, if a person is found murdered in his or her residence and the spouse is the prime suspect, a footwear impression located near the body may have little or no value if it is identified to be the shoe of the spouse. If however, the impression is found in the blood of the victim, the subject can be placed at the scene concurrent with or after the murder. Hence, the evidential value is far greater.

Barefoot Impressions

When a relationship has been identified between a shoe and an impression, it is essential to establish who owns the shoes, and even more critically, who was wearing them at the time of the occurrence. DNA analysis may provide the necessary link between an implicated shoe and the wearer by linking the sweat/epithelial samples taken from the shoe to the owner.

The configuration of the footprint (exclusive of friction skin minutiae) is also unique. Kennedy established a large database of 12,000 persons' bare footprints and a system for classification (Kennedy, personal communication 2009). Nineteen measurements and an outline of the impression provide a powerful basis for comparison. Other studies (Bodziak 2000, 381–85) have supported this finding. Software has since been developed which takes 150 separate measurements of the impression for comparison with an impression of separate origin (Kennedy personal communication 2009).

Barefoot impressions have considerable evidential value in cases where the foot impressions are distinct, but lack the ridge detail on which conventional impressions would be compared and identified. Similarly, sock impressions, while obviously lacking minutiae, are occasionally clear enough for comparison on the basis of size, shape, and other physical relationships.

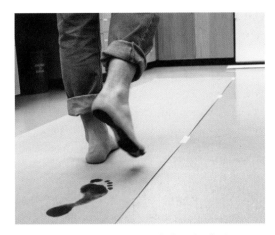

Bare footprints can be recorded in depletion, with successively less recording medium (ink) to obtain an optimal impression.

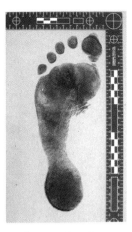

The bare footprint can then be compared to a latent impression on the basis of size, shape, and contour, even when no ridge detail is present.

Finally, if footwear connected to a crime scene becomes separated from the wearer, either by chance or design, there may be an impression of the foot on the insole of the shoe, which can be used to eliminate a subject as the wearer of the shoe or to establish correspondence and similarities between the two (Hammer, personal communication 2009).

Possible conclusions that follow barefoot impression analysis relate to one of two hypotheses (Kennedy, personal communication 2009):

- The impression *was made by the subject*
- The impression *was made by someone else*

In the best-case scenario, the evidence may give strong support to one or the other of these hypotheses, but conclusions of identification are not tendered.

Two-Dimensional Impressions

Two-dimensional impressions are defined as those having dimensions of length and width but not a significant depth (see Bodziak 2000). They can be found in and on a variety of substrates, all of which will determine the appropriate material and method of lifting.

Footwear impression evidence should be photographed prior to any attempt to lift or preserve it. There are several reasons this should be done. Photographs depict an accurate representation of what the scene looked like on arrival of the forensic investigator.

Information that can be obtained through photos include location of the footwear in situ, directionality and movement, gait, speed, matrix

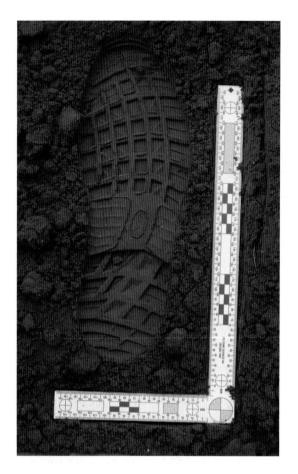

Photographing footwear and capturing this detail can be improved by using a few standard protocols.

- Camera should be mounted on a tripod and positioned perpendicular (90°) to the impression.
- ABFO (American Board of Forensic Odontology) ruler used—level with lower limit of 3D impressions.
- Oblique lighting introduced from varying locations around the impression at 45° angle.

transference, and number of suspects. Also, as with any form of physical evidence, photographs capture evidentiary detail in a nondestructive manner. Generally, any lifting and preserving technique will diminish detail or degrade the evidence in some way. The photograph is often the best representation of the evidence and any associated detail.

To assist in visualizing latent (invisible) two-dimensional footwear impression evidence, or enhancing details of three-dimensional footwear impressions (see following discussion), using grazed or oblique lighting can be a great asset. Forensic investigators can shine a light (flashlight or camera flash head), at an angle approximately 45° to the impression. This will cause latent impressions to become visible and enhance details in both two and three-dimensional impressions.

As with other types of evidence, numerous processing options exist and are largely selected because they are known by the forensic expert as being the best practice or providing the best results. As mentioned, the selection is dependent on the type of substrate and whether the impression is two-or three-dimensional. The following is a sampling of these varying factors and their recommended solutions.

Dust Impressions

There are two commonly accepted techniques for capturing dust footwear impressions. Because of the transient nature of dust impressions, they must be properly photographed prior to attempting any lifting or preservation techniques.

The first option is to place a sheet of black Mylar or metallic film over the impression. An electrostatic dust lifter is used to introduce an electrical charge to the film sheet, which in turn conducts the electrical current subsequently charging the dust particles that make up the footwear impression, resulting in the dust impression adhering to the underside of the metallic film.

The second option to capture this type of impression evidence is to use a *photographic subtraction technique.* This is a digital photographic method that involves photographing the two-dimensional impression

Subtraction Method

Since digital images are composed of numbers, mathematical operations can be performed on them. The following simple subtraction illustrates the technique:

$$
\begin{array}{r}
5 + 10 \\
- 10 \\
\hline
5
\end{array}
$$

A simple substitution in the values can thus be made:

$$
\begin{array}{r}
\text{SHOEPRINT} + \text{BACKGROUND} \\
- \text{BACKGROUND} \\
\hline
\text{SHOEPRINT}
\end{array}
$$

The process is illustrated by the photos at right:

A: A shoeprint on an obstructive background is captured in this image.

B: A second image of just the background is captured.

C: When the images are subtracted, the background is canceled out, leaving a much clearer image of the shoeprint.

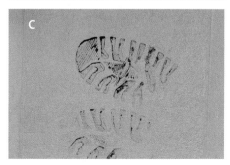

Footwear in grease developed with fingerprint powder.

and then digitally removing the interference presented by the background on which the impression sits.

Hence, if there is one image of a shoeprint on the disruptive pattern of a floor tile, and another image of just the pattern, in perfect register to the first, one can be subtracted from the other in the computer to give a much clearer image of the shoeprint (see Dalrymple et al. 2002).

Grease, Oil, or Moisture Impression

Fingerprint powder has an affinity to moisture. To enhance these impressions, magnetic fingerprint powder is applied with a magnetic wand/applicator. The footwear detail will develop similarly to fingerprint evidence. The impression can then be lifted by using gelatin lifters, fingerprint tape, or a liquid casting material such as dental stone, as in the Knaap process.

Iodine vapors or fumes can also be used over a latent footwear impression comprised of grease, fat, or other organic material deposits. It is also a viable option for footwear "wet marks." The resulting development will appear yellowish brown where the iodine is absorbed by the impression.

Blood

In cases where footwear impressions are in blood, chemical blood reagents such as amido black, leuco crystal violet (LCV), leuco malachite green (LMG), Bluestar, and others can be effective solutions to enhance partial or completely latent detail. These reagents should be limited to forensic investigators familiar with their usage and applications.

 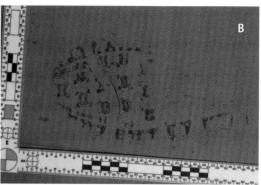

A. Shoeprint in blood is faint, with little detail visible.

B. After treatment with LCV, much more detail is apparent.

Soil Deposition

Where footwear impressions are soil depositions, forensic investigators may choose to enhance detail with chemistries that react with elements of the soil. The following is a selection of these chemical compositions and their reactive properties.

- *Potassium thiocyanate:* When sprayed onto two-dimensional latent soil impressions, this chemical reacts with the iron content in soil and enhances detail with an orange/red coloration.
- Bromophenol blue: *After spraying onto two-dimensional latent soil impressions, BP reacts with the pH levels of soil and enhances detail with bright blue coloration.*

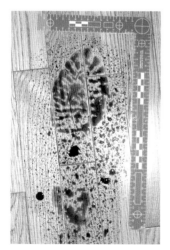

Footwear print in blood enhanced with LCV.

Footwear impressions in blood at a crime scene. Images courtesy of Toronto Police Forensic Identification Services.

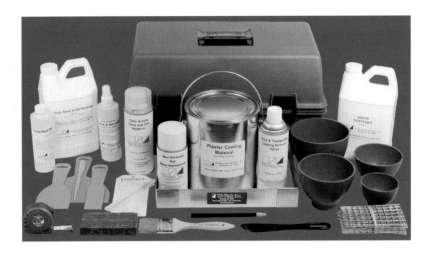

Casting materials, sprays, markers and trays form part of a footwear and tire track impression kit. Image courtesy of Tri-Tech Inc. All rights reserved.

Three-Dimensional Impressions

Footwear impressions are often seen embedded in a soft surface such as soil, sand, wet cement, snow, tar, and so on. The problem for the examiner is to preserve these impressions for analysis, interpretation, and presentation in court. Following is a simple overview of the ways in which casts are created from the molding of impressions found on different surfaces.

Soil

Footwear impressions in soil are commonly found at crime scenes. Because the majority of these impressions are found outdoors, they present challenges to the forensic investigator when lifting and preserving them.

Environmental conditions can impact how to best collect this evidence and may also affect the quality of the end result. Temperature, wind, and precipitation issues may need to be overcome and extreme cold temperatures may hinder casting materials from setting properly. High winds can distort the impression detail and add foreign debris like leaves, stones, and twigs into the impression.

Precipitation, however, can prove to be the most challenging. Rain can wash away detail or form a puddle in the impression; snow, sleet, or hail can obliterate, alter, or degrade detail and in some instances add unrelated artifacts to the impression.

The properties of the soil can also impact the impression quality. Soil with a high clay content can capture greater detail, whereas soil with a higher aggregate content will render less detail and be more fragile.

Soil impressions may offer considerable challenges to the forensic technician. As the impression dries out over time, the impression may crumble and fall apart. There may also be shrinkage, making accurate size comparison more difficult.

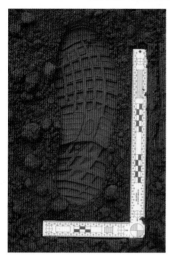

Footwear impression in sandy soil.

The standard process for capturing footwear impression in soil requires a plastic or zip bag filled with approximately 1.5 kg dry mix dental stone gypsum casting material.

Water is added to the powder and mixed until a smooth consistency is obtained, with a similar viscosity to pancake batter. The mixture is then poured into the impression, with caution to avoid distortion.

The mixture is spread, ensuring the entire impression is filled and void of any air pockets.

The dental stone is allowed to cure approximately 45 minutes before the impression is lifted.

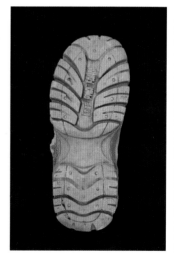

Excess soil is removed with water and a soft bristle brush after several hours.

Images courtesy of Toronto Police Forensic Identification Services. Photo credit John Doucette.

Tire track in snow, enhanced with Snow Print Wax.

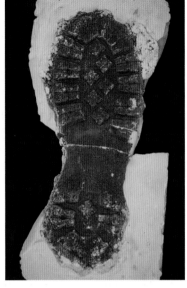

Footwear cast in snow after it has been captured in Snow Print Wax.

Snow

Photographing footwear evidence in snow provides certain challenges to investigators. The brightness and unified color of the impression can make it difficult to see and/or capture the shoe detail. In addition to previously recommended photography practices, the impression may demand additional techniques. Spraying a light coat of a contrasting color aerosol spray paint (like grey or rust-brown automotive primer paint, construction paint) enhances depth relief and impression detail.

An alternative option is to spray Snow Print Wax into the impression. This is an aerosol spray wax, colored to provide good contrast from the whiteness of snow, again enhancing depth relief and impression detail. Snow Print Wax also insulates the snow impression against the exothermic reaction commonly generated during the curing process of dental stone, a casting choice that is subsequently mixed and poured into the impression to replicate it.

Many other development and lifting techniques exist and are largely dependent on the matrix and/or substrate. Although three-dimensional footwear impressions are most often found in snow or soil, there will always be instances where a suspect steps into other soft materials, creating a mold impression. Wet cement, sand, or other soft substrates such as construction caulking, tar, chocolate, or cheese are certainly not as common but have been found on occasion.

Footwear impression photographed in snow.

Sulfur is heated in a pot until melted.

Sulfur in Snow Impression

Another choice for casting an impression in snow is sulfur. Powder or pellet sulfur (bright yellow color) is heated slowly in a pot, over low heat and in a well-ventilated area. Sulfur liquefies at approximately 116°C, turning to a dark amber color. Once completely liquefied, the sulfur is removed from the heat source and allowed to cool slightly, until crystallization forms around the edge of the pot, and the liquid begins to thicken. At this stage, the sulfur is poured into the snow impression, where it solidifies on contact, capturing the detail of the footwear before melting the snow.

The sulfur darkens as it melts.

The melted sulfur is allowed to cool slightly.

The finished casting.

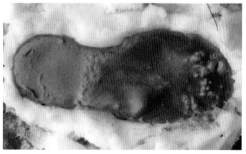

Sulfur mixture is poured onto snow impression.

Wet Cement

It would be impractical to attempt a casting technique of evidence in wet cement as this would likely result in obliterating any detail present. It is recommended to allow the cement to cure and then cast the impression using a pliable casting agent such as polyvinylsiloxane, Mikrosil or Reprorubber. These materials permit easy removal of the cast impression from the substrate. A hard casting material could bond to the cement and be difficult to remove.

Soft Substrates

Soft materials such as caulking, chocolate, tar, cheese, and so on may be better cast if the investigator employs ways to firm them prior to casting. Subjecting the substrate containing the impression to temperature change is an easy fix to many situations. All of these substrates will alter in texture and density when cooled, refrigerated or frozen. Utilizing these techniques will change the physical properties of the substrate, allowing the forensic investigator to easily cast the impression with hard or soft casting materials like dental stone, polyvinylsiloxane, Mikrosil, or Reprorubber.

Sand

Casting an impression from sand, like doing so from soil, is challenging and requires that the substrate be stabilized before casting material is poured. Eliminating or minimizing distortion of a sand impression and preventing its collapse can be aided by applying a sticky aerosol spray just prior to casting.

Two commonly accepted options are hair spray or wood sealants, such as clear lacquer or urethane. These products are available in aerosol spray cans and are best applied to the impression indirectly, that is, the impression is sprayed above its surface to allow the atomized liquid to fall onto it, rather than subjecting it to the pressurized propellant and possibly distorting the detail.

Sufficient time is required to cure or set, after which liquid dental stone is poured directly into the impression to cast it. Liquid dental stone should be applied from a close distance above the impression to avoid distortion, which could occur if poured from a height. Pouring the casting material onto a deflector (i.e., paint scraper, cardboard, etc.) in lieu of directly into the impression, to slow and control the flow, may assist in minimizing distortion.

Tire Track Impressions

Tire track impressions employ similar development techniques to those of footwear. Two-dimensional impressions may be further developed with magnetic fingerprint powder and a magnetic powder applicator. The pretense is that fingerprint powder will have an affinity to moisture (water, grease, oil, tire rubber) deposits within the impression. Enhanced tire track impressions can then be lifted using the Knaap method (pouring liquid dental stone on the impression and removing the cast once cured, securing the detail indelibly in the cast).

Three-dimensional tire track impressions can be collected with dental stone. Refer to the discussion of three-dimensional footwear impression casting for further details.

The constant breakthroughs and advances in many areas of forensic research reflect the interaction between technology and problem solving. Legal investigations almost wholly rely on newer and faster ways to isolate and analyze physical evidence to keep ahead of increasingly sophisticated crimes. Because forensic science is an eclectic field that continually borrows from other disciplines, there is always an abundance of methods and techniques to draw from, making this one of the fastest-growing areas of science to date.

Appendix

Case Studies

The following is a series of closed criminal cases in which the authors and contributors were involved as forensic investigators during their careers. The cases are intended to illustrate the various forensic tools and methods of analyses that were employed to solve each of the crimes in question. The names of the victims and their perpetrators have not been included to protect their families and next-of-kin. In some of the higher profile cases, details such as city names and places have been changed.

Case 1: Positive Identification after Intentional Dismemberment

In March 1988, two legs were found near Gananoque, Ontario, along the north shore of the St. Lawrence River. They had been severed at the knee. During the autopsy process, plaster casts were taken of the soles of the feet. It was hoped that in the future, they might be useful in the identification of the victim, thought to be a young woman. In the months that followed, other body parts were found in eastern Ontario.

Meanwhile in Toronto, weeks before the legs were found, a woman was reported missing. A dozen pairs of shoes were taken from her home for comparison with the plaster casts of the feet. Examination of the shoes involved cutting away the top of the shoes to expose the insole. All of the shoes were examined by laser. Fluorescing images of the foot were seen in two pairs of shoes, offering clear images of the ball of the foot and the toes. No ridge detail was visible. Efforts to locate a scientist with

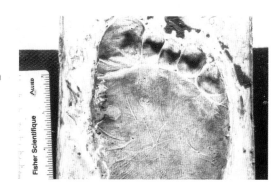

Plaster casts were taken of the bottoms of the victim's feet.

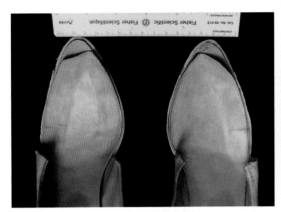

The insoles of the victim's shoes were examined. Nothing significant could be seen in ambient light conditions.

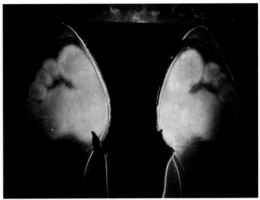

Laser examination of the insoles revealed fluorescing images of the victim's feet. No ridge detail was visible in these impressions. It was hoped that a forensic podiatrist could compare these images to the plaster casts of the victim's feet.

the expertise to compare the foot images to the plaster casts were unsuccessful.

The last pair of shoes examined bore white leather insoles with a pebbled surface. Traces of extremely faint ridge detail could be seen in room light. The insoles were fumed with iodine and photographed on high-contrast film, adding significantly to the clarity and extent of ridge detail. Comparison of these impressions to the detail in the plaster casts resulted in positive identification of the victim.

The focus was now on the victim's boyfriend. One day after the victim's identity was released to the press, he drove to a beach area of Lake Ontario near midnight, oblivious to the fact that he was under police

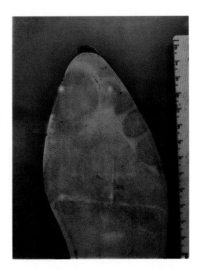

Iodine fuming and high contrast photography resulted in an image of clear and extensive ridge detail on both insoles. This resulted in the positive identification of the victim.

surveillance. He walked onto a pier with a bag containing something of weight. When he stepped off the pier sometime later, the bag was obviously empty.

As soon as the subject left the area, a police diver searched the lake in the vicinity of the pier and recovered four knives of various types and a cleaver. These were air-dried, treated by cyanoacrylate fuming, and sprayed with rhodamine 6G dye. One fingerprint was located and photographed on the tip of one of the knives. The suspect was subsequently identified as the source.

It was gratifying that cyanoacrylate and dye developed fingerprint evidence on a knife that had spent several hours in the cold waters of Lake Ontario. The suspect was later tried and found guilty of first-degree murder.

Five knives were recovered from the waters of Lake Ontario.

A latent impression, developed on the knife blade by cyanoacrylate and Rhodamine 6G, was identified as that of the suspect.

Case 2: Latent Palm Prints

Around 1980, an elderly woman of eighty-two years was assaulted in her home around 3 A.M. The attacker raped the woman and then tried to kill her by smothering her with a pillow. As he pressed the pillow down on her face, the victim stopped moving and pretended to be dead. Fortunately, the rapist thought he had succeeded in killing the woman and left the scene. After he left, the victim, feeling soiled, washed her nightgown and the bed sheets before calling the police.

The crime happened in a rural community with few resources; therefore, the local authorities requested the assistance of the Kansas Bureau of Investigation. The agent assigned found one suspect in particular who fit the description given by the victim and just happened to live across the backyard of the victim. The suspect was questioned and, after he passed a polygraph, eliminated from consideration. With very little evidence, the investigation was going nowhere.

The agent brought the crime lab the pillowcase that had been on the pillow used by the suspect in his attempt to smother the victim, in hopes that we could develop latent prints on the fabric. As far as we knew, latent prints had not been developed on fabric previously, but it was worth a try.

The pillowcase was old, having been given to the victim on her wedding day some fifty years earlier. It had remained unused and stored in a trunk since that time. About a week before the attack, the victim had

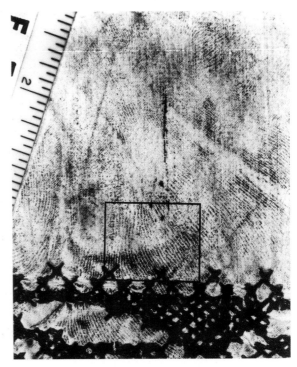

The palm print developed on the pillowcase by ninhydrin.

LATENT PALM PRINT   INKED PALM PRINT

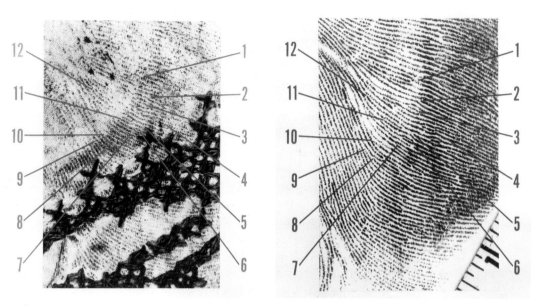

The charts illustrating the comparison and identification of the palm print.

taken the pillowcase from the trunk, washed it, hung it to dry inside her home, and then ironed it before placing it on her pillow. The pillowcase was linen fabric of about 120 threads per inch. The night of the attack was the first night the pillowcase had been on the victim's bed.

The pillowcase was processed by spraying it with a 6 percent solution of ninhydrin in acetone and then was allowed to hang in the processing room to dry. After one day of hanging, there was no indication of any print development. It was not until nearly a week of hanging that ridge detail appeared on the pillowcase. Examination of the ridge detail revealed a palm print of value for identification. The palm print was photographed using a #58 green filter and 4 × 5 black and white film.

Once the palm print was reported, the agent began to bring in known palm prints for comparison. On one occasion, the agent said he definitely had the right suspect since the individual had failed the polygraph. A comparison of the prints revealed this suspect was not the person who had left the print on the pillowcase.

After about six months of investigation, the agent brought the palm prints of the first suspect who had passed the polygraph and was therefore eliminated. A comparison of this suspect's palm prints revealed that he actually *was* the individual who had left the print on the pillowcase.

The information for this case study was provided by C. Carlson, supervisor, Fingerprint Identification Section, Kansas City Police Regional Crime Laboratory, Missouri.

Case 3: Identifying Evidence with Alternate Light Source vs. Laser

In the early 1990s, police located the home of a serial killer. After all contents had been removed, the house was examined by a forensic light source. Only small unsuitable fragments of fingerprints were located. The home was then examined with an argon-ion laser, becoming one of the first crime scenes scrutinized by a mainframe laser. Over the course of two days, over forty untreated fingerprints were located and photographed by laser.

Next, the door and window openings were sealed, and the home was filled with iodine vapor, revealing an additional four impressions. Finally, the walls, doorjambs, window frames, and cupboards were treated with ninhydrin, applied with a paint roller. Another sixteen impressions were located.

It is significant that not one of these impressions were visualized by just one technique, and that if sequential processing had not been employed, some of these impressions would have been missed. One cannot know or predict which fingerprints will be relevant to an investigation. It also reveals eloquently that lasers and forensic light sources are not the same thing, and although they may both be used successfully to excite detection chemistry like rhodamine 6G and indanedione, each has the potential to locate evidence missed by the other.

As in the case of the serial killer's house, examination of surfaces like this plastic bag by filtered lamp (505 nm) (left) periodically fails to reveal untreated fingerprints that are detected by laser (532 nm) (right).

Case 4: High-Velocity Impact

Two vehicles were racing on a city street when one struck a pedestrian. The driver claimed he was not speeding when the pedestrian was hit and killed. The car was taken in for forensic examination.

Typically, high-velocity bloodstains are associated with gunshots or power tools which result in aerosol misting—blood traveling in excess of 100 feet per second. In this case the vehicle was traveling fast enough when it hit the person to cause misting bloodstains down the side of the car. Note the picture with the scale in it. Bloodstains much smaller than 1 mm established that the vehicle was moving at a minimum of 100 kilometers per hour (about 60 mph).

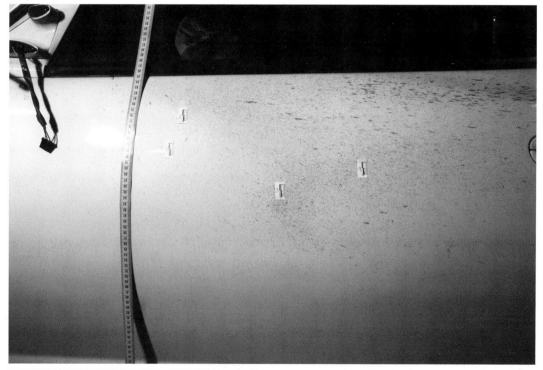

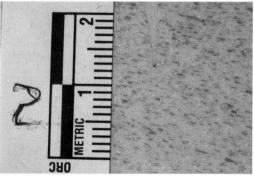

Fine blood misting can be seen on the door panel of the subject's vehicle.

Close examination reveals that the individual bloodstains are much less than 1 mm, confirming a high-velocity impact. Images courtesy of Scott Collings, Hamilton Police Service. All rights reserved.

Case 5: Suicide vs. Homicide

In the summer of 1989 the remains of an adult human leg washed up on the shores of Lake Eerie. Local police were called and the remains were taken to the morgue for further examination. Prior to this leg washing up, part of another adult leg and torso had come ashore not far from this location the previous week. It was assumed that the body parts were from the same individual. However, when both legs and torso were fully examined it was evident that they were from two different people. The torso and right leg had clear evidence of traumatic dismemberment; muscle, tendons and bone had been ripped and were ragged and uneven. This is often the case when bodies submerged in water have been caught in ship propellers and torn apart.

When the other leg part (also a right limb composed of the tibia and partial fibula) had been fully processed (the decomposed flesh was removed and cleaned to expose the ends of the bone) there were clear and even striation marks on the distal and proximal ends of the bones made visible under microscopic viewing. Both bones had all of their joint surfaces fully cut off, bearing these striation marks similar to those from saw blades. It was evident that the leg had been intentionally cut apart.

Meanwhile, the torso and full leg had subsequently been positively identified based on blood grouping (DNA typing was not used for identifying this unknown individual) and the marks of a premortem scar and tattoos. The individual had left a suicide note outlining his intentions to drown himself after consuming enough alcohol to keep him "underwater."

The partial limb still needed to be identified, but it was not until the following month when police in a nearby city began investigating reports of a missing woman. Her boyfriend was distraught, claimed they had a fight and "she ran off and never called or came back home." Neighbors claimed they had fought but did not see her leave the house. A witness claimed to have seen the boyfriend leave the house later that night carrying "a gym bag." The missing woman's young adult daughter, though she did not live at home, gave statements to the police attesting that her mother and boyfriend "fought all the time." As such, the boyfriend became their lead suspect. Traces of blood were found in the trunk of the car after police seized his vehicle. A hacksaw in the garage was seized, also bearing traces of blood, with a blade pattern that was ultimately matched to the saw mark impressions on the bone ends. The blood, tissue samples kept from the processed leg, and a blood sample from the missing woman's adult daughter were compared. Early DNA typing methods indicated a strong match between the blood found in the trunk and hacksaw and the tissue/blood samples from the leg. These all indicated biological relatedness to the daughter's DNA.

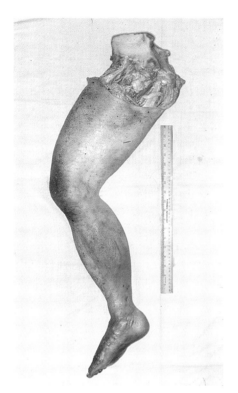

Traumatically dismembered leg remains .

Defleshed bone from the same remains reveals
the torn and ragged bone surface of
unintentional/traumatic dismemberment.

Case 6: Footwear Impressions in Blood

In the early 1990s, an elderly man was murdered in his residence. His throat had been cut, and the floor was extensively covered with blood. The brutal murder resulted in several boot prints recorded in blood on the painted wooden floor. Test impressions were made of the suspect's boots in both fingerprint ink on paper and powder on paper. Comparison of the test impressions to the blood prints from the crime scene revealed a high level of class agreement (tread pattern), but the numerous accidental characteristics did not appear in the same locations.

Fingerprint comparison differs sharply from shoeprint comparison in this regard. Fingertips are soft and very flexible. There will almost certainly be differences in appearance as well as spatial agreement between fingerprints recorded in different media, different amounts of media, or with different pressure. These differences in no way diminish the potential for positive identification, provided that there is continuous agreement of the ridge detail in identical sequence. Exact spatial agreement is not necessary and rarely exists.

In contrast, shoe bottoms are much more rigid. Footwear identifications are routinely illustrated by the overlay method, in which the spatial agreement of the class and accidental characteristics are displayed. Any significant difference in spatial agreement would therefore require an explanation.

Test impressions were taken again of the suspect boots, but this time using real blood (donated by a hospital lab) as the recording medium and painted wood as the substrate. The dynamics of blood as a record-

When a shoeprint is made in liquid blood, the viscosity of the blood may result in a very different impression from one created in another medium, like powder or ink.

ing medium were found to differ significantly from either of the techniques originally used to obtain comparison impressions. Both class and accidental characteristics in the blood recordings were found to be in agreement as to their size and location.

The boots were positively identified as the source of the bloody impressions, one aspect of the physical evidence, which led to a conviction.

Case 7: Paper Packets

The expression of a professional opinion can occasionally go beyond the presence of a fingerprint on an exhibit and the identification of the donor. This can have a significant bearing on the number and type of charges that the evidence supports.

In 1994, two people were charged with the trafficking of narcotics. A quantity of cocaine was found at a residence combined with other relevant items, including a set of weigh scales, a pad of multicolored paper, and paper packets (referred to as "coke decks") that had allegedly been used to contain and market cocaine. These consist of single pieces of paper approximately four inches square, which are folded to create a packet containing a premeasured quantity of cocaine for street sale.

Other similar packets containing cocaine were seized from another location. All paper items were then examined for fingerprints with ninhydrin, with the following results.

- Multiple identifications were made of two subjects on many of the paper packets.
- Numerous identifications were made of the same digit, at the same location on different packages, and at a similar orientation.
- Many of these identifications abruptly ceased along the fold lines in the paper packets.
- The fingerprint identifications were not visible when the package was closed.

The folded packages were compared to the pad of multicolored paper with the following results.

- The papers used to make the packages were the same dimensions as the pad of multicolored paper.
- The different colors of the packages were indistinguishable from the colors of the papers contained in the pad.

When this case was prosecuted in court before a judge alone (as opposed to a jury), the defendants were prepared (through their attorneys) to plead guilty to possession of narcotics, contending that the drugs found were for personal use. This is a far less serious charge than trafficking. The attorney did not accept the offer, and the case was heard.

In direct evidence, the fingerprint identifications were presented, and further opinions were expressed. Many of the impressions identified on different packets were

- of the same digit,
- in the same position and alignment,
- located along one side of the folds in the paper made during the creation of the packets,

- hidden inside the package when it was closed; and
- located on pieces of paper indistinguishable from papers contained in the pad seized in the residence.

Furthermore, the scales were located in the bedroom of one defendant, and the pad of paper was seized in the bedroom of the other.

These findings are consistent with the donors of the fingerprints preparing and filling the drug packets, using papers indistinguishable in size, weight, and color from papers located in the residence.

Though the defense attorneys did not object to the fingerprint identifications, they made vigorous attempts to attack the extended evidence, including the significance attached to the position of the fingerprints and the connection made by the similarity of the paper.

The narcotics officer stated in evidence that never in his experience had a simple consumer of drugs possessed at one time as many full packages of drugs. Also, the packages each contained, to a very precise degree, the same quantity of drugs.

The judge's decision included the following.

- Given the presence and position of repeated fingerprint impressions on the packages, the amount of cocaine on the premises, the location and existence of the scales, and the location of the paper pad, it is established beyond a reasonable doubt that there was trafficking at least intended in the possession of the cocaine.
- Both accused were found guilty of trafficking.

The fingerprint impression ceases abruptly and exactly along the line of the crease in the paper, consistent with the donor creating the package.

Case 8: Footwear Impression on Shirt

In 2004, a murder occurred in a residential community located in the east end of Toronto. During daytime hours, three armed assailants approached the victim's address and escorted him out at gunpoint. The suspects stripped the victim of his belt, using it as a restraint by lashing the victim's hands together behind his back.

The victim was escorted to the grass area that separates his property from the neighboring house, where he was forced to the ground. While laying face down on the grass, the suspects removed the victim's right shoe and sock and jammed the sock into his mouth to prevent him from calling out for help. At this time, one of the suspects stood on the victim's back and shot him in the back of the head. The projectile exited the victim's mouth and embedded into the ground several inches below the surface. As this was transpiring, other residents of the house arrived in a small car and were fired on through the windshield by the fleeing suspects. Neither occupant in the vehicle sustained injury.

Emergency medical services attended the scene and pronounced the victim deceased. The body remained on location pending arrival of the forensic investigators. While processing the scene, forensic personnel used a metal detector to locate and recover the projectile from the ground. A spent brass cartridge case was also recovered, situated atop the lower back area of the victim, on his shirt. An indentation of a shoe outline was visible on the back of the victim's ash gray T-shirt, but no class or individualizing characteristics were present at the time. The body was later bagged and removed to the morgue for further examination.

Forensic investigators attended the morgue and removed the victim's shirt. Precaution was taken to minimize degradation of the footwear impression. The shirt was laid flat and mounted onto a foam board to protect the impression pending further examination. The Ontario Provincial Police were contacted and assisted the forensic investigative team by processing the shirt with a spray application of potassium thiocyanate. This

chemistry reacts with iron content present in soil. The latent soiled footwear impression became visible and revealed numerous class and individualizing characteristics that were ultimately and positively matched to the shooter's running shoe. Had it not been for the application and reaction of this chemistry, footwear evidence vital to this incident would have been overlooked or unused.

Case 9: Anonymous Letters

Anonymous letters are among the most common and the most premeditated occurrences facing the identification technician. Usually minor in nature but malicious in intent, they can traumatize families and destabilize businesses. Accordingly, in the author's experience, success in these cases is significantly limited because of the following activities.

- The perpetrator takes pains to avoid touching the document or envelope, or licking the envelope flap or stamp.
- Letters are usually opened before their nature and content are known, often resulting in the handling by other persons.
- Typed adhesive labels are routinely substituted for handwritten addresses.

In one such case, a number of anonymous, threatening letters bearing self-adhesive address labels was received for fingerprint examination. The labels were removed from the envelopes by UNDU® adhesive remover, and the adhesive sides were treated with a mixture of Lightning Black Powder, Liquinox detergent and water. Two impressions suitable for comparison were developed on the adhesive side of one label, and were scanned.

Lightning Black and Liquinox detergent targeted the lipid component of the finger deposit on the adhesive side of the label. Any amino acids present are water-soluble and would be washed away in both the application and the water rinse. Thus, the envelope was then treated with indanedione, an amino acid reagent. Indanedione reacted with the amino acid content that had been transferred to the envelope.

Subsequently, several areas of ridge detail were developed on the envelope in the area protected by the label. The ridge detail ended abruptly along the border of the area previously protected by the label.

It was established through comparison that the impressions developed by indanedione on the envelope were mirror images of the detail devel

Fingerprint detail developed by Lightning/Liquinox on adhesive side of label.

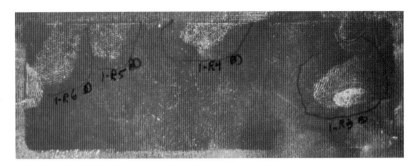

Area of envelope covered by label after indanedione processing.

oped on the adhesive side of the label; the obvious inference being that the print had been transferred to the envelope.

The impressions developed on the envelope by indanedione contained more detail than the source impressions developed on the adhesive side of the label by Lightning/Liquinox. Fortunately, the removal of the label with UNDU® did not destroy the impression on the adhesive side, or the detail transferred to the envelope.

A significantly greater weight can be ascribed to these impressions than any that might be developed on the remaining surface of the envelope. Fingerprints found on the envelope might have been placed there before it contained an anonymous letter, or may have been deposited by someone not involved in the action. This impression, however, indicates active participation in the sending of the letter.

Fingerprint on adhesive side of label.

Same fingerprint on envelope, mirrored after indanedione processing.

Bibliography and Suggested Readings

Alaoui, I.M., Menzel E.R., Farag, M., Cheng, K.H., Murdock, R.H. 2005. Mass spectra and time-resolved spectroscopy of the reaction product of glycine with 1,2-indanedione in methanol. *Forensic Science International*, 152(2–3), 215–19.

Alberink, I., Ruifrok, A. 2007. Performance of the FearID earprint identification system. *Forensic Science International*, 166, 145–54.

Almog, J., Frank, A. 1993. Modified SPR for latent fingerprint development on wet, dark objects. *Journal of Forensic Identification*, 43(3).

Almog, J., Springer, E., Wiesner, S., Frank, A., Khodzhaev, O., Lidor, R., Bahar, E., Varkony, H., Dayan, S., Rozen, S. 1999. Latent fingerprint visualization by 1,2-indanedione and related compounds: Preliminary results. *Journal of Forensic Sciences*, 44, 114–18.

Almog, J., Azoury, M., Elmaliah, Y., Berenstein, L., Zaban, A. 2004. Fingerprints' third dimension: The depth and shape of fingerprints penetration into paper-cross section examination by fluorescence microscopy. *Journal of Forensic Sciences*, 49 (5), 981–85.

Almog, J., Levinton-Shamuilov, G., Cohen, Y., Azoury, M. 2007. Fingerprint reagents with dual action: Color and fluorescence. *Journal of Forensic Science*, 52(2) 330–34.

Archer, K. 1998. 3-D craniofacial reconstruction (http://www.loonie.net/~karcher/thesis.html).

Artières, P. Corneloup, G. 2004. *Le Médecin et le Criminel*: exposition de la Bibliothèque municipale de Lyon, 27 janvier.

Ashbaugh, D.R. 1999. *Quantitative-Qualitative Friction Ridge Analysis: An Introduction to Basic and Advanced Ridgeology*. Boca Raton, Fl: CRC Press.

Beaudoin, A. 2004. New technique for revealing latent fingerprints on wet porous surfaces: Oil red O. *Journal of Forensic Identification*, 54 (4), 413–421.

Berger, H., de Waard F., Molenaar, Y. 2000. "A case of twin-to-twin transfusion in 1617." *Lancet* 356 (9232): 847–8.

Berryman, H., Symes, S.A. 1998. Recognizing gunshot and blunt cranial trauma through fracture interpretation. In *Forensic Osteology:*

Advances in the Identification of Human Remains (2nd ed.), K.J. Reichs (ed.), 333–352. Springfield, IL: Charles C. Thomas.

Bertillon, A. 1883. La Préfecture de Police à l'Exposition d'Amsterdam—L'Identification de Récidivistes. *La Nature–Revue Des Sciences*, 11(534), 197–203.

Bertillon, A. 1890. *Photography: With an Appendix on Anthropometrical Classification and Identification.*

Bevel, T., Gardner, R.M. 2002. *Bloodstain Pattern Analysis.* Boca Raton, Fl: CRC Press, pp 4–16.

Bindra, B., Jasuja, O.P., Singla, A.K. 2000. *Poroscopy: A Method of Personal Identification Revisited. Anil Aggrawal's Internet Journal of Forensic Medicine and Toxicology.*

Bisbing, R.E. 2004. *Fractured Patterns: Microscopical Investigation of Real Physical Evidence.* Westmont, IL: McCrone Associates.

Blake, T. 1999. DNA Genotyping, or 'Whose finger was it anyway?' In *Hordeum* (http:/hordeum.ocs.montana.edu/finger/finger.html). Bozeman, MT: Montana State University Dept. of Plant Sciences.

Bodziak, W.J. 2000. *Footwear Impression Evidence* (2nd ed.) Boca Raton, Fl: CRC Press.

Bonner, J. 2001. Looking for Faces in the Superbowl Crowd. Security Solutions, Access Control & Security Systems Integration.

Broeckman, A. 1996. *A Visual Economy of Individuals: The Use of Portrait Photography in the 19th Century.* Berlin: *Human Sciences.*

Butt, D. 2009. Investigating Internet child exploitation poses complex challenges. *Kid's Internet Safety Alliance.*

Caldas, I.M., Magalhaes, T., Americo, A. 2007. Establishing identity using cheiloscopy and palatoscopy. *Forensic Science International*, 165, 1–9.

Campbell, E. 1998. *A History of Dermatoglyphics, Palmistry & Character Identity* (www.edcampbell.com/PalmD-History.htm).

Cantu, A.A. 2001. Silver developers for the visualization of latent prints on paper. *Forensic Science Review*, 13, 29–64.

Cantu, A.A., Leben, D.A., Joullie, M.M., Heffner, J., Hark, R.R. 1993. A comparative examination of several amino acid reagents for visualizing amino acid (glycine) on paper. *Journal of Forensic Identification*, 43, 44–62.

Caplan, J., Torpey, J., eds. 2001. *Documenting Individual Identity: The Development of State Practices in the Modern World.* Princeton, NJ: Princeton University Press.Cassidy, M.J. 1980. *Footwear Identification.* Hull: Canadian Government Publishing Centre.

Cesarani, F., Martina, M.C., Ferraris, A. 2003. Whole body three-dimensional multi-detector CT of 13 Egyptian human mummies. *American Journal of Roentgenology*, 180, 597–606.

Cleary, E.W. ed.1972. *McCormick's Handbook of the Law of Evidence.* St. Paul: West Publishing. 524–542.

Coltman, C.A., Rowe, N.J., Atwell, R.J. 1966. The amino acid content of sweat in normal adults. *American Journal of Clinical Nutrition*, 18, 373–78.

Côté, J. 2003. *Wilfrid Derome: Expert en Homicides*. Montreal: Les Éditions du Boréal.

CPRC (Canadian Police Research Centre). 1993. TM-14-93—Vacuum Fingerprint Chamber Evaluation (http://www.css.drdc-rddc.gc.ca/cprc/tm/tm-14-93.pdf).

Crow, J.F., 1993. Francis Galton: Count and measure, measure and count. *Genetics*, 135, 1–4.

Cummins, H., Midlo, C. 1943. *Fingerprints, Palms and Soles*. Blakiston Company, Maple Press, p.22.

Dalrymple, B. 1979. Case analysis of fingerprint detection by laser. *Journal of Forensic Sciences*, July, 586–90.

Dalrymple, B. 1982. Use of narrow band-pass filters to enhance detail in latent fingerprint photography by laser. *Journal of Forensic Sciences*, October, 801–5.

Dalrymple, B. 1983. Visible and infrared luminescence in documents: Excitation by laser. *Journal of Forensic Sciences*, July, 692–96.

Dalrymple, B. 2000. Fingerprints (dactyloscopy) identification and classification. In *Encyclopedia of Forensic Sciences*. Academic Press, 869–77.

Dalrymple, B., Duff, J.M., Menzel, E.R. 1977. Inherent fingerprint luminescence—detection by laser. *Journal of Forensic Sciences*, January, 106–15.

Dalrymple, B., Shaw L., Woods, K. 2002. Optimized digital recording of crime scene impressions. *Journal of Forensic Identification*, November–December.

Dalrymple, B., and Smith, J. 2018. *Forensic Digital Image Processing: Optimization of Impression Evidence*. CRC Press, 2018.

Dauber, W. v. Merrell Dow Pharmaceuticals No. 92-102.1993. On writ of certiorari to the United States Court of Appeals for the Ninth Circuit. (http://www.law.cornell.edu/supct/html/92-102.ZO.html).

Davis, J.H. Bodies found in water. *American Journal of Forensic Medicine and Pathology*, 7, 291–97.

Di Maio, V.J.M. 1993. *Gunshot Wounds: Practical Aspects of Firearms, Ballistics and Forensic Techniques*. Boca Raton, FL: CRC Press.

Dumont, E.R. 1986. Mid-facial tissue depths of white children: An aid to facial feature reconstruction. *Journal of Forensic Sciences*, 34, 1214–21.

Eckert, W.G., ed. 1997. *Introduction to Forensic Sciences* (2nd ed.). Boca Raton, FL: CRC Press.

Evison, M.P., Finegan, O.M., Blythe, T. 1998. Computerized 3-D facial reconstruction. In *Assemblage* (http://forensic.shef.ac.uk/assem/evison6.wrl).

Fisher, J. 1994. *The Lindbergh Case.* New Brunswick, NJ: Rutgers University Press.

Freeman, M.D.A., Reece, H., eds. 1998. *Science in Court.* Aldershot, UK.

Galloway, A., Birkby, W.H., Jones, A.M., Henry, T.E., Parks, B.O. 1989. Decay rates of human remains in an arid environment. *Journal of Forensic Sciences,* 34, 607–16.

Galton, F. 1892. *Finger Prints.* London, Macmillan.

Gaviola, E., Strong, J. 1936. Photoelectric effect of aluminum films evaporated in vacuum. *Physics Review,* 49, 441–43.

George, R.M. 1987. The lateral craniographic method of facial reconstruction. *Journal of Forensic Sciences,* 32, 1305–30.

Gerasimov, M.M. 1968. *The Face Finder.* London: Hutchinson.

Grew, N. 1684. The description and use of the pores in the skin of the hands and feet. *Philosophical Transactions of the Royal Society of London,* 14, 566–67.

Gross, H. 1898. *Handbuch für Untersuchungsrichter als System der Kriminalistik*

Gross, H. 1909. *Enzyklopädie der Kriminalistik* (Encyclopedia of Criminology).

Guilbault, G.G. 1973. *Practical Fluorescence: Theory Methods and Techniques.* New York: Marcel Dekker.

Gunaratne, A. 2006. *Vacuum metal deposition.* BOC Canada, Peel Region Police Service, University of Toronto.

Gurdjian, E.S., Webster, J.E., Lissner, H.R. 1950. The mechanism of skull fracture. *Radiology,* 54, 313–39.

Hadlow, I. 2008. *Debating Ethics of DNA Database.* BBC News, January.

Hambridge, J. 1909. Fingerprints: Their use by the police. *Century Magazine,* 78 (6), 916–21.

Hammer, L., Kennedy, R.B. 2009. Footwear & foot impressions: Foot impressions and linking foot to shoe. In *Wiley Encyclopedia of Forensic Science.* A. Jamieson, A. Moenssons (eds.) London: John Wiley & Sons, 1244–48.

Hardwick, S.A. 1981. *A User Guide to Physical Developer—A Reagent for Detecting Latent Fingerprints.* Technical User Guide No. 14/81, Home Office Police Scientific Development Branch.

Hark, R., Hauze, D.B, Petrovskaia, O., Joullié, M.M., Jahouari, R., McCominskey, P. 1994. Novel approaches toward ninhydrin analogs. *Tetrahedron Letters,* 35, 7719–22.

Harkness, W.H., Ramsey, W.C., Ahmadi, B., eds. 1984. Principles of fractures and dislocations. In *Fractures in Adults,* Volume 1, C.A. Rockwood and D.P. Dean (eds.) Philadelphia: J.B. Lippincott. 1–18.

Herod, D.W., Menzel, E.R. 1982. Laser detection of latent fingerprints: Ninhydrin followed by zinc chloride. *Journal of Forensic Sciences,* 27, 513–18.

His, W. 1895. Anatomische Forschungen ueber Johann Sebastian Bach Gebeine und Antlitz' nebst Bemerkungen ueber dessen Bilder. *Abhandlungen der Saech-sischen Gesellschaft und Wissenschaften zu Leipz*, 22, 379–420.

Hodson, G., Lieberman, L.S., Wright, P. 1985. In vivo measurements of facial thicknesses in American Caucasoid children. *Journal of Forensic Sciences*, 30, 1100–1112.

Holck, P. 1997. Cremated bones. A medical-anthropological study of archaeological material on cremation burials. *Antropologiske skrifter* nr 1.c. Third revised edition. Anatomical institute, University of Oslo.

Human Genome Project (HGP) 2008.U.S. Department of Energy Office of Science, Office of Biological and Environmental Research. Human Genome Program.

INTERPOL. 2009. http://www.interpol.int/Public/ICPO/PressReleases/PR2009/PR200911.asp.

Jeffreys, A.J., Wilson, V., Thein, S.L. 1985a. Hypervariable minisatellite regions in human DNA. *Nature*, 314 (6006), 67–73.

Jeffreys, A.J., Wilson, V., and Thein, S.L. 1985b. Individual-specific fingerprints of human DNA. *Nature*, 316 (6023), 76–79.

Jelly, R., Lewis, S., Lennard, C., Lim, K., Almog, J. 2008. Lawsone: A novel reagent for the detection of latent fingermarks on paper surfaces. *Nanochemistry Research Institute* (Research Institute), 3513–15.

Johnson, A., Moise, K.J. 2006. Improving Survival in Twin-Twin Transfusion Syndrome. *Contemporary OB/GYN* December.

Kaye, B.H. 1995. *Science and the Detective: Selected Readings in Forensic Science*. Weinheim, NY: VCH.

Kennedy, R.B. 1996. Uniqueness of bare feet and its use as a possible means of identification. *Forensic Science International*, 82, 81–87.

Kennedy, R.B. 2000. Bare footprint marks. In *Encyclopedia of Forensic Science*. J.A. Siegel, P.J. Saukko, G.C. Knupfer (eds.) London: Academic Press, 3:1189–95.

Kennedy, R.B. 2005. Ongoing research into barefoot impression evidence. In Forensic Medicine of the Lower Extremity. J. Rich, D.E. Dean D.E., R.H. Powers (eds.) Humana Press, 401–13.

Kent, T. 1980. *Modified Gentian Violet Development Techniques for Fingerprints on Black Adhesive Tape*. HOSRDB Publication 23/82, Reprint of HOPSDB 1/80.

Kent, T., Thomas, G.L., Reynoldson, T.E., East, H.W. 1976. A vacuum coating technique for the development of latent fingerprints on polythene. *Journal of Forensic Sciences*, 93–101.

Kimura, S., Schaumann, B.A., Shiota, K. 2001. *Comparative Investigations of Human and Rat Dermatoglyphics: Palmar, Plantar and Digital Pads and Flexion Creases*. Japan: Anatomical Science International Publisher Springer.

Kollman, J. 1898. Die Weichteile des Gesichts und Persistenz der Rassen. *Anatomischer Anzeiger,*15, 165–77.

Kotz, J.C., Treichel, P., Townsend, J.R. 2008. *Chemistry and Chemical Reactivity*. San Francisco: Cengage Learning, 579.

Krogman, W.M. 1946. The reconstruction of the living head from the skull. *FBI Law Enforcement Bulletin*, 15, 1–8.

Kunkel, W.C., Lennard, C., Stoilovic, M., Roux, C. 2007. Optimization and evaluation of 1,2-indanedione for use as a fingermark reagent and its application to real samples. *Forensic Science International* 168 (1) 14–26.

Lacassagne, A. 1913. Les transformations du droit pénal et les progrès de la médecine légale, de 1810 à 1912. In *Archives d'anthropologie criminelle*.

Lacassagne, A. 1899. *Vacher: L'Éventruer et Les Crime Sadiques*. Lyons: A. Storck, Éditeurs.

Lander, E.S. 1998. Standards for DNA identification practice. In *DNA on the Witness Stand*. Genentech (http://www.accessexcellence.org/AB/WYW/lander/lander_5.html).

Lander, E.S., Budowle, B. 1994. DNA fingerprinting dispute laid to rest. *Nature*, 371 (October).

Lerner, L., Lerner B.W., Cengage, G. 2006. Integrated Ballistics Identification System (IBIS). *World of Forensic Science*, eNotes.com, 6 August (www.enotes.com/forensic-science/integrated-ballistics-identification-system-ibis).

Lerner, L., Lerner, B.W., Cengage, G. 2006. Alternate light source analysis, *World of Forensic Science*, eNotes.com.

Levinton-Shamuilov, G., Cohen, Y., Azoury, M., Chaikovsky, A., Almog, J. 2005. Genipin, a novel fingerprint reagent with colorimetric and fluorogenic activity, part II: Optimization, scope and limitations. *Journal of Forensic Sciences*. 1367–71.

Locard, E. 1930. The analysis of dust traces. *American Journal of Police Science*. 1, 276.

Locard, E. 1931–1940. *Traité de Criminalistique*. Lyon: J. Desvigne.

Locard E. 1939. *Manual of Police Techniques*. 3rd ed., Paris.

Lombroso, C. 2006. *Criminal Man*. Illustrated ed. Translated by M. Gibson, N. Hahn Rafter, Durham, NC: Duke University Press.

MacDonell, H.L. 1982. *Bloodstain Pattern Interpretation*. Corning, N.Y. Laboratory of Forensic Science.

MacDonell, H.L., Bialousz, L.F. 1971. *Flight Characteristics and Stain Patterns of Human Blood*. Washington DC: U.S. Department of Justice, Law Enforcement Assistance Administration, National Institute of Law Enforcement and Criminal Justice, 77.

Mann, R.W., Bass, W.M., Meadows, L. 1990. Time since death and decomposition of the human body: Variables and observations in case and experimental field studies. *Journal of Forensic Sciences*, 35, 103–11.

Mannheim, H. (ed.) 1972. *Pioneers in Criminology*. Patterson Smith, 2nd ed.

Maples, W.R., Browning, M. 1995. *Dead Men Do Tell Tales: The Strange and Fascinating Cases of a Forensic Anthropologist*. New York: Doubleday.

Mayer, J.C., Andreas, A. 1783–1788. *Anatomische Kupfertafeln nebst dazu gehörigen Erklärungen Anatomical*.

McClaughry, M.W. 1922. History of the introduction of the Bertillon system into the United States. *Finger Print Magazine*, 3 (10) 13–15.

Meier, R. J., Goodson, C. S., Roche, E. 1987. Dermatoglyphic development and timing of maturation. *Human Biology*, 59 (2) 357–373.

Menzel, E.R. 1979. Treatment with fluorescers. *Journal of Forensic Sciences*, 24, 582–85.

Menzel, E.R. 1999. *Fingerprint Detection with Lasers*. 2nd ed. New York: Marcel Dekker, CRC Press.

Merbs, C.F. 1989. Trauma. In *Reconstruction of Life from the Skeleton*, M.Y. Ìscan, K.A.R. Kennedy (eds.). New York: Alan R. Liss, 161–89.

Merkel, L. 2003.The History of Psychiatry. From PGY II Lecture Notes. September. (www.healthsystem.virginia.edu/internet/ … /history-of-psychiatry-8-04.pdf).

Microsoft Public Sector. 2006. Microsoft Technology helps in fight against child pornography. (http://www.microsoft.com/industry/publicsector/government/cetsnews.mspx).

Minutiae Magazine. 1994. Lightning/Liquinox, summer special, 24-7.

Modeste, K.I., Anderson, B. 2009. Using fingerprint powder to record friction skin details from a cadaver. *Journal of Forensic Identification*, 59 (3) 302–7.

Nafte, M. 2009. *Flesh and Bone: An Introduction to Forensic Anthropology*. Durham, NC: Carolina Academic Press.

National Institute of Standards and Technology. 1998. *Forensic Laboratories: Handbook for Facility Planning, Design, Construction, and Moving*. U.S. Office of Justice Programs, U.S. Office of Law Enforcement Standards.

National Research Council Report. 1992. U.S. National Academy of Science.

National Research Council Report. 1996. *The Evaluation of Forensic DNA Evidence*. The National Academies Press.

Nickell, J., Fischer, J.F. 1999. *Crime Science: Methods of Forensic Detection*. Lexington: University Press of Kentucky.

Oak Ridge National Laboratory. 1995. *The Case of the Vanishing Fingerprint*. (http://www.ornl.gov/info/press_releases/get_press_release.cfm?ReleaseNumber=mr19950327-00).

Oden, S., B. von Hofsten. 1954. Detection of fingerprints by the ninhydrin reaction. *Nature*. March.

Olsen, R. D. 1978. *Scott's Fingerprint Mechanics*. Springfield, IL: Charles C. Thomas Publishing.

Pounds, C.A., Griggs, R., Mongkolaussavaratana, T. 1990. The use of 1,8-diazofluoren-9-one for the fluorescent detection of fingerprints on paper: A preliminary evaluation. *Journal of Forensic Sciences*, 35, 169–75.

Pragg, J. Neave, R. 1997. *Making Faces: Using Forensic and Archaeological Evidence*. London: British Museum Press.

Proctor, A., Dale, M., Williams, J. 1998. Evidence: The True Witness (http://library.advanced.org/17049/ … cgi-bin/document_get.cgi ?path=/DNA).

Promega.com. 2007. *18th International Symposium on Human Identification*. Conference Proceedings.

Ramatowski, R.S. 1996. Importance of an acid prewash prior to the use of physical developer. *Journal of Forensic Identification*, 46, 673–77.

Ramatowski, R.S. 2000. A comparison of different physical developer systems and acid pre-treatments, and their effects on developing latent prints. *Journal of Forensic Identification*, 50, 363–84.

Ramatowski, R.S., Cantu, A.A., Joullie, M.M., Petrovskaia O. 1997. 1,2-indanediones: A preliminary evaluation of a new class of amino acid visualizing compounds. *Fingerprint World*, 23, 131–40.

Rawji, A., Beaudoin, A. 2006. Oil red O versus physical developer on wet papers: A comparative study. *Journal of Forensic Identification*, 56 (1) 33–54.

Reichs, K.J. 1998. Postmortem dismemberment: Recovery, analysis and interpretation. In *Forensic Osteology: Advances in the Identification of Human Remains*, (2nd ed.), K.J. Reichs (ed.). Springfield, IL: Charles C. Thomas, 353–70.

Reichs, K.J., Craig, E. 1998. Facial approximation: Procedures, problems and pitfalls. In *Forensic Osteology II: Advances in the Identification of Human Remains*, K.J. Reichs (ed.). Springfield, IL: Charles C. Thomas.

Renneville, M. 1995. Alexandre Lacassagne: un médecin-anthropologue face à la criminalité (1843–1924), Gradhiva. *Revue d'histoire et d'archives de l'anthropologie*. 17, 127–40.

Revue Des Deux Mondes. No ISSN 0750-9278-97. Paris.

Roux, C. Jones, N., Lennard, C., Stoilovic, M. 2000. Evaluation of 1,2-indanedione and 5,6-dimethoxy-1,2-indanedione for the detection of latent fingerprints on porous surfaces. *Journal of Forensic Sciences*, 45 (4) 761–69.

Ruffell, A., McKinley, J. 2008. *Geoforensics*. New York: Wiley-Blackwell.

Schmidt, C., Symes, S. (eds.). 2008. *The Analysis of Burned Human Remains*. Elsevier Press.

Sears, V.G., Butcher, C.P.G., Fitzgerald, L.A. 2005. Enhancement of fingerprints in blood, part 3: Reactive techniques, acid yellow 7, and process sequences. *Journal of Forensic Identification*, 55 (6) 741–763.

Shahrom, A.W., Vanezis, P., Chapman, R.C., Gonzales, A., Blenkinsop, C., Rossi, M.I. 1996. Techniques in facial identification: Computer-aided facial reconstruction using a laser scanner and video superimposition. *International Journal of Legal Medicine,* 108 (4) 194–200.

Smith, R. 1992. Demystifying Palm Prints. Report for Workshop.

Smith, T. 1999. Assistance and repression: Rural exodus, vagabondage and social crisis in France 1880–1914. *Journal of Social History.* 32 (4) 821–46.

Snow, C.C., Gatliff, B., McWilliams, K.R. 1970. Reconstruction of facial features from the skull; an evaluation of its usefulness in forensic anthropology. *American Journal of Physical Anthropology,* (33) 221–28.

Spitz, W.U. 1973. Drowning. In *Medico-Legal Investigation of Death,* W.U. Spitz., R.S. Fisher(eds.). Springfield, IL: Charles C. Thomas, 351–66.

Spitz, W.U. (ed.). 1993. *Medicolegal Investigation of Death,* 3rd ed. Springfield, IL: Charles C. Thomas.

Stewart, T.D. 1979. *Essentials of Forensic Anthropology.* Springfield, IL: Charles C. Thomas.

Stoilovic, M., Lennard, C. 2006. *Fingerprint Detection & Enhancement.* Workshop Manual. Australian Federal Police.

Turvey, B.E. 2008. *Criminal Profiling: An Introduction to Behavioral Evidence Analysis.* London: Elsevier.

Ubelaker, D.H., O'Donnell, G. 1992. Computer assisted facial reconstruction. *Journal of Forensic Sciences,* 37, 155–62.

U.S. Department of Justice, Federal Bureau of Investigation. 1998. *CODIS Program Overview.* Washington, DC, October 8.

U.S. Department of Justice, Federal Bureau of Investigation. 1998. *DNA Database Press Release.* National Press Office. Washington, DC, October 13.

U.S. Department of Justice, Federal Bureau of Investigation. 2006. *CODIS Program Overview.* Washington, DC, August 7.

U.S. Department of Justice, NIJ. 2002. *DNA Initiative.* (http://static.dna.gov/tables/articles_all.htm).

U.S. Department of Justice, NIJ. 2009. *DNA Field Experiment.* (http://www.ojp.usdoj.gov/nij/topics/forensics/dna/propertycrime/welcome.htm#majorfindings).

U.S. Department of Justice, NIJ. 2009. *DNA Initiative.* (http://static.dna.gov/tables/articles_all.htm).

U.S. Department of Justice, NIJ. 2001. *Electronic Crime Needs Assessment for State and Local Law Enforcement.* April Report. (http://www.ojp.usdoj.gov/nij/pubs-sum/186276.htm).

U.S. Department of Justice, Office of the Inspector General Audit Division. 2006. *Combined DNA Index System Operational and Laboratory Vulnerabilities.* Audit Report 06-32. van der Lugt, C. 1997. Ear Identification, presented at the conference for Shoeprint and Toolmark Examiners. Noordwijkerhout, 24 April.

van der Lugt, C. 2001. *Earprint Identification.* Den Haag: Elsevier Bedrijfsinformatie.

Vanezis, P., Blowes, R.W., Linney, A.D., Tan, A.C., Richards, R., Neave, R. 1989. Application of 3-D computer graphics for facial reconstruction and comparison with sculpting techniques. *Forensic Science International,* 42, 69–84.

Wagner, E.J. 2006. *The Science of Sherlock Holmes.* Hoboken, NJ: John Wiley and Sons.

Welcker, H. 1883. *Schiller's Schädel und todenmaske, nebst mittheilungen über Schädel und todenmaske Kants.* Braunschweig.

Wertheim, K., Maceo, A. 2002. The Critical Stage of Friction Ridge Pattern Formation. *Journal of Forensic Identification,* 52 (1) 35–85.

Wiesner, S., Springer, E., Sasson, Y., Almog, J. 2001. Chemical development of latent fingerprints: 1,2-indanedione has come of age. *Journal of Forensic Sciences,* 46 (5) 1082–84.

Wilkinson, D. 2000. Spectroscopic study of 1,2-indanedione. *Forensic Science International,* 114, 123–32.

Wonder, A. 2007. *Bloodstain Pattern Evidence.* Elsevier Academic Press.

Xiques, P. 2006. *War on Crime: Technically Speaking.* Oak Ridge National Laboratory Report (http://www.ornl.gov/info/ornlreview/rev29_3/text/war.htm).

Index